What Do I Say?

The Therapist's Guide to Answering Client Questions

Linda N. Edelstein
and
Charles A. Waehler

WILEY

John Wiley & Sons, Inc.

Copyright © 2011 by John Wiley & Sons, Inc. All rights reserved.

Published by John Wiley & Sons, Inc., Hoboken, New Jersey.

Published simultaneously in Canada.

For general information on our other products and services please contact our Customer Care Department within the United States at (800) 762-2974, outside the United States at (317) 572-3993 or fax (317) 572-4002.

Wiley also publishes its books in a variety of electronic formats. Some content that appears in print may not be available in electronic books. For more information about Wiley products, visit our website at www.wiley.com.

Library of Congress Cataloging-in-Publication Data:

Edelstein, Linda N.
    What do I say? : the therapist's guide to answering client questions / Linda N. Edelstein, Charles A. Waehler.
        p. cm.
    Includes bibliographical references and index.
    ISBN 978-0-470-56175-1 (pbk.); 978-1-118-06146-6 (ePDF); 978-1-118-06147-3 (eMobi); 978-1-118-06148-0 (ePub)
    1. Counselor and client. 2. Psychotherapist and patient.   I. Waehler, Charles A.   II. Title.
    BF636.6.E34   2011
    158'.3—dc22   2010051401

Printed in the United States of America

V10002771_072618

To my clients, past and present, because I admire their courage, honesty, hope, and hard work. —L.N.E.

To my students, with thanks for all that we have learned together, and for the places we will go. —C.A.W.

Contents

Preface

For many years we have consulted with each other about our work as psychotherapists, teachers, and supervisors. We have always agreed on how much we enjoy working with new professionals and having a hand in the next generation of clinical work. Last year, we discussed writing down answers to clients' questions to arm therapists because we knew that questions and answers is a topic that is rarely written about, despite therapists' anxious concerns. When we seriously got down to writing this book, we realized that rather than arm practitioners as if they were going into battle, we wanted to empower therapists to view questions and responses the same way they see other collaborative pieces of clinical work.

Most books about the psychotherapy process devote a couple of paragraphs to admitting that clients ask questions and that these questions probably have significant meaning. These comments also suggest that we ought to use clients' questions effectively in the growth and healing process. It is rare, however, to find a full discussion of questions. Specific suggestions for answers are even more uncommon. Instead, we have seen that serious conversations about how to respond to questions are left to supervision or thrown into courses as a byproduct of other work, if at all. But we knew from our own clinical experiences, from teaching, and from consulting to other clinicians that clients ask a lot of questions, often very good questions. Unfortunately, therapists can feel flummoxed when this happens because they haven't had opportunities to sort out their concerns, beliefs, and practices.

The more we consulted with other therapists and with students about the idea of a book about clients' questions and therapists' responses, the more we uncovered all kinds of previously unspoken feelings, mostly discomfort and apprehension. Concerns such as "I don't want to lead my client down the wrong path," "I won't know the answer," "I'll reveal too much," "I'll look stupid," "I'll feel stupid," and "I'll say the wrong thing" came from both novice and experienced therapists. We began to think that being asked questions by clients conjures up images of the horrible third-grade teacher who put you on the spot, or the mean kids who snickered, or the parent who quizzed you during dinner. Questions then begin to feel like an inquisition, and responding becomes a competitive win-or-lose game. But therapy isn't a test; it's not even a quiz—it is a relationship. For better or worse, you and your client are tethered together, and if either of you fail, both of you fail.

We know that, as mental health service providers, your effectiveness is related to how comfortable and competent you feel in the room with your clients. If you are anxious, distracted, or fumbling around for what to say, your ability to be attentive to your clients—to be a healthy and professional person in the room—will be compromised. At these confusing times, you wish that you could have a quick consultation with a supervisor or colleague. Later, in the car or in the shower, you come up with an ideal response and wish you had thought of it earlier. We wanted to write a book that helps mental health professionals feel confident during anxiety-provoking situations with their clients.

This book is set up so that both beginning students and more experienced practitioners can think about their interactions with clients' questions. We want this to be the book that therapists wished they had read before they sat across from a client and felt overwhelmed by inadequacy. At one time or another, every therapist has wondered unhappily, "Why didn't my supervisors or professors prepare me for this?" We hope to serve readers in ways similar to the ideal supervisor, who helps formulate the words that express what the therapist wanted to say. Lonnie, a Smith College MSW graduate, called this book, "a supervisor in my backpack."

We conceptualized this book as practical and friendly, and we have tried to write it in that spirit. We imagined that we were sitting around with some of our favorite graduate students and colleagues and having fun with the ideas. Linda actually had dinner parties with her team of graduate students where they shared their developing thoughts. Charlie talked about these issues with his colleagues in a group private practice and reviewed them with his advanced practicum classes.

We also surveyed graduate students and asked them, "What client questions make you apprehensive?" We received about 70 generous replies with hundreds of questions that would give even the most seasoned professionals reason to pause and reflect. We used the questions generated by the surveys, added ones from our own combined half-century of practice, and went to experienced colleagues for even more questions. We gathered an excellent, super-sized collection that we grouped into logical categories. We could have simply considered ways to respond to client questions that would get you past the awkward moments, but to do so would be similar to telling you to close your eyes during the scary part of a movie. Instead, we have devoted this book to thinking about ways to use client questions to enhance therapy.

First, we address ways to think about client questions and potential therapist responses in terms of general constructive strategies. To this end, we talk about some big-picture considerations as well as make focused observations about language and word use.

Second, knowing that clinicians are frequently faced with questions on specific topics, we have organized the questions and responses into 23 of the most commonly asked subject areas. We move through these 23 topics in an organized manner, asking numerous questions, examining underlying issues, proposing possible responses, and ending with further thoughts and references for additional reading. We present our rationale and thinking behind the responses. Some questions and their answers are challenging because the context is complicated, whereas others are more straightforward. These are all meant as jumping-off points for our readers. The ideas are useful to consider ahead of time so that you are more at ease during sessions. We have written in a conversational tone and illustrated our ideas with examples from our own lives and work, and from the experiences of our guest clinicians, both seasoned and brand new. In reading the experiences of others and writing down our own, we relearned that many experiences are common and, although we need to treat our work seriously, we are better off when we take ourselves lightly.

In reading, we expect that you will skip around to topics that challenge, confound, or confront you. If you do jump around from topic to topic, please recognize that certain themes could easily be considered in all chapters (e.g., ethics), but they are not repeated in every applicable chapter. Several topics, like diversity and boundaries, have specific chapters of their own and also are germane to all other areas.

Although we want to inform, even prod, you by the considerations we have brought into this text, we don't want you to use the proposed responses in a cut-and-paste fashion with your clients. To do so would take away your individuality and the special quality that emerges from forging unique relationships with clients. Instead, we trust that you will modify, individualize, and personalize your responses. Our language can be easily incorporated into a therapy conversation, but we know that good therapy is not done by following a script. Although thinking ahead can be helpful, therapy evolves from the interactions in session. You respond in the moment to a client's very personal, idiosyncratic statements, and no two sessions are ever alike. As you personalize the elements in the book, you will become increasingly spontaneous and confident.

The material in this book comes from a variety of theoretical orientations. Some theories emphasize different aspects of client treatment, but many elements, known as *common factors* in the literature, cut across different orientations. These elements account for a great deal of the successful change we all work toward with clients. We have used therapist responses that fit into a common-factors approach. You may notice that two core ideas related to psychotherapeutic work permeate the book:

1. The more that our clients know about their affective, cognitive, and behavioral thought patterns, beliefs, attitudes, hopes, desires, and fears, the more gain is possible in psychotherapy.
2. The positive, constructive, respectful, attuned relationship created between you and your client is at the heart of the change process.

With these two ideas in mind, you will see that we use some psychodynamic terms because we were both trained and continue to be informed, particularly at the conceptual level, by theories that appreciate the power of our clients' internal dynamics and irrational conflicts. Linda considers herself a feminist therapist, and Charlie describes himself as an integrative, multitheoretical therapist. We both value clients' cognitive, affective, and behavioral learning. We appreciate their contextual, cultural, and systemic concerns, as well as individual differences, and have integrated aspects of the major theoretical orientations into our work and into our attempts to formulate consistent, well-considered responses.

We are also informed by the Presidential Task Force on Evidence-Based Practice in the American Psychological Association (2006), which created a policy statement that says, in part, "Evidence-based practice in psychology (EBPP) is the integration of the best available research with clinical expertise in the context of patient characteristics, culture, and preferences" (p. 284). This sentence reflects the three components that help direct successful therapeutic interventions: empirical evidence (broadly defined), clinical expertise, and client characteristics.

With regard to empirical evidence, we have reviewed the literature and, not surprisingly, little experimental data exist that have examined the dialogue of questions and responses. We have enjoyed and absorbed the theoretical discussions when we could find them, reviewed the research and and practice recommendations, and then attempted to present the material in ways that mirror the actual activity and flow of the therapeutic session or supervisory discussions. At the end of each chapter, we have included sources that might be interesting to our readers.

Clinical expertise, our own and others', heavily guided our responses to questions. We tried hard to capture everyday examples of queries and, more importantly, to examine what clients reveal with their questions. In doing so, we hope to expand your therapeutic understanding of material that can help clients change.

With regard to client characteristics, in specific chapters you will see some references to individual differences such as race, religion, sexual orientation, age, socioeconomic status, privilege, or ability, but more often, you will read many comments urging you to appreciate each client. We also know that our readers are individuals with as much variety as our clients. In this way, each therapeutic relationship reminds us that people connect despite their perceived differences. In Chapter 18, Individual and Cultural Differences, we have included many of the specific questions that come up with regard to individual differences.

You will notice that we chose to alternate our description of therapists and clients as male or female rather than addressing them in the text as him/her or he/she. We certainly recognize that clients and therapists can be either gender, but including he/she or him/her all the time is awkward and changes your experience as a reader. We hope this does not inadvertently promote any gender stereotypes. Also, we have included many examples from clients and clinicians. Most clinicians are identified and clients' identities are changed (although we have permission to use their stories) to ensure confidentiality.

If you want to get in touch with us for questions or comments, Linda is available through email, l.edelstein@sbcglobal.net or through her blog, www.lifeaintforsissies.com, where you can join the conversation. Charlie can be reached at cwaehler@uakron.edu.

Linda N. Edelstein, Evanston, IL
Charlie A. Waehler, Akron, OH

Acknowledgments

Linda

I never wanted to write a book about therapy, unless it was a mystery novel, so when Charlie and I came up with this idea about questions and answers, it was an unexpected gift. During the writing, I've had the opportunity to think back over the years and reflect on many significant moments in treatment. I've also gotten clearer about some ideas that matter to me. I've been a therapist for a long time, and this book became the culmination of teaching, clinical work, reading, conversations, and personal thought. Mostly, it has been a lot of fun.

Even with Charlie, a co-author who envisioned the book just like I did, writing is a notoriously solitary process, but I have received a lot of help. I want to thank my dynamic graduate student team of Damon Krohn, M.A.; Jessica Bell, M.A.; Elizabeth Marklein, M.A.; Dina Zweibel; and Greg Rizzolo. The team independently researched chapters, generated original ideas, and added information and liveliness that would have been missing otherwise. In the very early stages, Luna Sung worked on preliminary versions of the chapters about prejudice and stigma.

My writing group is made up of loyal friends who are also esteemed colleagues, Margit Kir-Stimon, Ph.D.; Melissa Perrin, Psy.D.; and, for awhile, Joan Liataud, Psy.D., all of whom remained on call for reading, editing, and complaining. I want to thank Nancy Newton, Ph.D., my comrade on many projects over the years, who has generously and endlessly been able to take my thinking to more creative places and pull me out of mental mud. Additional thanks go to my office partner, Patty Shafer, Ph.D., who was willing to talk with me about clinical work and theory; Keira Dubowsky, who helped with the cartoons (that never made it to the final version of the book) and other creative ideas; and Jennifer Dubowsky, M.S.O.M., who very patiently listened to the process of writing and encouraged everything, including the website and blog so that we can continue the dialogue.

Also, special thanks to friends Anita Adams, M.B.A.; Ken Adams, J.D.; Karen Drill, M.A.; Janna Dutton, J.D.; Eve Epstein, J.D.; and Hedda Leonard, who were all very kind to me, made themselves endlessly available to discuss this project, and who are probably as happy as we are that the book is done.

Charlie

Those of you who know me well know that I am a collector. I like to cling to valuable thoughts, ideas, and wisdom, as well as relationships, connections, and all sorts of experiences. This book has provided a wonderful opportunity to sort through many different ideas, combining and reworking them with novel notions to give them new life and energy: that has been a joy for me. Most joyful among these has been the opportunity to create new connections with students who provided invaluable assistance in identifying, exploring, clarifying, and energizing ideas that have enriched this material. Chief among these people has been Sam Gregus, whose blend of curiosity, wisdom, hard work, and good cheer kept advancing the work. Other students who assisted in a variety of activities have included Zack Bruback, M.A.; Sara Carnicom; Jill Hendrickson, Ph.D.; Jennifer McDonnell; Lindsay Newton; and Jennifer Underwood. Colleagues who have also been of assistance have included Mark J. Hilsenroth, Ph.D.; and James L. Werth, Ph.D.

I also want to acknowledge the support and understanding I have received from my immediate and extended family as I have taken private time to work on this material. I hope that all the delayed gratification necessitated by the work will prove worthwhile. I also appreciate the support and understanding from my professional colleagues and graduate students for the time and energy that has gone into this project. Thanks, too, to Linda, who has again proven to be a great fellow traveler.

Linda and Charlie

Early in the process, we were guided by Margaret Zusky from John Wiley & Sons, who led us to our editor "in perpetuity" Rachel Livsey. We have been very lucky to work with Rachel, who commented on all aspects of the project with laser-like accuracy. Also, thanks go to senior production editor, Kim Nir. To gather client questions, we surveyed graduate students in Ohio, California, Illinois, and Virginia. They filled out surveys and provided us with hundreds of examples of questions that make them anxious. We used many of them. This also helped us to realize that we wanted to gather more clinical examples than those we could cull from our own careers, so we asked other students and colleagues to share their experiences as guest clinicians and they graciously consented. Their contributions have made the book richer than it would have been otherwise. We are grateful to the people who allowed us to use both their stories and their names: Jeremy Bloomfield, Psy.D.; Margit Kir-Stimon, Ph.D.; Carol Kerr, Ph.D.; Damon Krohn, M.A.; Elizabeth Marklein, M.A.; Mary Miller Lewis, Ph.D.; Nancy Newton, Ph.D.; Melissa Perrin, Psy.D.; Hinda Pozner; Abbey Prujan, M.A.; Lee Rodin, M.S.W.; Tammi Vache-Haase, Ph.D.; and Naomi Woods.

Particular thanks to Carol Kerr, Ph.D., who advocated for and wrote most of the chapter on Individual Differences. Thanks also to Mark Epstein, J.D., a mental health lawyer who reviewed the chapter on Confidentiality, and Meghan Roelke, Psy.D., who distributed surveys to her class at The Chicago School. At the completion of the writing, before publication, we had the good fortune to be reviewed by six anonymous clinicians and educators who read carefully, commented artfully, and brought some new ideas to the project.

To our clients from whom we have learned much and who have allowed us to use their questions and experiences, thank you. We hope we have been faithful to the spirit of our collaboration.

PART

1

Client Questions
in a Broad Context

INTRODUCTION TO PART 1

Eileen dropped heavily into the chair and opened her second session with questions. "When will I stop feeling so guilty? Will I ever get over this? How do I forgive myself?"

Zac, her therapist, was stumped. These direct questions prompted a flood of racing thoughts that filled his mind. Which approach would be best? Should he answer the question, pose questions himself, or explore, but how could he make the transition into meaningful exploration? Or would it be better to use reflections like "You've had another rough week," or take the question at face value and provide information? And if he did try to answer the question, what was the correct answer? He didn't want to sound glib or provide false reassurances; at the same time, she was asking for a reason to hope. He knew what some theories said about processes of guilt and forgiveness, but Eileen was her own unique individual. Their therapeutic alliance was new and untested. How could he prompt further examination without making her feel dismissed or put down? How could he use this moment to gain credibility and trust as an empathic listener?

Eileen might be 30 or 70 years old. She might be in prison for murdering her child or feel guilty because she has fallen in love with her coworker. She may be reacting to a transgression that occurred 2 weeks ago

1

or 20 years ago. Zac might be analytic, eclectic, cognitive-behavioral, or feminist. What remains a constant is that clients ask questions, and clinicians often find themselves wanting to know more about how to reply in ways that are thoughtful and intentional. This isn't an unusual example. Zac knew that Eileen's questions revealed some of her most intimate struggles and intense emotions. He was also filled with his own thoughts and feelings. He wanted, as most clinicians do, to engage Eileen, to respond in ways that deepen their dialogue, and to provide clarity and hope to his client.

As caring, social beings, people who have chosen to become mental health practitioners are usually pretty comfortable conversing with others. We all practice active listening skills such as empathic paraphrasing, open-ended questions, and nonjudgmental reflective statements to encourage therapeutic conversations. We have learned various intervention techniques so that we can help guide clients to be more effective in their lives. At times we stumble through these skills. Everyone does. But for the most part, we feel confident knowing what to say and what to ask in order to interact therapeutically with our clients. And then a client asks a direct question.

Direct questions, even when they are innocent and innocuous, often catch us off guard. When the question feels challenging or intrusive, self-protection is often the natural first reaction, and we want to shut the conversation down. Our sense of control has been upset; it feels like the tables have been turned. After all, aren't *we* the ones who get to ask the questions?

We have each been in practice for more than 25 years, but it isn't hard to recall our jumbled reactions from the client questions of earlier days. In answering their questions, we wanted to be brief, but not simple; to engage our client's curiosity, but not parrot back the question; to avoid giving direct advice, but not sidestep a request for assistance. We wanted to sound wise but knew that how we sounded was less important than promoting our client's therapeutic goals. Good manners said that we ought to be polite and forthcoming, but this is therapy, and the goal is additional exploration of our client's own ideas. We wanted to examine the overt and covert meanings of the question, but not become interrogating detectives; and we wanted to express ourselves without making the conversation about us.

In short, we wanted to practice our craft well and that made us anxious, particularly when we were faced with difficult questions. So, for better or worse, we responded and moved on, but we were sometimes left believing that we could have been more effective. We knew that there would be other questions from other clients, and we wondered what a more experienced therapist might have been able to do. We realize now that we had the skills; we just hadn't focused them on responding effectively to questions. With all our training and reading and clinical placements, no one had ever addressed answering questions as a significant aspect of everyday therapy. We hope to change that.

WHY DO CLIENTS' QUESTIONS CAUSE APPREHENSION?

Answering clients' direct questions can be perplexing for several reasons. Consider your own practice, and see if any of these seven reasons apply to you:

1. *Client questions represent a shift away from the normal therapeutic pattern in which the therapist asks the questions.* When this activity is reversed, you may feel like your role has been usurped, leaving you perplexed, unprepared, and feeling like you have lost control of the process and content.
2. *Client questions reflect different motives.* They can be variously intended as inquisitive or invasive, engaging or deflecting, polite or intrusive, clarifying or complicating, solicitous or dismissive, congenial or offensive, curious or aggressive, innocuous or challenging, helpful or obstructive. And this list is not exhaustive. Many questions represent a combination of several of these motivations and a variety of complicated communications—no wonder they can be disconcerting.
3. *Questions can make you feel very responsible, and although you want to be helpful, you are rightfully reluctant to take on the influential role inherent in providing a specific answer.* If you believe that you help your clients when you promote autonomy, critical thinking, and self-examination, then providing simple answers to questions is nearly impossible.

4. *You will not always have the answers.* Optimal answers to client questions are always going to be highly personalized and idiosyncratic to what is going on with this client at this time in his life. It is daunting to think about having to answer and address all these unique meanings.

5. *You may have recognized that many answers take the focus and energy of the session off the client and put it on you.* This isn't the attention you want.

6. *Because your answers reveal much about you, they also highlight the nonclient, nontherapist relationship.* You may not want to head in that direction.

7. *As you probably know from answering questions tossed out by family and friends, there is a serious possibility to disrupt the relationship with the wrong answer.* Potential misunderstandings abound.

Your ability to respond effectively is enhanced by increased awareness, knowledge, consideration, and experience. Clients' questions and your responses can be used constructively when you are prepared. The many questions and potential responses we offer in the 23 topic chapters provide ways for you to think about the attitudes and strategies that work best for you as you receive client questions, clarify them, and respond successfully, turning the interchange into effective psychotherapy.

Charlie

Toward the end of every intake interview I conduct, after I have spent most of our time asking questions and exploring the client's answers, I say "I have asked a lot of questions here. I wonder if you have any questions for me?" Usually after brief reflection, most clients respond "No, none that I can think of now." Sometimes I get a general, appropriate question along the lines of "So what do you think is going on?" or "Is there any hope for me?" or "What do we do now?" Sometimes I get a question like "Why did you ask me about . . .?" or "What is your training to do this work?" or "Have you ever seen anyone like me?" I believe that client questions yield additional information with which to formulate beginning diagnostic impressions. As important as this information can be, when I invite questions my main goal is to communicate my desire to have the client be a fully involved, valued participant in the therapeutic process and to authorize him to ask questions and be curious in our work together.

Clients want to know that they are understood. You can show understanding in many ways other than directly responding to questions. When a client asks plaintively, "Do you know how painful relationships can be?" he does not want his therapist to say, "Yeah, I've been married 15 years and at times it's really hell. In fact, recently we have been going through a tough patch involving . . ." as a response. He also doesn't want to be met with silence. He wants empathy and understanding. He also wants a smart, sympathetic ear that will help him explore and clarify his struggle. We hope that you will neither dismiss questions nor answer them reflexively without exploration. Appropriate statements in this example involve words like "I can see that you are struggling now. Tell me about your relationship." or "What has become painful for you at this time?" or "Relationships can certainly be painful; what's going on for you?"

WHAT DO THE DIFFERENT THEORIES ADVISE?

Various theories have good reasons for proposing seemingly contradictory advice about answering client questions—they work with different models that believe in distinctly different strategies for change. With the exception of psychodynamic and psychoanalytic theorists, almost nothing has been written directly about responses to client questions. Because this book focuses exclusively on that topic, we have little guidance, but we also have no shackles. It is an opportunity to examine the basic principles of different theories and extrapolate reasonable ideas about their attitudes toward answering client questions.

You probably have opinions about the major theories—the ones you like and those that leave you cold; the ones whose principles make intuitive sense and others that require intellectual stretching. You may even consider yourself a firm disciple of one theory. As you read about the theoretical approaches to answering questions, you may find, as we have, that your philosophical leanings don't match exactly to your practice when it comes to answering questions. Don't worry; as you get further into the topic chapters, you will be increasingly able to discern what questions you want to answer, how you want to answer them, and why you are making that particular choice.

We begin with traditional psychoanalytic perspectives, because they are clearly stated. This view says that therapists should resist answering direct questions and instead promote their client's fantasy. The less the client knows about the therapist, the more the client is able to generate fantasies regarding the therapist. Clients are told this information at the beginning of treatment so they are not dismayed by a lack of response coming from their analysts. Both parties agree that these fantasies become valuable therapeutic material. The alliance between the analyst and client is based on many factors, but therapist verbosity is not one of them. The technique reflects the underlying theory. Freud encouraged therapists to be neutral with their patients, so as to reflect nothing but what was shown to them (Freud, 1912/1959). Orthodox analytic perspectives about client questions have traditionally tended to see them as resistance, defensiveness, or avoidance. If that is your view, you might interpret a question with "You would find it easier to have me talk than you." or "You would rather have me explore this topic than you doing it." or "You are avoiding talking about *your* life."

Greenson (1967) suggested that, from the analytic point of view, the first time a client asks a personal question, you encourage him to explore his reasons for asking. After listening to the client's associations, Greenson would explain to the client that by processing the question's meaning instead of answering, he and the client could gain a greater understanding of the significance of the question. Furthermore, he informed clients that most of their questions would not be answered so he did not appear unnecessarily cold and unresponsive. The second time a client asked a question, he remained silent. So, if you are strongly analytic, you have a model that provides clear reasons and guidelines for responses.

Other psychodynamic clinicians take a softer approach. Langs (1973) cautioned that unnecessarily frustrating responses to realistic and appropriate questions may serve the therapist's defensive and hostile needs, rather than the positive work of the client and the therapy. Langs maintained that realistic and reasonable questions may have deeper implications, but he urged clinicians to maintain a reasonable and human balance between a direct answer and the need, when indicated, to analyze rather than respond to the question. Today, many self-psychology and relational psychology practitioners would agree. If you believe that replying to some questions more directly, especially early in therapy, will encourage engagement with treatment and with you, then you have support. Feldman (2002) suggests that, in the initial stages of therapy, useful responses both validate the client's curiosity and encourage further exploration in ways that are consistent with how the therapy process will be approached in future sessions.

Wachtel (1993) contended that a categorical refusal to answer certain client questions creates an implicit power struggle and adversarial relationship that may inhibit the client's connection with the therapist, stop questions about the therapeutic process, and diminish your client's willingness to share her wonderings with you. He stated, "One should not equate answering the question with abandoning one's interest in understanding its meaning and, conversely and equally importantly, one should not assume that the only way to discover its meaning is to refuse to answer it" (p. 225).

Much has happened in psychology since Freud's 1912 dictum to "be impenetrable," but not with regard to answering questions. Glickauf-Hughes and Chance (1995) noted that, "the few guidelines that are provided for responding to clients' questions derive from Freud's emphasis on therapist abstinence in the therapeutic relationship" (p. 375). If, like us, you are eclectic or work from other models, your guidance comes from extracting ideas from existing theoretical principles in specific models that make sense to you and your work.

Carl Rogers was a psychologist in the humanistic tradition and the father of client-centered therapy, which had its roots in Freudian thinking. Client-centered theory has many factors in common with other major viewpoints but also diverges significantly. Practiced with less orthodoxy today than it was in the 1960s and 1970s, Rogerian thinking has received little credit for the powerful influence it has exerted on many of the relational and humanistic approaches that are popular today. The hallmark of Roger's client-centered therapy is a nondirective approach that is based on the belief that each individual is basically responsible for himself and capable of coming to his own healthy decisions. For example, even out of context, we imagine that if a client asked, "Are you gay?" Rogers would have recommended a response such as, "You wonder if I am gay." In adhering to theory, the answer would be nondirective and unanswered. There will be occasions when you have what Rogers referred to as "those troublesome questions from the client," when your client wants to know your convictions about how people ought to act or what they should believe and "you begin to wonder. The technique is good, but . . . does it go far enough! Does it really work on clients? Is it right to leave a person helpless, when you might show him the way out?" (Rogers, 1946/2000, pp. 420). If you believe that people have the potential to work out their own answers, and will do better with no intercession from you, then you have no need to answer most questions.

Pure behaviorism, as practiced by B. F. Skinner in the 1970s, was both a psychological approach and a philosophical belief that thoughts and feelings could not be verified and, as such, were not scientific. From this perspective, answers to questions would be irrelevant. Techniques that resulted in measurable behavior change were the focus. It is rare to find many radical behaviorists today. Out of behaviorism, beginning in the 1960s, writers such as Aaron Beck and Albert Ellis guided that branch of psychology toward what we now refer to as cognitive-behavioral treatment (CBT).

Cognitive-behavioral theories approach psychotherapy and client questions from a perspective that is quite different from the psychoanalytic and psychodynamic approaches. The basic belief is that psychological disorders involve current, conscious dysfunctional thinking, so CBT theory and techniques seek to challenge and modify a client's dysfunctional thoughts and behaviors. In keeping with the theory, CBT practitioners use a variety of techniques, including the Socratic dialogue (questions that guide clients to become active participants in finding their answers, often by examining cognitive and behavioral evidence), assignments, journaling, relaxation techniques, thought-change records, role-plays, generating alternatives, and other strategies. Treatment is usually of shorter term than that of most dynamic or feminist models and discourages dependency on the therapist. This is not to say that the therapy relationship is ignored, but rather that CBT relies on non-specific elements of the therapeutic alliance such as rapport, genuineness, and empathy. Questions are met with empathy and pursued with regard to the client's thoughts and the subsequent impact on behavior. The same question that was asked above, "Are you gay?" would be answered, or not, and then examined with a goal of understanding thoughts and behaviors; for example, whether the client thinks that a gay therapist would be better able, or less able, to help. "Tell me your thoughts about gay therapists" might be a suggestion from a CBT clinician who is interested in whether the client thinks that similarities in sexual orientation is a good thing, or not. The clinician pursues the implications of these thoughts. For example, does the client only feel comfortable hanging out with gay (or straight) friends? Does the client gauge the merit of the treatment based on certain characteristics of the therapist?

Questions about the therapist and the therapeutic relationship, fodder for psychoanalytic therapists who attend strongly to transference and counter-transference, would be noted by CBT practitioners but not addressed directly and certainly not elevated to center stage. If techniques are the mechanisms of change, then it isn't surprising that the literature does not speak to responses that explore the therapeutic relationship. Instead, writers might encourage client questions that help clarify the strategies in which they are engaged. In deciding how to respond, CBT practitioners may feel comfortable disclosing their solutions to problems or providing didactic comments because the client is learning new strategies. However, questions that seem to be off-task are inconsequential to the treatment.

In his article on neutrality, Greenberg (1999) noted that the clinician invariably participates somewhere in her client's schema of relationships. So, we urge practitioners to consider your place in your client's world and participate with awareness and intention. Going even further with the idea that a clinician will occupy a significant place in her client's set of relationships, humanistic and feminist theoreticians contend that a real relationship, in addition to the therapeutic relationship, exists between therapist and client, and this relationship is an important ingredient of therapy. This observation makes treatment a collaborative endeavor in ways dissimilar to both analytic and cognitive-behavioral therapy. Feminist therapies (there is not just one) grew out of the women's movement of the 1960s, when some psychologists promoted the idea that a client's personal experience was embedded in political situations and reality, and was not simply a function of unresolved internal conflict or dysfunctional cognitive patterns. Feminist therapy is technically a practice driven by eclectic theory and informed by feminist philosophy and scholarship. It grew out of the dissatisfaction with societal rules that blocked men and women's potential for growth and development. The writers encouraged awareness of factors that were external, as well as internal, to clients' lives and experiences.

Laura Brown and Lenore Walker are two writers who have clarified tenets of feminist therapy theory. Walker defines them as egalitarian relationships; power; enhancement of women's strengths; non-pathology-oriented and non-victim-blaming; education; and acceptance and validation of feelings. There are feminist therapists who are psychodynamic, cognitive-behavioral, behavioral, and eclectic. The theoretical underpinnings blend with the basic tenets of feminist therapy to determine how you think about and answer questions.

Again, until now, no one has written specifically on what these tenets mean in the context of answering questions, but the basic principles of the feminist models provide some information. When you consider an egalitarian relationship as being significant for the therapist and her client in order to model personal responsibility and assertiveness, answering some questions directly is appropriate. Another principle, that of teaching clients to gain and use power, also encourages direct answers on the part of the therapist, because this teaches the client that she will be able to elicit responses. Finally, acceptance and validation of your client's feelings lends itself to value appropriate self-involvement, which removes the we-they barrier of traditional therapeutic relationships. For these reasons, feminist therapists may be more willing to directly answer the question "Are you gay?" Then, depending on their theoretical views, they could pursue a discussion.

Because of these ideas about collaboration and empowerment, notions about self-disclosure and answering questions are different from the other theoretical viewpoints and have caused some conflict in feminist therapists who are also psychodynamic clinicians. Some disclosure in response to client questions may promote the desired goal of having a therapist-client relationship that is closer to egalitarian and therefore more empowering to clients, but it does not further analytic principles of encouraging fantasy. Practically, therapy lives in the grays, not in black or white. Decisions such as when and how to disclose can be unsettling to all therapists, who are often forced to come up with their own sense of when to answer, taking into account their personal experiences, as well as their client's personality, problems, history, and the multitude of other individual and cultural factors that must be considered.

You can see that the placement of boundaries in answering questions depends, to a great degree, on your theoretical viewpoint and is also influenced by the client, the problem, the relationship, and the myriad of factors that go into making all your clinical decisions. In this book, we take a middle-of-the-road perspective in deciding how to respond to client questions. From this perspective, client questions are received, explored further when appropriate, and understood collaboratively. When properly received and responded to, client questions represent an opportunity to promote further client understanding as well as advancing a healthier appreciation of, and attitude toward, increased personal curiosity and self-understanding. Whatever your responses are, you play a key role in what happens next in your client's development, so try to be clear in your own mind about the interactions that you establish.

REMEMBER, IT'S NOT ABOUT YOU

At times we were tempted to use the phrase "Remember, it's not about you" to begin each chapter in this book. Whether a client's question is reasonable or flattering, intrusive or insulting, personal or generic, it is not about you. The question may say something about you and may be quite insightful, but as your client's production, it remains primarily about her. Questions, how many or how few, reveal information about the questioner. You can learn a great deal about your client's personality and coping style from the quantity of questions she asks.

Linda

I used to treat a man and his wife who were very different in their personalities and approaches to the world. He was aggressive, independent, and, in his words, "walked to the beat of my own drum." His wife was very gentle but independent. He never had questions for me; he wanted to talk about himself and went out of his way to tell me that "I don't want any input from you; I just want to think out loud." On the other hand, she had a million questions for me and about me. They were ostensibly in treatment to discuss child-rearing disagreements, but one dynamic that underlay their stated objectives was that she was, not surprisingly, overly concerned with others and what they thought and, also not surprisingly, he was guilty of not listening to anyone else, making unilateral decisions, and doing things his way with little regard for her wishes. Their approach to asking me questions was instructive and reflected other aspects of their attitudes toward their children, business associates, and the community.

Therapy is about both of you working to understand your client. As you will see in the topic chapters, this means that sometimes you answer questions directly whereas at other times you won't. Sometimes you will answer a question from one client and not answer the same question when it comes from another client. You respond in ways that are sensitive to and personalized for this client.

With regard to the statement "It is not about you," think of a continuum of answers from "Me" at one end to "Client" at the other. Good therapy always spends more time on the client end of the continuum. Responses to client questions will always have the intent of bringing understanding to the client's life and pursuits. Unavoidably, there will be times when conversations will be about you. You will have emergencies, need to reschedule because of a family problem, take a vacation, or recover from an illness, and it may be appropriate to provide your client with legitimate information about you. There will be other times, for valid reasons, when you must put your needs before your client's. It is better to cancel a session with a client than to fake your way through a meeting when you are sick or distracted by other pressing issues.

GUIDELINES FOR ANSWERING QUESTIONS

In responding to clients, your attitude is as important as your words. Therefore, when questions present possibilities to advance your client's treatment goals, we encourage you to do the following:

1. *Receive the question respectfully.* Your client has taken a risk by asking a question, and you want him to know that you are receptive to his questions. Be sure that you understand the question; paraphrasing is still the best way to clarify your comprehension.

Charlie

I was at a wedding and involved in a discussion about traditional values and the role of marriage. The group was large, and after several different, strong opinions (including my own) had been proposed, two women who had staked out a position quite different from mine asked "What are you?" I have learned that answering "psychologist" can become a conversation stopper or lead to lots of bad jokes, and I could see that this discussion clearly was primed for that. In some situations, I say "teacher" or "writer" or "social scientist" to avert the jokes. While I was trying to figure out what response I wanted to give to this question, one of the women jumped in and said, "Because she is a Taurus and I am a Gemini." I really misunderstood that question.

Paraphrasing invites your client to rephrase, clarify, correct, or to consider the question in broader or deeper terms. This often leads him to shed more light on the query or examine the question further.

2. *Promote your client's curiosity about the question whether you decide to answer it or not.* You can always provide encouragement by asking your client to elaborate on the question. Clients need support in order to allow themselves to ask questions, be open to new information, and to wonder about novel ways to look at themselves and their undertakings. If they feel ridiculed, the conversation withers rather than opens up. In the outside world, people often find themselves in situations where not knowing is shameful. Therapy is a place where not knowing is expected, acceptable, and just another step toward figuring things out.

3. *Answer your client sufficiently to keep her engaged.* What constitutes sufficiently will vary with different questions and different clients. One-word answers rarely feel sufficient, but a 10-minute monologue is overkill. You can check back with your clients to assess the adequacy of your response, but it will probably be obvious as you observe what your client does with your response—ignores it, works with it, or amends it.

4. *Explore possible underlying and idiosyncratic meanings with your client.* You are presented with a chance to teach lifelong self-observation skills. You want clients to internalize a process of raising questions about their lives, thinking through their problems, and valuing themselves in ways that will sustain them over the long haul. If you want clients to become increasingly self-reflective, model inquisitiveness.

At the same time as we suggest guidelines, we also recognize that there is no formula for answering questions. Your choice of answer depends on the question, the client, the relationship, your comfort, the point in treatment, and your goals. In the chapters that follow, you will see ample illustrations of types of questions, types of responses, and the rationale for responding as we did. Generally, there are seven possible directions to take when you respond to client questions, and you have the skills for each.

1. Answer simply and directly and let the question go. Like Freud's famous quote, "Sometimes a cigar is just a cigar," some questions are just questions.

   Examples of questions in this category: "Where do I sit?" "Is another time available on Tuesday?" "Pretty tulips, where did you get them?"

2. Answer and relate the question back to your client's life, turning the question into a discussion that is pertinent to your client.

   Example of a question in this category: "Did you have a good Mother's Day?"

   Examples of a response: "Thanks, the day was lovely. We had a great brunch. How was your Mother's Day since your mother moved to Arizona?"

3. Inquire about the question and then answer (if needed) and use the question to reflect on your client's life in the present.

   Example of a question in this category: "Why did you go into this field?"

   Example of a response: "I'm glad to answer, but I'm curious about what made you ask that question today?"

4. Inquire about the question and don't answer because it is getting too personal (it is your decision about what questions are "too personal") and use the question to reflect on your client's experience.

   Example of a question in this category: "How old were you when you first had sex?"

   Example of a response: "That's a question I am going to pass on answering. Can I assume that you have been thinking about age-appropriate sexual behaviors?"

5. Interpret the client's motive for the question because the answer is usually irrelevant.

   Example of a question in this category: "My marriage counselor has a much larger office than you do. Are you thinking about moving?"

Example of a response: "Perhaps you are worried about which therapist is more skilled. Could that be your concern?"

6. Refuse to answer and set a boundary.

Example of a question in this category: "Have you ever been sexually assaulted?"

Example of a response: "I know that this is a profound concern of yours, but I'm sorry, there are areas of my life that I do not discuss."

7. Explain or educate while refusing to answer.

Example of a question: "How do you manage this with your husband?"

Example of a response: "Marriage is so complicated, and relationships are all unique. We ought to concentrate on your life." or "It can be distracting to focus on me, and I don't think it will help." or even, "I may have a couple of suggestions, but let's look at your situation first."

Most of all, your response to questions is determined by your clinical assessment of the client, the specific question in context, and the possible motives behind the question. As those factors change, you might understand the question differently and alter your response.

The questions that your client asks are important; so are the questions that you ask yourself:

"What is in my client's best interest at this time?"
"What is comfortable for me?"
"What lies behind the question?"
"Is this simply a way to make a further connection with me?"
"Does the question reveal some issue for my client?"
"Is my client expressing reservations about me?"
"Is this an angry, hostile, or veiled attack?"
"Is it important to have tighter boundaries, or looser ones?"
"Am I less worried about the individual questions and more concerned about the excessive number of questions?"
"Are the questions deflecting attention from my client?"
"Is my client asking in order to normalize his own experience?"

"Is my client challenging boundaries to see how far I will go?"

"Is this a simple question that has no major significance?"

"Is my client trying to figure out another point of view or determine what is normal?"

"Is my client trying to be socially appropriate and doesn't really care about my vacation/floral arrangement/new jacket?"

You will not be flooded with questions. Responding to client's questions will take up a small portion of your clinical life. Unfortunately, the anxiety that client questions cause occupies more space than it deserves.

STYLE AND LANGUAGE CONSIDERATIONS

We have been careful to choose accessible words for this book, just as we do in treatment, in order to ease conversations. In writing, we have avoided jargon and tried to use the words and tone that we often use with our clients, in supervision, and in consultation with respected students and colleagues. We have made these decisions based on our desire to have you think about, amend, own, and use these ideas with your clients. Some of our most powerful therapeutic instruments are words, so in this section, we focus our attention on language and phraseology that helps clinical work.

As we put together the responses to questions in the topical chapters of this book, we noticed that style and language are consistently woven together. Style refers to the way you select and arrange your answer so you will be heard and understood. Language considerations include attention to the specific words and phrases; it is an area for awareness, not carelessness. Clients listen closely to your language and remember what you say to them. In fact, some people will repeat your exact words back to you, even years later.

Style and language considerations are not unique to answering questions but are important during those dialogues, because those are moments when clients may be open to new ideas. Therefore, you want to proceed with intention when you respond to client questions. We highlight some basic practices that can be forgotten in stressful situations. Some general ideas about style and language when you answer client's questions include: take time to formulate your response; be transparent;

use metaphors and analogies; practice the soft sell; lead with positives and speak to strengths; use client language when possible; clarify jargon: yours and theirs; avoid sarcasm; and use a few key words that can make a difference.

Take Time to Formulate Your Response

Being asked a question can make you feel like you are being put on the spot, so you feel pressured to reply immediately. Take your time. Sometimes a delayed answer is the best one. When you take your time, you model deliberation. This gives permission to your client to do the same. Your thoughtful pacing may be one of the most therapeutic aspects of the interaction. To do so, you can pause and reflect before responding, or muse out loud, "Let me think for a moment about how to best respond to that."

Be Transparent

Let your clients in on the thinking that leads to your responses. By being transparent about your thought process, you can increase the likelihood that your clients will learn the same method. When you offer the evidence that you used to reach your response, you show that you use a reasonable process that clients can learn and practice on their own. For example, when a client asks, "Should I quit my job?" you can respond using information you previously acquired and synthesized with today's problem: "You liked your job until you got new responsibilities. It could be helpful to talk about that shift; maybe it will clarify your options."

Use Metaphors and Analogies

Metaphors can provide a new way of looking at a situation. By objectifying the issue at hand, metaphors allow the message to bypass entrenched dysfunctional patterns and provide a chance to think about the problem in a fresh way. This helps clients gain a different perspective on themselves, their situations, and their resources, and allows clients to entertain alternative strategies and pose solutions to their problems.

Clients like metaphors because they are slightly distant from personal material, can be interesting and involving, and are less threatening and confrontational than direct statements. Metaphors simultaneously conceal and reveal. Metaphors and analogies can also appeal to people who are less amenable to oral communication and instead need visual or kinesthetic cues for them to be more involved in the therapeutic process. They can be important in working with difficult clients to enhance rapport, to make points, and to convey information in a nonconfrontational manner. The effectiveness of analogies is enhanced by choosing images that connect with the language and interests of your client, so that it relates to everyday activities.

Charlie

Jim's wife insisted he get therapy in order to save their marriage. She experienced him as rigid, cognitive, and instrumental. Jim and I talked about his approach to life and the success it brought him in his management position in a complex education system. When we got around to discussing his style at home with his wife and kids, he asked, "What's wrong with solving problems the same way at home?" This was a great question for him, bringing out both his confusion about life as well as his emotional frustration about adaptive and nonadaptive activities. I knew Jim was an avid golfer, and I said, "Jim, how many clubs are you allowed to carry in your golf bag?" At first he shook his head as if to reorient himself to this seemingly tangential question, and then he responded "Fourteen." I went on to say, "Would you ever consider playing a round of golf with only one club?" At this point, Jim got it. Smiling, he said, "Of course not. There is always a situation that requires different demands. Sometimes you need muscle and sometimes you need finesse." I could see him begin to think about interpersonal flexibility in the same way. We used this analogy of "the other clubs in my bag," and it served us well. Jim worked at being more versatile in interactions with his wife and family. Even his golf game improved, because he became more willing to shape his shots to suit the course and was more forgiving of himself when he made mistakes.

Practice the Soft Sell

Aggressive, high-pressure promotion of an idea is rarely effective in responding to client questions. Everyone has had the experience of entering a store to buy one item and being followed, badgered, and otherwise pressured to consider purchasing a ton of other things. Offering ideas in treatment has to be different from commission sales. Hard-sell responses can irritate clients, who then resist all therapeutic services by simply not returning to therapy. You might be able to convince a client of a certain position or belief in the short run, but words like "You must" or "You have to see" or "Any reasonable person in your position" remind clients of demanding parents and bosses. Furthermore, the ethical responsibility to promote client autonomy can be violated by the hard sell. Even more practically, if clients haven't owned the idea you are promoting, it won't stick.

Lead With Positives and Speak to Strengths

When you respond to client questions, and particularly when you respond to a query about a difficult concern, begin with a statement that lets your client know you are on his side. When your client understands that you are not there to cut him down, you have a better chance for collaborative conversations. It is helpful to acknowledge the adaptive context, contemporaneous or historical, of his actions rather than simply focusing on his shortcomings and maladaptive qualities. Similarly, you can note the strengths in a particular personality trait that may have gone awry. For example, "It seems like your positive quality of being open to others and interested in many different people can set you up for some very painful experiences."

Use Client Language When Possible

Use the language and terminology that your client uses. Changing your client's phrase from "cop" to "police officer," "daddy" to "father," "fight" to "argument," "disagreement" to "difference of opinion" changes the meaning, and although we might be all about changing meanings, language shifts disrupt the flow of the conversation. Clients use language in ways that is both important to them and that reveals their makeup. By staying with their words, you promote therapy as a deeply personal experience.

Linda

I worked with a vibrant 28-year-old woman who came in to treatment because she was mildly depressed. In the first session, she described her many varied activities and concluded with the off-handed comment, "I never drink with people I don't trust." I had never heard anyone phrase their drinking rules in that way, and my stomach knotted up. I filed the words away in my mind. Her nightmares started immediately and, three sessions later, she described an "incident" that happened 11 years earlier. She had gotten drunk while she was on a trip with her high school club and had been raped. Before she revealed the assault, I didn't know what secret she had carried for 11 years, but her language told me to listen hard to every discussion about alcohol and trusting people.

In the conversation where she told me about the sexual encounter, I mistakenly used the phrase "date rape" and she leaped off the couch in anger. I was startled by her reaction, but it certainly highlighted my error in thinking that we had conceptualized that encounter in the same way. For 11 years, inside her head, she had used the word "incident," never *rape*. The word *rape* conjured up an image of a victim, and that was not an accurate representation of her. The word was not used again until she introduced it months later when she felt strong and confident.

The exceptions to following your client's choice of words might be when the language obscures the meaning of the words (e.g., "hook up" means different sexual behaviors to different people), is disrespectful, ("my #%&*$% sister"), or when you are not comfortable with that particular characterization ("your snotty receptionist").

Clarify Jargon: Yours and Theirs

Lack of clarity and precision muddles therapy. You are in a profession where lots of terms can deliver many different messages. Because we seek greater understanding, you need to make sure that you and your client agree about terms and their meaning. For example, we have both listened to enough different translations of "borderline" or "abusive" that now we always ask for clarification. Jargon can act as a shortcut, and clients assume that you know exactly what they mean, but you don't. For our part, we attempt to use psychological terminology with clients sparingly. Generally, it is best to use only ideas that can be explained in plain English.

Avoid Sarcasm

Sarcasm is very common in casual conversations and can be a tempting response to some questions, but it is a form of humor that uses sharp, cutting remarks or language that mocks, wounds, ridicules, or shows contempt. It doesn't have a place in therapy. When you respond, you model interpersonal communication skills that clients will adopt and use outside of therapy. If you slip and inadvertently communicate in a sarcastic way, you can observe your own words aloud and rephrase them in a way that models comfortable self-reflection and self-correction.

When It Comes to Words, Saying Less Is Often More

Think about the point you want to make, choose your words carefully, and say them kindly. Using many words to respond can actually obscure clarity in your message rather than add to it. More words can often mean that you end up tripping over them and then the focus turns to you while you clarify your thoughts. Let your client be the person to add details and depth.

A Couple of Key Words

Therapy is an intimately collaborative process. Your words convey to your clients that they are not alone. The therapeutic relationship is based on "we" so use it, for example: "What can we learn about you from your reaction to the new rules at work." "We" goes a long way toward promoting the accurate notion that you and your client are working in a partnership. In the terminology of Harry Stack Sullivan, using the word "we" elevates you to being a fellow participant observer with your client.

If "we" is a word to include, "should" is a key one to eliminate. Should conveys the opposite of collaboration. Should reaches directly into your client's highly idiosyncratic, often dysfunctional, system of judgment.

We can assist clients by helping them identify their shoulds, to recognize their source, their functionality, and the degree to which they want to maintain or alter these schema for their personal well-being, but becoming our clients' next oppressive dictator is a position to avoid.

How Will I Know if My Responses Are Effective?

Once you take seriously the importance of answering questions in ways that further treatment, you will also become curious and concerned as to whether your responses make a difference. In general, we would look for the following indicators to let us know if a response is on the right track:

1. The response expands the *breadth* of material explored by the client so that she says *more* about her life and personal undertakings.
2. The response promotes the *depth* of areas explored so that a response leads your client to feel feelings *more deeply* and think *more complexly*.
3. The response helps promote the *connectedness* the client feels with you, so that your working relationship is further developed or maintained.

These considerations apply across theories. For brief examples, depth and breadth might be revealed in examination of relationship patterns (interpersonal therapy); cognitive distortions and positive thoughts (cognitive); family patterns (psychodynamic); systems awareness (feminist); knowledge of self and increased authenticity (humanists); or recognition and acceptance of individual and cultural differences (multicultural). Also, whichever your theoretical orientation, the third indicator of a successful response, greater connectedness, provides trust and security to proceed regardless of your techniques.

FURTHER THOUGHTS

In the previous sections, we suggested ways to think about and respond to client questions. We also recognize that each therapist needs to develop, own, and deliver her statements with a personal therapeutic style. Additionally, we also know from experience that each therapy is quite individualized and idiosyncratic: No two therapies are alike. Therefore, we expect that each therapist will consider our ideas in the context of her training and standards of care, as well as her clientele and what is effective with each client with his particular problems, culture, and individual differences. With these general ideas and particular considerations in mind, we move to 23 chapters that cover hundreds of commonly asked questions.

PART

2

Client Questions
and Responses
by Topic

INTRODUCTION TO PART 2

The clinical world changes when you leave the classroom and are at a placement. It changes even further when you start your job. The world of theory meets reality, sometimes in a collision rather than as a friendly greeting. As you work with clients, there are days when the discrepancy between ideas and real people seems unbridgeable, and you wouldn't be shocked if your head exploded and a million pieces of theory littered the room. Luckily, it doesn't take long before you begin to choose and select ideas and ways of understanding your clients. From then on, your identity development as a clinician becomes a smoother, more integrated, if ongoing, process and you move toward fulfilling your ambitions, dreams, and expectations. You become a clinician as you live out your commitment to and involvement in defining your new self. Your identity evolves as you acquire new skills, test ideas and techniques, gain confidence as you meet new challenges, make mistakes and recover, and discover what you do and don't believe. You have something very valuable in common with your clients: you are both trying very hard to become the best of you.

CHAPTER

1

The Early
Sessions

In these early sessions, you and your client are still strangers to each other and are at the start of a unique, intimate, life-changing relationship. Clients begin to develop a sense of you, just as you learn about them, and together the two of you begin to define the relationship. These first conversations set the stage for all the meetings that will follow.

Linda

Yesterday I received a voice mail from a woman who had been referred to me by a colleague. In the original message, she said, "I want to know if you have openings in your practice, but I also want to ask you some questions about your experience and your background." Her choice of words made me sit up and take notice. When I returned the call, we first talked about scheduling, then she asked, "Can you understand what it is like to be a working mother?"

(continued)

"Yes, I can," I answered. "Is being a working mother some of the reason that you want to come in?" "Maybe. My husband thinks so," she replied. Pause, tension in her voice. "But do you know what it is like to be a working mother?" she persisted. Phone questions from strangers, without context or visual cues, can be especially challenging.

That moment was a decision point. Do I answer directly or not? I already said that I could understand. I could reflect her concern by commenting, "Being a working mother must be very important to you," but what would be the point, so I answered, "Yes, I have been a working mother most of my adult life." Her voice relaxed, the tension was gone. Whether I had been a working mother or not, a direct answer was better than having her come in, ask again in a dozen ways, and perhaps be disappointed. There was an unspoken need for her therapist to be a working mother. If I had not been a working mother, I would have said, "I am not a mother but have worked successfully with many women who are." In this chapter and all those that follow, the best advice we can give you is to listen to what is said, and listen even harder for what is *meant*.

It isn't unusual for clients to have questions before they even come in to your office. Answer some of them, particularly if the questions are pressing, are about factual information, or are about business details. Other more clinical queries can be met with, "Let's save that for our meeting." When you answer questions, you demonstrate that you will try to be forthcoming and sensitive to their needs. But more complex questions, such as requests for specific treatments, medication referrals, or queries that require deliberation on your part, belong in your office where you have privacy, time, and attention. From the beginning, your communications reflect your attitude about boundaries, professionalism, and thoughtfulness.

Some clinicians would argue that Linda gratified the client with her answer on the phone, and they would have been right. But more important than a minor gratification, why wouldn't she answer that question at that time? By responding directly to the content and to the client's obvious concern, Linda had decided that the answer mattered, was not harmful, and that being a working mother/therapist was probably a deal breaker for this client just like being a Christian therapist, or a gay therapist, or a cognitive-behavioral therapist would have been for someone else. The importance of being a working mother was probably one reason that a colleague made the referral. This brings up a second point. Potential clients often look for therapists who meet certain criteria: older, younger, male, a behaviorist, a suburbanite, a *whatever* therapist. They imagine that they will be more comfortable or be understood better by a therapist who has those characteristics. Maybe they are correct and maybe not, but when we make referrals, we try to honor the requests and respect their legitimacy so that the client can comfortably begin treatment.

"Are you a working mother?" is only one example of the thousands of questions you will receive during your career. Whatever questions that you answer, or don't answer, we believe that your attitude in these early sessions is particularly important and that you remain polite, warm, and respond to questions such as "Where should I sit?" or "Did you take the photos in your waiting room?" as you would in any social situation. You want your clients to be comfortable.

Your answers in the beginning of treatment must keep two different, occasionally colliding agendas in mind: doing the business of therapy and beginning the emotional work of therapy. Portions of the early sessions may feel like they are exclusively business, but both lines of work go on simultaneously. If you can't talk straight about business, how can you talk about other delicate or emotionally charged concerns? If you can't hear your clients' fears and worries about pouring out intimate life details to a stranger, how effectively will you hear their other emotions later on? The manner in which you handle any topic early in treatment sets the tone for future interactions. The responses in this chapter address the inescapable fact that, in the beginning, you and your client are unfamiliar to each other, but you are prepared to engage in difficult, personal conversations. Clients ask some questions directly, whereas others are unspoken. Both types of questions deserve attention, and your replies are not simply answers to the content. Your responses begin to create a climate in which clients can express themselves and personal discoveries are encouraged.

In the early sessions, clients ask business and technical questions while others lurk just below the surface and include "Will this be a safe place for me?" "Can I trust you?" "Why am I talking to a stranger?" "Will you understand me?" "Am I normal?" "Am I a freak?" "What is going to happen?" "Is this going to be a waste of my time and money?" "Will you read my mind?" "Will you try to tell me what to do?" "Will you like me?" "Will I like you?" "Will you judge me?"

Some of these unspoken questions may be broached directly by gutsy or experienced clients, but whether or not they are asked aloud, these worries still swirl through your clients' heads. These same questions may arise in other contexts later on, and we will address them again as they apply to other topics, but here is where they are asked or not asked and answered or not answered for the first time.

QUESTIONS

If you work for an agency or other organization, they probably have rules and procedures about the early sessions, such as an initial evaluation, note taking, supervision, taping, fee setting, and insurance. Our ideas and suggestions about the early sessions are designed to complement your school or agency policies and give you some additional ways to think about clients' questions and your answers. The following questions are answered in the Responses section:

> **"What are your fees?"**
> **"Do you have a sliding scale?"**
> **"Do you take insurance?"**
> **"How often do we meet?"**
> **"Do you take notes?" "May I see them?"**
> **"Do you tape sessions?" "Why do you tape sessions?"**
>   **"May I tape sessions?"**
> **"What is your philosophy/theoretical orientation?"**
> **"How long does therapy take?"**
> **"What should I talk about?" "Where should I begin?"**
> **"Will you ask me questions?"**
> **"Do you understand what I'm talking about?"**
> **"Are there many surprises in therapy? Do you find hidden**
>   **memories?"**
> **"Can you help me?"**

RESPONSES

The first four questions—"What are your fees?" "Do you have a sliding scale?" "Do you take insurance?" and "How often do we meet?"—are primarily business and can be treated in a straightforward manner, but keep in mind, when you discuss appointment times and fees with clients, you set down your first expectations of your clients. Conversely, they also begin to gather a great deal of data about who you are and how you conduct yourself.

"What Are Your Fees?"

Do you set fees and collect payments or does someone else do that? If you set the fees, keep it clear. "Each session is $$. Sessions are XX minutes long. I prefer to be paid at the end of every session." or "I will bill you at the end of every month and would like to be paid during that following month." or "Our bookkeeper will be sending you the bill. Her name is Ms. X, in case you want to talk with her. She also handles credit card payments." Even if you don't collect the money, we believe it is preferable for you to retain some responsibility for fees, such as monitoring payment, because it is integral to treatment.

"Do You Have a Sliding Scale?"

Some therapists and agencies do, but others do not. Perhaps there is a discounted fee for students; maybe Medicare or Public Aid will be billed. Be clear about your policy and sensitive to the implied request for financial consideration. You could respond in a way that recognizes the unspoken issue, "I do (or I don't) have a sliding scale. Do you anticipate that you will have difficulty paying the fee?"

"Do You Take Insurance?"

Again, clarify the policy and explain your expectations. "Yes, I take Red Star insurance and I bill them directly. You are only responsible for your co-pay and any other charges, like a deductible, that they do not cover." or "No, I do not take insurance payments but will provide you with a bill that you can submit on your own." Whatever policy you or your organization has devised, make a habit of spelling it out plainly because this is a likely area for later confusion.

Many therapists prepare written lists that answer frequently asked questions about business-related concerns. They give this paper to each new client at the initial session. Printed materials are time efficient and clients can review them at their leisure, but papers don't replace discussions that are essential to building the process and the relationship.

"How Often Do We Meet?"

We tend to see people weekly, at least, at the beginning of treatment. If asked about meeting less often because of financial concerns, we say, "It might be better to save your money until you can come in weekly for a couple of months. If we meet less often in the beginning, we will never get to know each other well enough to make real progress, and instead we would spend all of our time playing catch up. It is not a good use of your hard-earned money. Later, we can be more flexible with sessions." If you have another policy, explain it to your client and add your rationale. This response explains why regular meetings are important. You also have the opportunity to explain your policy about missed sessions or late cancellations.

If the client asks, "How often do we meet?" because she is in crisis and fearful that she will not have enough time with you, you are answering an entirely different question. Then, we advise you to deal with the anxiety and come up with a plan that does not leave her without help in a crisis. That may involve an interim phone call, the number of a crisis line, or enlisting the support of her family, friends, or other professionals.

"Do You Take Notes?" "May I See Them?"

The next questions are less straightforward than the previous ones: "Do you take notes?" "May I see them?" "Do you tape sessions?" "Why do you tape sessions?" "May I tape sessions?" On the surface, the answers are simple; however, we would be wondering if, below the surface, the client is experiencing some anxiety and concerns about confidentiality or fears of being judged. In asking these types of questions, clients may also be wondering, "Can I trust you?" "Why am I talking to a stranger?" "Who do you talk to?" "Do you have a supervisor?" "Do you review your notes?" "Will this be a safe place for me?" You have to choose whether you also want to address the unasked questions when you answer. Whatever you decide, keep the underlying concerns in mind.

Answer clearly and explain that, "Yes, my notes are locked away and are used to help me remember material so that we can do our best work here." When clients ask about reading your notes at the very beginning of treatment, the question refers more to your policy than a request to read your file. "If you have any questions about my thoughts, I'm happy to answer them. I don't show my notes to anyone. You could legally request to see them, but I prefer that you do not. Are you worried about something?" Particularly in the beginning, when you are new to your clients, their apprehension or worry is at a peak. Trust begins now and becomes stronger as you continue. Also at this time, expressly stating who will have access to your notes and records in court-referred or non-voluntary cases acknowledges the reality of those situations and begins a relationship free from secrets or surprises.

Charlie

I have clients who jot down a thought or two during sessions, and I also write a few words or draw an idea for them on paper and hand it to them, but only Kathy started her sessions by opening her notepad and picking up a pen to signal that she was ready to keep a written record of our interactions. "I don't trust my memory. I want a record of our session so I can think about it." I initially found this process jarring. I had to resist the temptation to "play to the notebook." That is, I would often feel disappointed when I said what I thought was a kernel of wisdom and she did not write it down, whereas I was dismayed when she would jot down something that seemed rather inconsequential to me. (Heck, for all I know she was writing up her grocery list during our sessions.) Over time I got used to her keeping her own notes in our sessions, and I have wondered why other clients haven't done something similar.

"Do You Tape Sessions?" "Why Do You Tape Sessions?" "May I Tape Sessions?"

If you tape sessions, explain why, who listens to the tapes, and when they will be destroyed. You can ask, "What are your worries about taping?" and you may want to go further and wonder, "Are you worried about our sessions being listened to or evaluated?"

Linda

I had one client, a dedicated researcher, ask if *he* could tape our sessions. I was startled. I asked him why he wanted a recording, and he said, "I plan to listen to it during the week." I was skeptical but I agreed, saying, "I'll try it, but if it inhibits my comfort during the session, we stop." That was fine with him. He did tape and did listen during the week to remember the topics we talked about. Taping, listening, and reviewing information turned out to be very much in keeping with his personality and his approach to learning. I forgot about it. More often, this scenario happens in reverse. The clinician tapes the session, with varying degrees of self-consciousness on the parts of both participants, and the clinician reviews the recording later alone or with a consultant.

"What Is Your Philosophy/Theoretical Orientation?"

This question usually comes from clients who have some knowledge of treatment, have been in therapy previously, have read about it on the Web, or have been coached by experienced friends. They are not always sure why they ask you, but understandably, they are hoping to learn more about the work you will do together.

It's a good idea to develop an answer and keep it jargon free; clients don't want a lecture. Charlie usually answers, "I take a pretty psychodynamic and interpersonal approach to understanding the roots of what you are struggling with, and then together we will identify the best approach to help you move past your concerns." Linda also believes in keeping the answer brief and says, "I was trained psychodynamically and believe strongly that understanding is the key." For more sophisticated clients, she might add, "I especially like the feminist theories, relational psychology, and have been won over by the benefits of cognitive psychology."

Then, it is useful to illustrate how your theoretical viewpoint or techniques are specific to your client's situation. Calling up information that you previously received, you could explain, "You've said that you worry about failing at your job, so we would want to understand your thinking—what strategies you use, where they came from, how they serve and don't serve you, and what you might want to change about them." or "You said you are tired of being a doormat but don't know how to change, so our job is to understand what makes it difficult for you to speak up." In order to set the stage for the work to follow, you might add, "Everyone develops patterns of behavior. These may have started a long time ago, so we need to explore what gave rise to them and also what keeps them in place." If you plan to use specific techniques, this is a good time to describe them and explain how they fit into your treatment philosophy and, more importantly, why they are helpful to this client's particular problem. In general, in the first meeting we attempt to provide each client with our initial impressions or hypotheses about our understanding of their problems and how we plan to approach it, and then we ask, "How do these ideas sound to you?"

Clients want to get a sense of you (although some have probably Googled you before stepping a foot into your office), so many of these early questions or comments are wondering, "Who are you?" or "What are you going to do to me?"

"How Long Does Therapy Take?"

If you have a specific time limit, say, "We have 10 sessions, so we will focus on one problem that you choose to concentrate on." Or, if it is your placement, "We can work together until June but, if it seems wise to stop earlier, we will. We will decide that together." If there are no external constraints and you are not working within a time-limited model, you can say, "We will decide together when we are through. We will know when that time comes—you will be less troubled by the problems that brought you in."

"What Should I Talk About?" "Where Should I Begin?"

The last set of questions is more complex than those posed previously. In these questions, we can sense the client's apprehension, inexperience, or curiosity. All convey an element of fear. "What should I talk about?" "Where should I begin?" "Will you ask me questions?" "Do you understand what I'm talking about?" "Are there many surprises in therapy? Do you find hidden memories?" "Can you help me?"

We begin first interviews with the request for clients to talk about "What has brought you in?" or "What made you call at this particular time? or " I'd like to hear about the problems that brought you in." At some point, Linda also adds a simple framework, "We have 45 minutes to talk. I will watch the clock to make sure that you have time to ask me questions and I have time to give you some of my initial thoughts." Then she carefully follows the client's story. She also leaves time for handing out her take-home data form, setting the next appointment, and stating a few basic rules. If you work in an agency and have a long intake form that is required immediately, fill it out first, before you begin talking more freely. "Let's take care of this form so that it doesn't get in the way of our discussion." Also, if you are only doing an intake and will not be the therapist, say so at the outset: "I am here to get a sense of your problem and take care of the paperwork. Afterward, you will be given a therapist to work with on a regular basis."

The same question, "What should I talk about?" would be answered differently in later sessions. In future meetings, we would respond, "As you sit here, what's on your mind?" or "What are some of the things that are going on with you?" If we have already begun an important topic, we say, "I didn't think that we finished with the discussion from last week when we talked about person/event/emotion. What do you think?" or "You opened a number of doors last week; we can go through any of them." During these early sessions, and later on if it is true, you can suggest, "I thought that last week's conversation was very important, and it doesn't seem to me that we finished talking about family/mood/situation." If a topic is consistently avoided, you eventually have to say, "We haven't talked about your father/children yet. Have you noticed that?" If "What should I talk about?" is asked following a particularly difficult session, it is also a good idea to inquire "What was your reaction to last week's session? It seemed intense to me."

"What should I talk about?" asked by a hostile, or court-ordered, or family-mandated client requires some acknowledgment of the circumstances by suggesting, "I know it is not your choice to be here, but we could begin by talking about the *problem/behavior* that brought you here." When a person is an involuntary client, maybe even hostile, it is best to deal with that dimension of treatment up front. You can say, "I'm beginning to think that you don't want to be here," if you are testing the water. However, if you already know of your client's reluctance, go for it and say, "We both know that you don't want to be here" or "I understand that you are very reluctant" or "I know that therapy isn't your choice, but I want us to figure out ways to make it work for you."

"Where should I begin?" is a common question asked at the beginning of treatment. If your client is very anxious, be prepared to offer more structure. That may also be true in nontraditional settings. If your client is naïve about therapy, provide a beginning idea. When your client is struggling with what to say, you don't want to set off a panic attack; you want to get her talking freely. You can ask, "What is most pressing?" or "What brought you in at this particular time?" It is a good idea to begin with events that can be answered easily and successfully, for example, "Did something specific happen that brought you in?" or "We can start with some history. Tell me about yourself, where you grew up, that sort of thing." If the presenting issues are rather vague or long-standing, it can be useful to ask, "What led you to call me this week?

All of these suggestions can help clients learn to talk about themselves, but ultimately they are responsible for what they present. They know their concerns better than you do, and they will have to live with the results of their decisions. You can gently remind them of their responsibility by saying, "You know what is disturbing you better than I do. You are the pilot. I am your co-pilot." We want to let our clients know that although therapy is hard, active work, they are not alone. We frame our answers to begin to establish a collaborative relationship.

We always ask about prior experiences with therapy. We want to know if they found treatment helpful—a good sign for us—what they remember, what they learned, and what they thought was most useful. We are also concerned with any aspects of treatment or the treatment relationship that the client found unhelpful. Perhaps the most frequent complaints are that the prior therapist spoke too little, leaving the client feeling alone and unheard, or the therapist spoke too much, talking about herself and again leaving the client alone and unheard. We never badmouth previous treatment, even if it is tempting, unless an ethical or legal violation has occurred.

"Will You Ask Me Questions?"

"I can always help you if you get stuck, and I certainly have questions to ask, but you know your problems and your mind better than I do, so I will let you take the lead in the topics that we discuss." If this question persists week after week, we would probably inquire, "You often want me to ask you questions. Do you generally have trouble getting started?" We would also wonder if this client is generally hesitant to offer information. Perhaps he has learned that it is safer to respond than to initiate. It's an idea to keep in mind. Beneath questions that indicate reluctance, you may find unspoken concerns like, "What is going to happen?" "Will you read my mind?" "Will you judge me?" which are fears related to exposure. When clients talk freely, they begin to uncover new thoughts and put ideas together in new ways. It can be exhilarating or unnerving, or both. As experiences, thoughts, and feelings are revealed, your client becomes increasingly naked to both of you, so your reception and support is essential. Your honest, sincere curiosity about your clients is a wonderful gift and an important process to model for them.

You can see from our suggested responses to the last several questions that we try to provide answers while setting the stage for future sessions, explaining our expectations of treatment to our clients, gently making it apparent that entering treatment is an important responsibility, and hoping that we are beginning a strong collaboration.

"Do You Understand What I'm Talking About?"

This question asks you for more than reassurance; it asks you to summarize or reflect on the significant points that were brought up. When a client works to explain her world, she wants to know that you have understood. You can say, "I heard the following important concerns . . ." When you have reflected the main points, and perhaps addressed elements that put her story in perspective, she feels validated and usually amends those aspects of her narrative that need modification.

There will be times when the question, "Do you understand?" cloaks concerns about "Am I normal?" and more seriously, "Am I a freak?"

These questions can be answered, "I'm going to try my best to understand you. Tell me when I slip up." Or, if the client asks directly, "Am I normal?" we might reply, "I don't really use words like *normal*. I simply want to understand what is troubling you." or "You came here because you have some problems you want to work on. That takes courage." If your client has a good sense of humor, you might say, "Normal is a temperature." And, clients don't usually refer to themselves as freaks unless their self-image contains a deep flaw. Ask about strong characterizations such as "freak." "That's a strong statement. Why would you say that about yourself?" or "You seem to see yourself as a freak. I don't, but I want to understand where these ideas come from." More important than your specific words, your behavior demonstrates your desire to understand.

"Are There Many Surprises in Therapy? Do You Find Hidden Memories?"

The implication of this question, or others like it, may be that there is another, as yet unspoken, problem or that your client fears that he may uncover some long-repressed memory. Occasionally, it means that he is worried that you could plant some false memory during the course of therapy. These types of fearful questions often arise after a news story breaks in the media in which some innocent person is blindsided by previously unknown experiences. Words of gentle reassurance are in order, but don't make empty promises. You might say, "We will begin with the problems that we know about. If other concerns emerge, we will be ready to understand them as well. Hidden memories are unusual."

Near the end of the first session, it is a good idea to invite questions by saying, "I've been asking you questions; do you have any questions for me?" Sometimes, clients are startled. They did not come in with questions for you; they expected to be answering, not asking questions. In these instances, you can reassure them, "That's fine. This is not your only opportunity. If and when you have questions, feel free to ask them." When clients do have new questions for you, they tend to fall into several categories: they may want to discuss business details; they may want to know more about you (see Chapter 2, Experience, and Chapter 10, Personal Questions); and they may want to know what is going to happen (see Chapter 3, The Therapeutic Process).

Once in awhile, a client aggressively turns a question on you. Aggressive questions that occur in early sessions are rare but worth mentioning. Sometimes, it is not one hostile question but an excessive amount of questioning that reveals hostility, aggressiveness, anxiety, or it may be a way to deflect attention away from himself. These situations are disconcerting because you are thinking about ways to be helpful and suddenly you are met with aggression, resistance, or a mixture of both. Whatever the origin, you still have to deal with it. Start by assuming some fear or anxiety and answer one or two of the legitimate questions before observing, "You have a lot of questions. Are you worried about starting therapy?"

If, over time, the questions become a way for your client to avoid talking about himself, getting excessive advice, or demonstrating excessive concern with others, we would respond differently. First of all, we would tuck this hypothesis into our memories, because it may be a helpful theme later on, but in the moment, we might say, "I think you would rather talk about me than about you." Or, regarding the questions of a personal nature, say, "Wait, this is your session." or "Let's get back to you."

Every once in awhile you will get a straightforward aggressive challenge such as, "How do I know you are any good?" or "What makes you think that you can help me?" These questions are rare but, in the early sessions, they deserve an answer. "As we work together, you will decide the degree to which you trust me." or "You'll have your answer in a couple of weeks of working together." or "I've helped other people; why would it be different with you and me?" or "I'm not alone in this room; we are working together to help you." If you can remind yourself that your client has entered a process that will make him feel intensely vulnerable, your compassion will outweigh your defensiveness or your desire to aggress.

Linda

In all sessions, there is always the potential for one of my least favorite types of question, referred to as the doorknob question. It can be sprung after the first session or at any other time but is particularly disconcerting in the early weeks. For example, after an initial session filled with disclosures of childhood beatings, adolescent aimlessness, suicidal thoughts, and adult depression culminating with some wife swapping, Mike walked to the door, put his hand on the knob, turned around, and asked me, "Do you think I'm crazy?" I answered, "You have a lot of problems and we have serious work to do, but you're not crazy." He grinned. Other doorknob questions can only be answered with the promise that, "That question is too important for a quick response. We ought to start with it next time."

"Can You Help Me?"

While all of these questions and answers are going on and you are trying to figure out your client's problems, assess the severity and complexity, and decide how to be helpful, you also have another very important task in the early sessions. You have to give your clients realistic hope; you have to convey your confidence that, if they have courage and work hard, they can change their lives for the better. In that, you answer the most basic question, "Can you help me?" with the very honest response, "Together, we can help you."

Earlier in this chapter, we referred to underlying, unspoken questions and fears but rarely addressed them directly in our answers. During these early sessions, there is little point in answering most of these worries immediately. Concerns such as "Can I trust you?" or "Will you judge me?" and others are answered through your attitudes, behaviors, and as the trustworthy relationship develops.

FURTHER THOUGHTS

"The first step toward getting somewhere is to decide that you are not going to stay where you are."

—Unattributed

The initial meetings are a unique period of therapy—an encounter of strangers. As a therapist, over time you will come to know your clients deeply, but the first couple of meetings are about gathering information, entertaining tentative impressions, and beginning an alliance. For your clients, the early sessions are about getting comfortable with you and with this strange process. Many clients are anxious to get the first meeting over with, feel some relief, and leave with the hope that together you can make important changes. After the first session, more of the process is exposed, no matter what theory you work in. Your client learns more about the role of being a good client, and you become more secure in what you have to offer. But don't forget, in these early sessions you have a lot to offer as well—careful listening, nonjudgmental support, empathic understanding, thoughtful inquiry—all of which can be therapeutic.

Second meetings especially can be odd, because clients often have given you a lot of personal information, so they flop down and look at you as if to say, "Okay, I did my work last time, now it's your turn to work your magic." Continue to listen and conceptualize; don't try to become a magician.

Never lose your appreciation for the apprehension that clients feel upon entering into what is often a very foreign and threatening process to them. Always, always remember that it takes courage, and usually a large dose of discomfort and confusion, for clients to come in, talk to you, expose themselves, and ultimately create new understandings.

SUGGESTED READINGS

Feldman, T. (2002). Technical considerations when handling questions in the initial phase of psychotherapy. *Journal of Contemporary Psychotherapy, 32,* 213–227.

Ivey, A., & Ivey, M. B. (2003). *Intentional interviewing and counseling: Facilitating client development in a multicultural society.* Pacific Grove, CA: Brooks/Cole.

Pomerantz, A. M. (2005). Increasingly informed consent: Discussing distinct aspects of psychotherapy at different points in time. *Ethics & Behavior, 15,* 351–360.

Pomerantz, A. M., & Handelsman, M. M. (2004). Informed consent revisited: An updated written question format. *Professional Psychology: Research and Practice, 35,* 201–205.

Sue, D., & Sue, D. M. (2008). *Foundations of counseling and psychotherapy: Evidence-based practices for a diverse society.* Hoboken, NJ: Wiley.

Wachtel, P. L. (1993). *Therapeutic communication: Knowing what to say when.* New York, NY: Guilford Press.

Weiner, I. B., & Bornstein, R. F. (2009). *Principles of psychotherapy: Promoting evidence-based psychodynamic practice.* Hoboken, NJ: Wiley.

CHAPTER

2

Experience

Experience is never free. We paid with our sleepless nights, misgivings, and risks that failed or succeeded. We had days when we doubted our entitlement to sit in the clinician's chair, but the work rewarded us with some wisdom, insight, and confidence. While you are earning the history that will reassure you that you are a talented clinician, you are likely to judge yourself harshly. Therefore, as your confidence is developing, here is a kinder way to think about experience. You don't judge your clients; you admire their willingness to work honestly and be vulnerable to self-discovery. You are not disgusted by their lack of self-knowledge; you are impressed by their courage to step into unknown spaces. Treat yourself with similar esteem and respect.

Linda

In some situations, the question "Are you a student?" sounds more like an accusation than a query. I remember a fellow student years
(continued)

ago who developed the half-truth answer to the question, "Are you a student?" by tossing it back philosophically as, "We are all students, aren't we?" and there were occasions when I admit to using it. Another version of the answer was, "Yes, I am in training." Somehow, "in training" sounded better than "student," a label that conjured up recurrent nightmares of forgetting an assignment, losing the class location, or otherwise being unprepared and inept. All of these efforts speak to the desire for credibility.

Because they are seeking your help, clients will ask questions about your professional experience. Over time, the answers get easier, because you have taken advantage of opportunities to learn more, so you gain confidence in your areas of expertise. The horrified question that one graduate student asked, "What about clients who have more experience with therapy than I do?" sums up a fear of students and early-career therapists. And, it is true that some clients will have had more years in therapy than you have had in coursework, supervision, and practice. There is absolutely nothing you can do about it except to learn with them. The topic of experience is huge at the beginning of your career when you worry that you have little to offer.

It doesn't feel like there is anything noble about being a beginner—at anything. It is often embarrassing to be a novice. These feelings of insecurity can reemerge later in your career when you are faced with new issues or challenges. You will be confronted by complex clinical situations, be blindsided by events that you did not anticipate, have your work reviewed by others, and may have your clinical assessments disputed by clients and colleagues. If you decide to be a therapist who keeps an open mind and open heart to your client's experience, you are agreeing to spend your professional life at a certain level of unknowing.

All too often, students and early-career therapists suffer from the Impostor Syndrome. A description of the Impostor Syndrome has found its way onto Cal Tech's counseling website, www.counseling.caltech.edu/articles/The%20Imposter%20Syndrome.htm, which defines it as "a collection of feelings of inadequacy that persist even in the face of information that indicates that the opposite is true. It is experienced internally as chronic self-doubt, and feelings of intellectual fraudulence." Even Wikipedia.com has a page about Impostor Syndrome, so you know that you are not alone when you expect someone to tap you on the shoulder and call out, "What, are you kidding?" These pervasive reactions highlight the importance of being able to answer, or not answer, questions about your professional experience without being defensive.

Experience is important, but it isn't everything. Studies in this area demonstrate only a slight or moderate correlation between certain markers of professional experience (e.g., years in practice) with successful outcomes. What is likely to be more important than some external markers of professional practice is the personal experience that your client has with you at any given moment during your work together. The honesty, directness, connection, availability, curiosity, sensitivity, and trustworthiness that you demonstrate in the room with your client trumps the diplomas that you have hanging on your wall.

Confidence inspires confidence, so even if you don't have the full measure yet, enter the therapy room knowing that you are well-trained, will work hard, and will get consultation when you need it. During your years of training, you have gained experience asking questions, listening actively, and being fully present. Confidence doesn't mean that you know everything or that you are perfect. Confidence means that you have the right to acknowledge that you are prepared intellectually and emotionally and believe in yourself.

When clients question your experience, they are also admitting that they can no longer help themselves and need assistance. They hope that you can help them—and you can.

QUESTIONS

There is nothing terribly complicated about answering factual questions about your experience; it's simply uncomfortable to do so at the beginning of your career. Certain questions never cease. Clients ask about your qualifications because they are concerned about being understood and receiving adequate care. Therefore, the goals of the answers that we suggest are to create honest, comfortable responses for you and simultaneously to address your client's underlying questions of, "Do you know what you are doing?" and "Can you help me?" Remember that these questions from clients are only partially about you. Psychotherapy is a mystery to them, so they are curious and may wonder "What's the purpose of counseling?" or "Are you as unprepared for this as I am?" or "Can I trust you with my feelings?" The following questions are answered in the Responses section:

"What is your training?" "What are your credentials?"

"Are you a student?"

"Are you getting a doctorate?"

"Do you have special areas of expertise?"

"Have you ever treated anyone with my problems?" "Can you
   fix my (symptom)?"

"How long have you been practicing?" "How long have you
   been in this field?"

"Have you been in therapy?"

"Have you ever had (my problem)?" "What makes you think
   you can understand what I am going through?"

"How old are you?"

RESPONSES

The first three questions—"What is your training?" "What are your credentials?" and "Are you a student?"—are the easiest to answer directly. "I am a graduate student in psychology/social work/counseling." You may want to mention the name of the school. You may feel better adding, "I am in my third year of training." If you are out of school, you can say "I am not a student. I had 2/3/4/5/6 years of training in school, and I have been working for 1/2/3 years." To demonstrate that you understand the concern, you might ask, "Are you worried about my ability to understand and help you?" Don't pull out your resume and read to them line by line; that may calm your anxiety but not theirs.

Clients have the right to know certain things about you so that they enter treatment as informed participants. Informed consent is the translation of ethical principles into definite requirements. Historically, informed consent meant that you wanted the client to consent to proceed with treatment, but today it means that you disclose information that allows clients to participate knowingly. We have an obligation to make certain information available to clients so that they can make an educated decision about the process in which they will be participating. Many counselors hand out printed descriptions regarding elements of informed consent. All of the professional organizations have descriptions and information that is available to you, including American Counseling Association at www.counseling.org/resources, American Association for Marriage and Family Therapy at www.aamft.org/resources, National Association of Social Workers at www.socialworkers.org/pubs, American Psychiatric Association at www.psych.org/, and American Psychological Association at www.apa.org/.

When clients persist in asking detailed questions about ethics or credentials at the beginning of therapy, we explain, "I promise to save time for your questions about me, but let's begin with you so we both have a sense of where we are going. Okay?"

Charlie

When I began my first placement as a doctoral student, I was assigned to a pleasant couple who were struggling to manage their children's behaviors. During our first meeting in October, I stated that we would be able to work together through May. They asked how I could be so certain, to which I responded that I was a student in training, and May was when my placement ended at the agency. "Student? Oh, huh," was their response. I read their downturned glances as, "Hmmm, he will be of little value, competence, or skill. We are guinea pigs in the hands of this novice." We met together twice a month for the next few months, and in the back of my mind, I always imagined their sense of disappointment at getting a beginner.

With about a month left in my placement at this agency, I again mentioned my planned departure by reminding them, "As I said at the beginning of our work together, I will be leaving in about a month, as my training here will be over." They responded, "Training, what training? You didn't tell us that you were a student."

(continued)

I realized that my being a student had never really registered with them, and they had not seen me as incompetent nor poorly prepared. If I had been able to see that my insecurities were enhanced by their feelings of incompetence as parents, I would have been a more confident, effective therapist with them.

Charlie's example brings up another important point about experience. Early in your career especially, but it goes on forever, you will find yourself strongly identifying with some clients' problems, whether it is about low self-confidence, bad relationships, anxiety, or any other concern that emerges from your work together. You may be snagged by your own insecurities, like Charlie's experience. Also, your misplaced empathy and over-identification can show up more subtly, such as joining in a client's helplessness and despair. Either way, your effectiveness goes down if you get stuck in your world and your problems. This is the first place, but there will be others, where we pull out the well-worn admonition, "Clinicians need their own therapy."

"Are You Getting a Doctorate?"

Just answer simply with your professional degree. "I am." or "No, I am going to get an M.S.W./M.A./M.S." or "No, I've finished school and have my M.S.W./M.A./M.S." And, if it is true, explain, "I haven't decided about a doctorate. I'm enjoying the work I do now." Professional degrees usually mean more to us than to our clients, who rarely understand the differences among training programs.

"Do You Have Special Areas of Expertise?"

If you are in training, you probably don't have any special expertise yet, but you certainly have interests that are developed, and you can mention those. "I'm particularly interested in trauma or the psychology of men." or whatever it is that fascinates you, if it is relevant. If you are out of school, you may want to note, "A good deal of my training has been in cognitive-behavioral therapy." or "I've begun to specialize in OCD." or "I find myself drawn to couples therapy." or "I work primarily with children under the age of 13." Be honest. Also, consider your past jobs and where you are going professionally.

"I worked with children before I went to school and am specializing in that." or "I work with adults only and find that cognitive-behavioral therapy is very effective." If your interests and expertise match nicely with your client's stated problems, you might note that, for example, "I'm particularly interested in life transitions, and I believe that fits very well with the issues we have been discussing." or "I work with dialectical behavior therapy, and I believe that will be very helpful with your concerns." Even with areas of expertise, you are always treating a person, not a part or disorder.

"Have You Ever Treated Anyone With My Problems?" "Can You Fix My (Symptom)?"

Many people can have depressive symptoms or relationship problems or conflicts with family members, but their problems never seem identical to those of any other client. We are not working on a line of cars where the goal is similarity and all parts are interchangeable and any changes or upgrades are illustrated in a manual. Perhaps the best way to answer this question is to clarify the client's basic problems and comment on their uniqueness, thereby addressing both your understanding of the general dynamics and the importance of their individual personality and history. For example, "Yes, I have worked with other people who suffer from depression/are distressed by a breakup/have terrible bouts of anxiety. However, you are more than a collection of symptoms, and we will work together to figure out what helps you feel healthier." You can add specifics such as, "You have suffered some very important losses lately." or "You have coped well until this year." or sadly, "You have struggled with this problem for a long time, sometimes effectively and sometimes it has gotten the better of you." You may also want to address this question directly by asking, "Are you afraid that no one can help?" or "Are you concerned that I can't help?" Not to belabor the car metaphor, but it is useful to dispel the notion of fixing clients. If you want to fix people, you are headed for serious disappointment. This field is more like doing collaborative, complicated puzzles; it takes attention, tolerance, patience, cooperation, and cannot be completely controlled.

These questions also speak to your responsibility to learn more about the problems facing your client. This might mean getting help from supervisors, teachers, consultants, colleagues, books, and other resources. In order to treat Mai, a young adolescent, Linda steeped herself in information about Cyndi Lauper, including reading teen magazines, because the 13-year-old identified strongly with the pop star. Weekly, they talked about Mai's problems through discussions about Cyndi's life.

"How Long Have You Been Practicing?"
"How Long Have You Been in This Field?"

These are also business questions, but they don't feel like it when you are new. Instead of seeming like neutral curiosity, they can make you feel like your competence has been called into question. Occasionally, the inquiries are meant to dig at you, but unless you know for sure, you might want to ask, "Are you concerned about being in competent hands?" but first, answer, "I worked before grad school and have been practicing during the 1/2/5 years in my program." or "I've been doing clinical work throughout grad school." or "I did 1/2/5 years of clinical work in grad school and have been out since X."

"Have You Been in Therapy?"

This is not a frequently asked question, and we strongly recommend keeping your own therapy experiences private, maybe forever, but certainly until you know your client very well. Rarely can this question be answered affirmatively without an elaborate explanation that puts all the focus on to you. This information is not included in informed consent guidelines and, more significantly, it is not in the best interest of the client to have information about your treatment. You can respond, "I am a strong believer in therapy, but I don't discuss my personal experiences in that area." Keep the focus on your client; disclosure about a personal matter like therapy shifts the interest to you and burdens them with fantasies of your problems.

We also know that some clinicians are trained to normalize the experience of entering therapy and to let clients know that having their own therapy is a valued, essential component of their training. In these instances, you could say, "I am a believer in therapy and was trained in a program that encouraged/insisted on students having therapy. I certainly have used (would use) therapy."

"Have You Ever Had (My Problem)?" "What Makes You Think You Can Understand What I Am Going Through?"

Your answers here are dictated by your clinical judgment rather than by law or ethics. These questions are better answered by acknowledging the underlying concerns. "Maybe your question is whether or not I will understand (your problem)." or "I understand about depression/anxiety/ losses and believe that I can help you." or "You will know by the end of this session whether you feel comfortable and want to continue in treatment with me." We also do not believe that it is usually helpful to share your own struggles, such as, "Yes I have also suffered from a major depression/substance abuse." Stay in your chair. If the client presses you on your personal experience, you can respond, "I get it. You want to know that I will understand your (problem). I *am* pretty good at understanding, and you will be able to make sure that I get it."

Remember, everyone who has had an alcoholic father, a death in the family, an abusive relationship, a panic attack, or other problem has had a different experience from others who ostensibly went through a similar concern. Certainly, much of your understanding comes from events that occurred in your own life. More understanding comes from the universality of some experiences. However, your deep comprehension will come through your connection to your client and the cooperative, working relationship that you build together.

"How Old Are You?"

Children and adolescents often ask this question. We answer directly and in language suitable to their years. They probably ask about age because adults commonly ask them about age, and because everybody over 16 looks old to them. Unless you have strong reasons to do otherwise, answer and ask, "Does that seem young/old to you?" They are probably wondering about you; if they ought to place you more with older sibs or with moms and dads. Children and adolescents also feel free to pursue information, and it comes from curiosity more than challenge or skepticism; they are used to adults of all varieties.

It's doubtful that an adolescent or adult client cares about your exact age. More likely, you are being asked because you seem young or old to them. Younger clinicians get the question far more often than older therapists, but older therapists get the same question for the same basic reason, "Will you understand me?" You can respond, "I'm glad to answer, but why do you ask?" or "I'm not sure how my age matters, but I want to hear what you are worrying about." or "Am I a surprise? What were you expecting?" or "What were you hoping for?" Often, the age issue needs to be expressed and then it can be dropped, particularly when your client realizes that age doesn't influence your ability to listen and understand. Don't back away from the age question. After the question is asked and you have acknowledged the concern, you can respond, "Of course you want a competent therapist. Let's talk about why you are here, and we will be better able to assess if I can be of help to you." Skill and understanding does not particularly correlate with age.

Naomi Woods, a first-year graduate student

As a beginning therapist, and fresh from undergrad, I look my age—and counseling is a field where a few gray hairs serve you well. One question that I dread, and which has haunted me when clients terminate abruptly, is "How old are you?" When I first started seeing clients, I would straightforwardly answer, "I'm twenty-three." But my supervisor encouraged me to probe beyond the question. How was the client feeling about my age? Were they afraid that, because I was so young, I would be unable to help them? I was so nervous about them asking that I never delved into the feelings behind the question, and I think I lost several clients because of my lack of confidence.

We have also heard clients say that they are glad to see their therapist's youth (to therapists we supervise, not to us) because "that means you have been trained in newer techniques and you are not stuck in any old-fashioned ways."

FURTHER THOUGHTS

"Experience is not what happens to you. It is what you do with what happens to you."

—Aldous Huxley

As a clinician, you never have enough experience because each person you work with is unique. You learn from all of your clients: sometimes, you relearn ideas that you've previously thought about; at other times, you have new encounters. The person you see tomorrow will have a story unlike the one you heard today, and the two of you will create a different relationship. The same factors that make the practice of therapy endlessly fascinating also make it profoundly humbling.

Early-career clinicians and students worry about their lack of experience. Don't let your self-doubt interfere with your work. There can be advantages to having less experience: you have fewer expectations about people and the process, and that openness can be helpful to clients; you don't fall back on old stories (or clichés) because you don't have them yet; and, maybe most importantly, you are very present in the room and carry hope that positive change is possible. The ability to work hard and develop a trusting relationship does not correlate with experience. We value experience, but it isn't everything. Experience can provide a secure, accumulated base of knowledge on which to rely, but we also know that the freshness and wonder of the process was strongest when we were starting out.

You gain experience as you practice your craft. In school, in workshops, and through books, you learn theories and methods, but until you practice these activities, they don't belong to you. You are a renter, not an owner. You can gain additional fundamentals of clinical work through self-reflection, but you have to give it a try in the real world, over and over, sometimes succeeding, sometimes making mistakes, getting constructive feedback from others, and always building your knowledge and your identity as a clinician. You will claim your profession as a therapist through practice, continued learning, attention, and an open mind.

SUGGESTED READINGS

Ackerman, S., & Hilsenroth, M. (2003). A review of therapist characteristics and techniques positively impacting the therapeutic alliance. *Clinical Psychology Review, 23,* 1–33.

Fisher, C., & Oransky, M. (2008). Informed consent to psychotherapy: Protecting the dignity and respecting the autonomy of patients. *Journal of Clinical Psychology: In Session, 64,* 576–588.

Sandell, R., Carlsson, J., Schubert, J., Broberg, J., Lazar, A., & Blomberg, J. (2002). Varieties of psychotherapeutic experience. *European Psychotherapy, 3,* 3–16.

Sandell, R., Carlsson, J., Schubert, J., Broberg, J., Lazar, A., & Blomberg, J. (2002). Varieties of therapeutic experience and their associations with patient outcome. *European Psychotherapy, 3,* 17–35.

CHAPTER

3

Therapeutic
Process

It's always an honor to be invited along on a client's journey. Over the years, that fact never changes. People come in and want to know what therapy will be like, but it's impossible to predict any client's personal experience. Along the way, they discover or rediscover themselves and come to their own understanding of therapy. Throughout, you remain close to your clients' experiences and become a strong partner in their development.

Linda

Every week for an entire year, when I met Ed in the waiting room and walked him back to my office, he said, "I've got a joke for you," and proceeded to tell me some hilarious joke and I laughed heartily. Then we entered my office, settled down, and talked about his sad, confused feelings and messed-up relationships. Ed allowed himself to be exposed and often ashamed during these conversations. Then, the session ended and he left. I never referred to or interpreted the presession jokes. I always understood that when we walked in and walked out we were two equal adults. He was a grown man who could entertain and amuse me. Although, in clients' minds, the therapy process goes on seven days a week, at home, in the shower, in the car, and in other conversations, the sessions remain safe because they are physically bound by the walls of the consulting room.

People take risks when they enter therapy because they are stepping into unknown personal territory, and neither of you can predict what will be uncovered. Clients sign on to a process that most of them don't understand. Different theoreticians and researchers who study the process emphasize different elements of therapy as responsible for growth, so it is reasonable that your clients wonder what will happen during these meetings and how their lives will change. Most experienced clinicians believe that clients' understanding and investment in the process is increased when they have some knowledge of what will happen. The therapy process is your domain. You can be more forthcoming in explaining this area than when you are venturing into worlds that belong to individual clients. Neither of us has ever tried to fully describe the process to clients, but we keep the elements—relationship building, assessment, goal setting, intervention, and termination—in mind as we answer their questions.

Relationship building refers to the rapport and therapeutic bond that develops between the two of you. Assessment, which includes formal and informal means of information gathering, involves determining the psychological status of your client through observation, interview, life history data, or assessment instruments. When you set goals, the two of you think through the cognitive, behavioral, and/or affective changes to be made. As with assessment, the formality of goal setting can range from formal contracts to informal, shifting agreements. Intervention includes the techniques you use to meet the agreed-upon goals and can range from interpretation and empathy to didactic statements to structured plans that involve work both in and out of sessions. Finally, termination is the last portion of your time together during which the two of you usually focus on review and separation.

By definition, the process is dynamic. The relationship will change, as all relationships do; your clients' initial goals may be modified as they understand themselves better and feel increasingly safe with you; and your interventions evolve as you deal with the situations discussed in your office. Therapy grows and changes just like other healthy endeavors.

QUESTIONS

By the time a client has found his way into the seat across from you, he has probably exhausted his personal resources, attempted many solutions, and made an effort (maybe many efforts) to get help. As clinicians, we take these efforts very seriously, so when clients want to know what is going on or what will happen next, we want to answer in ways that set realistic expectations, provide hope, and explain enough about the therapeutic process to have an informed partner in the room.

The counseling process will remain a mystery to most of your clients. We have all studied the process in depth and it still feels confusing at times. That's okay. You probably drive a car expertly without having had an extensive education about its assembly. Similarly, people can be successful clients without the readings, but many are curious about what to expect and want confirmation that you will be a good guide. At first, the process may be disruptive to some clients, but as they continue, they realize that self-awareness leads to greater, long-lasting security. The following questions are answered in the Responses section:

> "Why is it different to talk to you than to my best friend?"
> "Would I be doing the same things if I was working with a different therapist?"
> "I don't believe in all this therapy crap. What do you think about that?"
> "Is this like the television shows?" "Are you going to be like Dr. Phil or Dr. Laura?"
> "What if I don't have any big problems, but I just want to feel better about myself?" "What is it exactly that we do here?"

"How are you going to help me?"

"Will I cry?"

"What if I lie to you?"

"Is this what I'm supposed to be talking about?"

"Is this what we are supposed to be doing?"

"My friend called me passive-aggressive/paranoid. What does that really mean?"

"Can I see you more often than once a week?"

"Are you going to give me tests?"

"Are you going to give me a diagnosis?" "What do I have? Is it permanent?"

RESPONSES

"Why Is It Different to Talk to You Than to Talk to My Best Friend?"

This question is a good reminder that the relationship between you and your client is important during all phases of treatment. We are impressed by the thorough and consistent research evidence that supports a strong correlation between having a positive therapeutic alliance and positive client outcomes in therapy. The personal, human connection, regardless of different perspectives of psychotherapy, is at the core of clinical work.

Clients don't know it when they first walk in, but they are about to create a very important, unusual relationship. They simply feel grateful when the two of you work well together; you conceptualize it as a positive therapeutic alliance. Comparing you with a trusted friend is reasonable, and you can clarify the nature of treatment by saying, "Talking to your best friend can be very helpful, but that doesn't make it therapy. It means you are lucky to have a good friend." or "You come in here as an expert about your life. I come in here trained with knowledge about therapy. We put these two pieces together. That doesn't happen outside." You may also want to acknowledge the uniqueness of the therapy process, for example, "Because you can trust that everything that we talk about will stay in this room, our relationship is pretty unique." or "This relationship is confidential. You can't always be sure of this with other relationships." You provide the nonjudgmental context that allows your client to be open to previously hidden, frightening aspects of herself. You offer the necessary emotional support and aid the process of self-examination.

You can also draw other comparisons to friendship. "Even when friends love you and want desperately to help, they have their own agendas and they often want a certain outcome. I want us to understand what is going on for you, and I don't benefit other than seeing you work in your own best interest." or "In here, the focus is on you; we don't split the session with half for your problems and half for mine." This safety and attention promotes the therapeutic alliance, which, just like other important relationships in your life, you must build, maintain, and modify during the entire time that you work together. We offer this array of potential answers so that you can respond to the question and also intentionally clarify the nature of the alliance with this client.

Every once in awhile, this question, "Why is it different to talk to you than to talk to my best friend?" will be hostile. Perhaps you are working with someone who was coerced into treatment and doesn't care about an alliance with you. She may be indifferent, aggressive, or unable to form attachments; this may be temporary or permanent. You will feel differently about these clients, and you may be disappointed, but your work remains the same.

"Would I Be Doing the Same Things if I Was Working With a Different Therapist?"

Acknowledge the type of treatment that you do; you don't have to explore what everyone else might do. For example, "We are going to work in a method called cognitive-behavioral therapy." or "I believe in working toward understanding your life and family history as the first step to change. Other therapists work in different ways." But clients are not only asking about your technique; they wonder what to expect from the relationship, so consider addressing that matter, too. "Therapy has similarities to other relationships. Think of it this way: You go on a trip with one friend and have a certain experience. If you go on the same trip with a different friend, you will have an experience that is similar in certain ways and different in others. Not always better or worse, but the two of you create something unique." You have answered your client's question and simultaneously drawn attention to the uniqueness of the relationship that you create together. The process is an evolving interaction of relationship and technique.

"I Don't Believe in All This Therapy Crap. What Do You Think About That?"

Lack of knowledge about the counseling process doesn't stop clients from anticipating their experiences. When you receive questions like the ones that follow, you are hearing their expectations and uncertainties about treatment. "I don't believe in all this therapy crap. What do you think about that?" and "Is this like the television shows?" and "Are you going to be like Dr. Phil or Dr. Laura?" are questions that speak to general expectations, although in different ways. Usually, expectations remain vague but can be inferred through these types of questions. You can redress any misconceptions and clarify the reality of the therapy process with your responses.

There are many expectations embodied in this dare. This client expects little help, perhaps because of pessimism, excessive independence, or difficulty being collaborative; it is too soon to tell, but you are being challenged to defend your work. This is a great example of a question that does NOT require engagement. You are not in the room to arm wrestle or defend your profession. In fact, the opposite response might be more effective. File away the information you have received. This pattern will repeat later on, and you will have more to work with at that time. Right now, it is enough to understand that this client will confront you and is skeptical about treatment. As treatment unfolds, you will learn more but, for now, reply with, "You're allowed to believe whatever you want. Let's talk about the problems that brought you in, and then later on you can decide what you think about therapy."

What follows is a terrific example of the launch of therapy. The client is simply being himself; the experienced psychologist has insight into the situation and how to handle it.

Jeremy Bloomfield, Psy.D.

Steve is 55 years old, an executive with a furniture company, and has a serious anger problem. His wife called for him, and on the phone,

(continued)

she recounted several incidents in which he felt hurt, blew up in anger, and alienated himself from others, quitting committees and leaving social groups. Steve showed up for the appointment. He was very reasonable in our meeting and acknowledged his anger, saying that he cannot calm down until he physically breaks something. If he is home, he has another solution—he stares into the mirror and castigates himself. During the course of our meeting, I also realized that he is very rule driven; he lives by his rules, including a self-imposed punishment of putting $100 into savings when he loses his temper.

At the very end of the first session, Steve stared at the chair I was sitting in and said, "One thing that is going to drive me crazy is the tag hanging from the bottom of your chair. The only reason it says not to remove is for the retailer, not for you. You know that you can remove it?" The session was over, and I acknowledged his comment, but I did not add to the dialogue nor respond to the implied directive to remove the tag. I felt comfortable knowing that I didn't need to do anything, but I've been thinking about his comment since he left. It intrigues me. This was only a first session, so I have to think even more carefully about how to respond. Do I remove the tag? If I remove the tag, does that say that he intimidated me or that I will shy away from evoking his anger? Or, if I remove the tag, does it say that I heard his concern and will respond to his needs?

My initial idea was to do nothing, see how he responds, and allow the issue to remain alive. It would be easy enough to bring attention to his concern about rules and tags and even to relate this to his struggles with anger. Yet I feel there is something important about the bind I'm in, and so I think what I will do is present both sides of the dilemma to him (instead of mulling over my choices), and we can talk about it and explore his ideas and decide what to do together.

An experienced clinician like Jeremy thinks about these odd comments, like a removable tag. He knows that he has gotten a small glimpse into Steve's thinking and will use that information, one way or another, to help the treatment.

"Is This Like the Television Shows?" "Are You Going to Be Like Dr. Phil or Dr. Laura?"

Therapy is private, often secret, and difficult to describe even when you try, so people don't know what to expect. They may have gathered all of their beliefs about treatment from TV and the movies, the media version of counseling where every problem is solved in one hour, minus commercial breaks. Whenever a successful show features a therapist, clients talk about them. Often, the associations are favorable, like the therapist in *The Sopranos* or in *In Treatment*. However, you will also hear about a movie therapist who sleeps with her clients or another who turns out to be a serial killer, so ask for details. References to TV and movies reveal clients' expectations. You can ask, "There are a lot of television shows and movies that feature therapy. Which ones were you thinking about?" You will gather needed information from your client's answer. Then, you are in a position to address the comparisons, fears, or hopes. Once you have a sense of her expectations, you can explain the differences between the TV therapy and your work together.

"What if I Don't Have Any Big Problems, But I Just Want to Feel Better About Myself?"

This is another question that speaks to misinformed expectations, as do the variations, "Do I have to be crazy to be in treatment?" or "Are my problems worthwhile?" or "Should I take care of my problems myself?" You didn't arm-wrestle the challenging client, and you don't need to oversell this one; just reassure him that therapy is not just for so-called crazy people and, "Of course you are allowed to want to feel better about yourself." or "You don't need big problems to be here." Or, address the unspoken fears of dependency by saying, "It can take more courage to get help than to go it alone." Then turn it back to him and get to work: "What do you want to feel better about?" or "Tell me some of the things that you want to change." You can build on his hopes and model an attitude of openness as you encourage him to settle in so the two of you can talk about any and all facets of his life.

"What Is It Exactly That We Do Here?"

When clients ask this question, there will be days when your mind snaps to the response, "Your guess is as good as mine," but that is inaccurate and glib. It does, however, speak to the complexity of the process. When a client is new to treatment, answer generally, for example, "We talk. We discuss the things that bother you, and together we try to understand and then figure out what to do." If you plan to use specific techniques, describe them to your client. Explain your treatment protocols, such as hypnotherapy, time-limited CBT, interpersonal process therapy, or others in a way that presents your reason for the selection, lets your client know what to expect, and explains the procedures. If you have not decided what technique is most suitable with this client, you may need more information before you answer: "Tell me more about your problem, and then I'll be in a better position to answer this question with you."

"How Are You Going to Help Me?"

More than asking for a technique, this question is usually about sharing fears and confusion. "As you talk in here and we know more about you and your life, we can better understand what distresses you. Then, you can make clearer decisions about what to do." People often feel lost at the start of treatment, and it is your job to remind them "You are not alone. We will work together."

On the other hand, if this question is a sincere inquiry about your plan for treatment, in the spirit of informed consent, you have an ethical obligation to also provide the client with alternatives to therapy with you, such as medication, therapy with another person who would undertake a similar process as you, therapy with a person who might undertake a different technique, or no treatment of the current concerns. When a client is engaged with you, our experience tells us that he is not looking to change therapists; after all, he could just stop coming in. He is seeking greater understanding. Explore the context for the question and answer him honestly. Your openness matters.

Charlie

At the end of intake sessions with clients I sometimes say: "One way to think about what we do here is a jigsaw puzzle. Today we started to look at many of the pieces. We turned some of them over, and we put some colors together into piles with similar colors. As we continue to work together, we will look for straight-edge pieces or similar colors to put the picture together so it makes more sense for both of us and we know more of what things look like for you." This explanation seems to resonate with clients by giving them something familiar with which to compare treatment, and likely something with which they have had success. It also does so in a way that they can appreciate that the process will take time and progress may come in fits and starts. For the appropriate client, I sometimes add: "Lots of people are like a thousand-piece puzzle, you are more like a three-thousand one," and people seem comforted that they are seen as complex and their problems are not minimized.

In deciding the answer to "How are you going to help me?" you will also take other variables into account. For exmaple, your client's level of functioning, the setting, the treatment modality, and your client's ability to think abstractly will all influence your response. If, and it is uncommon, the question "How are you going to help me?" is aggressive, you are better off observing that aloud before continuing, for example, "You sound skeptical." or "You don't sound hopeful."

"Will I Cry?"

This question always seems best to answer with, "Probably, and that's okay, we have tissues. You may experience all kinds of feelings, and they are all okay." This response normalizes the client's emotions and gives him permission to cry without feeling ashamed. Over time, therapy evokes the range of feelings from sadness and loss to anger to happiness and to a sense of confidence. All emotions have their place in your consulting room.

"What if I Lie to You?"

This is a fascinating question because really proficient liars don't inquire first. This is a client who is struggling with his levels of disclosure. "You can. I'll never know and I'm not here to be a cop. But it makes absolutely no sense to lie to me—it would be like lying to yourself." or "How

can we ever help you if you lie?" or "Therapy is a place that teaches people how to be honest; it is a better way to proceed." or "You don't seem
like a professional liar to me. I can only guess that you are deciding how
much to trust me." And you might follow with, "That's a strange question; what made you ask it?" In supervision about specific cases, clinicians have asked each of us if we think that their client is lying to them.
We advise them to work with the material that their client presents,
today's truth, lies, or a mixture of the two. As you come to believe that
your clients have the major responsibility for the course of treatment,
you will relax about issues of veracity.

"Is This What I'm Supposed to Be Talking About?"
"Is This What We Are Supposed to Be Doing?"

You have spent years training to be a therapist, and you want to be
a good one. The person sitting across from you wants to be a good client.
Some will have questions that speak to a concern or fear about being
a good client. The questions in this section are about the process, but
this question and others also reveal naiveté. They need to be answered
with reassurance and without subjecting your client to extensive lectures. Treat these questions as examples of anxiety and respect the power
of encouragement. "You are talking just fine. If I have a question or want
to switch our direction, I'll jump in." or "I want you to talk about the
matters that are present in your head, so this is good." or "Yes, this is
what we are supposed to do; talk, figure things out, and try to understand
your thoughts and feelings."

Similarly, queries like, "Is now a good time for me to be in therapy?" can be confidently responded to: "I'm sure this is a good time to
be in therapy or you wouldn't have taken the trouble to get started."
Validation of your client's experience goes a long way. If she reveals self-
doubt, file this information away for a later conversation. Some of the
most courageous people you will ever meet will be seated in your office.
Acknowledge health, good decisions, and spunk when you see it. Clients
are probably already well aware of their foibles and don't need more
reminders. Your words assure clients that, although they have to do the
heavy lifting, their efforts do not go unnoticed.

On the other hand, if, "Is this what I'm supposed to be talking about?"
or "Is this what I'm supposed to be doing?" occurs later intreatment and

reflects a lack of involvement in the change process, you might answer differently. You can speak to her potential (rather than your own frustration): "Although I do hear you talk with greater clarity than when we first began talking about this topic, I also hear some reluctance to going further." or "That makes me wonder if you could be achieving more in this area if you took more risks/extended yourself further. What is holding you back?" Clients with whom you have established trust will experience your accurate challenges as empathic understanding rather than impatient attacks.

"My Friend Called Me Passive-Aggressive/Paranoid. What Does That Really Mean?"

With the final set of questions, your client is asking about a specific dimension of the process, that of assessment. "My friend called me passive-aggressive. What does that really mean?" "Are you going to give me a diagnosis?" "What do I have? Is it permanent?" "Are you going to give me tests?" "Can I see you more often than once a week?" Whether you do a formal assessment or not, the notion of judgment or evaluation is in the room, needs to be addressed, and can be done in ways that provide additional benefits to the treatment process.

You can ask for the story behind this lay diagnosis, and then you will gain a real example from your client's life that provides information. Anytime a client brings in third-party reports about behaviors in her life, whether it is a promotion at work, election to a leadership position in an organization, or feedback from a partner, you have an opportunity to compare these views with your own observations. Whether the outside diagnosis is accurate or not, it probably has some relevance and can help both you and your client further understand some aspect of the client's personality, behavior, or relationship.

Choose the important aspects of the story and say, "When you didn't return your friend's phone call, your behavior struck her as passive-aggressive, meaning that you acted in a hostile way but cloaked it in passivity. Does that make sense? Do you think that you do things like that?" Or, for "paranoid" we might say, "Sounds like when you were questioning the motives of your coworker, your friend thought you were reading too much into his action. Do you think there is anything to that?" Examine the behavior, whatever the supposed diagnosis is, with a nonjudgmental attitude, and the two of you can puzzle over it together. Use the story and leave the DSM on the shelf.

"Can I See You More Often Than Once a Week?"

At this point, we are considering this as another assessment question. There are good reasons for a client to suggest additional sessions either temporarily or permanently, but, if you work for an agency, be sure that it is okay before you commit. Either way, attempt to discover your client's motivation. "It may be possible, but why are you suggesting it now?" or "How do you think it would be useful for us to meet more often?" or "Tell me how this idea came about." Then you can decide, knowing that treatment is more intense when you meet with greater frequency. If you think the intensity will not be useful, you could use the analogy of not being able to do an intense physical workout every day without hurting yourself, as people's muscles need time to recover from being stressed. Or, if increasing the frequency of session seems unwise for any number of reasons, say, "Let me think about it and get back to you next week." or "I understand your thinking, but we are better off keeping this schedule because you seem to have plenty to be working on between sessions." If meeting more often is indicated then, "That seems like a good idea to me. Let's try it and see if twice a week works."

"Are You Going to Give Me Tests?" "Are You Going to Give Me a Diagnosis? What Do I Have? Is It Permanent?"

These questions all have a medical feel, such as a patient asking her physician, "What affliction do I have and what pills do I take?" If you assess clients with instruments, explain the procedures and move forward with them. If not, say, "No tests, we talk to get our information. I'm certain that we can uncover all that we need to know." Questions about diagnosis are asked because of curiosity, fear, and insurance. Explain your procedures about diagnosis. When you decide what that diagnosis is, talk it over with your client. Use plain language, back up your conclusions with information you have received, and be respectful. "I will be putting a diagnosis of XXXX on your insurance form/agency record/file. What this means is . . ." Be sure to check in with your client about what she is learning and understanding because these unfamiliar terms describe personality traits or behaviors that have great importance to her.

Charlie

I always share with my clients the diagnosis that I will submit to their insurance agency. I believe they have a right to this information. I use both official and plain language in ways that communicate my understanding of their struggle and have found that clients are usually relieved and gratified by having me communicate an accurate understanding of the concern with which they have been wrestling for some time. One time when I was sitting across from a muscular, tattooed man who suffered from extreme outbursts of destructive anger, I had doubts about whether he would find my diagnosis of intermittent explosive disorder comforting, or whether he would use his massive forearms to rip my head off. I began by saying: "Luke, there are at least three disorders that might describe to your insurance company what you are being treated for." I described how he might fit an adjustment disorder with mixed emotional features or dysthymic disorder (with agitated symptoms). I went on to say: "I think the most accurate diagnosis would be intermittent explosive disorder, which means . . . ," and I explained my differential diagnosis. I feared that he would act out his pathology in that moment, but instead he leaned forward and said with relief: "Oh, thank god!" After I asked what he meant, he explained: "I figure if you have a name for this condition then I am not the only one who suffers from it, and I also have to figure that you have some way of helping me get over it. I should have come here a long time ago."

Your client may come in and tell you that he has received one or more diagnoses previously. We listen to the names of these diagnoses and add the information to our own thinking. You can respond by commenting "Does that diagnosis seem like it fits you?" or "I'll keep that in mind and we can talk about it whenever we need to." Diagnosis is important for treatment planning and whenever you are working with medications. You don't have to feel chained to a previous diagnosis, but another clinician, who was also working hard, came to this conclusion, so it is worth some contemplation.

The fears and hopes revealed in all of these questions allow you to clarify and encourage collaboration and to address the responsibilities that each client must accept. In responding to the questions about the therapeutic process, instill your answers with equal parts of optimism, encouragement, and the reality that it is difficult to feel, think, and behave in new ways.

FURTHER THOUGHTS

> "It's not too difficult to get the skeletons out of the closet with people, but to get the gold out is a different matter. Psychology is the art of finding the gold of the spirit."
>
> —Robert Johnson

You cannot appreciate the exposure that your clients will endure in order to grow until you have tried it yourself. As therapists, we need to experience our own therapy in order to identify with the process and with our clients' experiences of trying to reveal themselves to us and to themselves. We don't want you to become clinicians who "do" something to others; we want you to be in a relationship that appreciates and relates to the other person's struggle.

Linda

I began my own therapy during graduate school, and the night before my first session, I spent most of it in the bathroom throwing up. I knew that I would take therapy seriously (that was me); I had no idea what I would talk about, and I was terrified. Now, looking back, I realize that on some level, I understood my life was going to change.

Within limits, therapy is a unique, unpredictable process. We educate people a bit in order to get a collaborative relationship going, but the whole of it cannot be taught—it needs to be lived. People learn by participating, by testing a new hypothesis about their own life or trying a new behavior and seeing what happens. Therapists who want to control the process can stifle much of the spontaneity with too many instructions, too much education, and too much talk. If you listen closely enough, clients will tell you, one way or another, where the damage has been done and what they need in order to adapt and grow. Through your attention, work, and commitment to the process, you communicate to clients, "I see you as a person of value."

SUGGESTED READINGS

Ablon, J. S., Levy, R. A., & Katzenstein, T. (2006). Beyond brand names of psychotherapy: Identifying empirically supported change processes. *Psychotherapy: Theory, Research, Practice, Training, 43*, 216–231.

Hilsenroth, M. J., Cromer, T., & Ackerman, S. (in press). How to make practical use of therapeutic alliance research in your clinical work. In R. Levy, J. Ablon, & H. Kaechele (Eds.), *Evidence-based practice and practice-based evidence: Psychodynamic psychotherapy in process*. New York, NY: Springer Press.

Martin, D. G. (2010). *Counseling and therapy skills* (3rd ed.). Long Grove, IL: Waveland Press.

Prochaska, J. O., & Norcross, J. C. (2002). Stages of change. In J. C. Norcross (Ed.), *Psychotherapy relationships that work: Therapist contributions and responsiveness to patients* (pp. 303–314). New York, NY: Oxford University Press.

Waehler, C. A., & Lenox, R. A. (1994). A concurrent (versus stage) model for conceptualizing and representing the counseling process. *Journal of Counseling and Development, 73*, 17–22.

Weiner, I. B., & Bornstein, R. F. (2009). *Principles of psychotherapy: Promoting evidence-based psychodynamic practice* (3rd ed.). Hoboken, NJ: Wiley.

CHAPTER

4

Expectations
About
Change

You have a lot in common with your clients. During clinical training, you have to give up some aspects of who you have previously been in order to find out who you might become. In therapy, your clients will have to face the same sort of change. Many of the familiar personal attitudes, beliefs, and behaviors that keep them comfortable have to be reevaluated and, in some instances, surrendered. At these times, when clients are required to change, they realize their attitudes and behaviors are not like a pair of slippers they are able to slide on and off but are more frightening to shed and difficult to alter. Knowing this, you can be more empathic to your clients and the difficulty of their work.

Linda

I used to tell a lie (I don't say this anymore) to clients in the beginning of therapy. It would occur after we had talked about aspects of their lives that they said they wanted to change, whether it was emotions, personal behaviors, or interpersonal relationships. If someone asked, "What if I don't like the change?" I often responded, "Then you can change back." This is not true. They certainly can continue to change, but the idea of undoing change, as if you were untying a shoe, is equivalent to unknowing. How can you reclaim unknowing?

Your beliefs about change will determine your attitude about answering questions. You want to instill hope in your clients, and they need it, but be careful about making prognostications such as, "It takes at least 21 days to change a habit." or "it takes a year to solidify new behaviors." Until you know your client, understand the desired change, the history of the behavior, the type of experience being addressed, and contextual factors, it is unhelpful to talk too much about internal resolve, environmental adjustments, awareness, focus, willpower, commitment, practice, or perseverance.

We don't expect you to be locked into one theory exclusively, and we don't know many people who are, but theory does provide a perspective from which to conceptualize client dynamics. There are many good theories about how people change. However, answering questions about change and what clients can expect is far less intellectual and comes from joining with their individual experiences and their struggles to feel, act, and think differently. People who are successful in many areas of their lives still need your help with problems they cannot sort out on their own. They may be disappointed in themselves for being unable to make changes, so they often come in reluctantly. Their questions about change are usually appeals for assistance and reassurance that they are not incompetent or helpless.

QUESTIONS

Clients ask many questions about how therapy will help them to change their lives, but there isn't much variety to these inquiries. The following questions are answered in the Responses section:

"Why is change so hard?"

"I know my behaviors aren't working for me, so why do I continue with them?"

"Will I get better?"

"Will change be gradual or happen with one big event?"

"How does this change thing work, anyway?"

"Why do I fall back into my old habits so easily?"

"How does this change thing work, anyway?"

RESPONSES

In the suggestions that follow, we provide ways to address your client's wish to be in a different place in her life. At these moments she needs understanding and appreciation for her dilemmas and an understanding of the humility that comes with being imperfect. As her partner in change, you are invested in her ability to move forward, whether it is to let go of thoughts and behaviors that restrict her or to courageously reach out and develop more of her potential. The fears and hopes revealed in these questions allow us to encourage optimism and simultaneously address the reality that it is difficult to feel, think, and behave in new ways.

Charlie

I like to think about change in psychotherapy as not just giving up bad habits or practices, but instead adding skills and options for clients to use when appropriate. I sometimes tell clients, "It is like you are a house with many rooms, some of which have been feared and avoided and explored less than others. I don't see our work as trying to pick up this house and move it to a whole new foundation in a new location, but instead we want to make the house more comfortable and gain access to the previously feared rooms." When clients think about the process as growth rather than destruction, they can relax knowing that they will not be asked to uproot all they know for something that is totally unfamiliar.

"Why Is Change So Hard?"

Even if clients do not directly say so, they quickly understand that change is a difficult undertaking. It takes diligence to change patterns of thinking, feeling, and behaving. As therapists we can help acknowledge and normalize that reality. "Change is often hard. It means that we have to give up some of our old ways of thinking or doing things and that happens slowly. There are losses involved in change." or "As human beings we often like things to be the same, we like consistency and having something that we can count on, even when it is not ideal."

One of the elements that appears fairly consistently in theories about change is that if a client believes that she is capable of changing, she has a better chance to accomplish her goal. You can help her to believe in herself by identifying areas of her life in which she has been successful. "What were some of your past successful experiences with making changes?" or "What elements of your life have you been able to change?"

"I Know My Behaviors Aren't Working for Me, So Why Do I Continue With Them?"

You may want to remind your client that, "If it was easy, you wouldn't have come in. You would have already taken care of it." or "We are all creatures of habit. It takes time to learn new ways." Your client can change more easily when she: has an emotional relationship with you that helps fight demoralization; is in a setting that allows expression and understanding; and has trust and hope of improvement through the treatment you suggest. Answer in a way that your client can understand: "We make change happen when we work well together, when you trust me and I understand you. Then, you can speak freely, have less fear, and feel safe. When that happens, you are able to think and feel differently about your problems, which, in turn, permits you to think and act in new ways."

Linda

Occasionally, when a client asks "Why is change so hard?" I've said, "Insight and understanding in therapy is similar to the real world
(continued)

when I walk into my kitchen and realize, 'Hmm, this is dirty and needs heavy cleaning.' Knowing the problem exists, being dissatisfied, and understanding the solution still doesn't make my kitchen clean. I have to get out the rags and cleansers and scrub." Personal change cannot be outsourced.

"Will I Get Better?"

First, reflect your client's worries: "Are you feeling hopeless?" or "You have low confidence that you can change your life/get away from these nagging feelings." As you empathize with his fears, you both will learn more about the concerns that underlie this question.

Many studies have consistently concluded that therapy helps. Some of these studies use objective, independent measures and others use subjective ratings. Some have thousands of subjects and others report on the progress of a single individual. The vast majority of people report making at least some gains whether they are in the areas of feeling better, acting more effectively, or thinking more rationally. Sharing your digested version of the empirically supported material can be the right answer for some clients. "Yes, the data support the idea that most people benefit from psychotherapy, and I am confident that we will see that here as well." or "There are many studies you can read that have concluded that therapy helps."

"Will Change Be Gradual or Happen With One Big Event?"

Not surprisingly, clients worry whether they are changing fast enough, whether the change is good enough, if they are changing in the right direction, and who they will be at the end of the process. You can't predict any client's outcome, but you can certainly reassure him that, "Change is a highly personalized experience. It usually happens in gradual steps, but it can occur with big leaps forward and big leaps sideways and short slides backward. We might see the whole variety, and we will pay attention to all of it so that you can avoid going back to old, ineffective, ways. The important thing is to undertake movement in the right direction."

Charlie

Paul had spent the first several months of our therapy together lamenting the negativity that pervaded his household. He took full ownership of his contribution to this ongoing problem, but he also saw little hope for change unless his wife would change along with him. This was unlikely because they had been in couples counseling for more than two years before he began seeing me individually. As Paul somberly reviewed his relationship, I responded with lots of empathy, understanding, contextual explanation, and historical review.

Finally, at one session Paul announced as he sat down: "I am ready to be a joy-filled person." He went on to say, "I am going to turn my 'I have to' statements into 'I get to' ones, and my 'I must' statements into 'I can' statements." You would have thought that we had been doing extensive cognitive-behavioral treatment, but he seemed to have done that on his own by reading between the lines of our work together. He began to believe that he had both the responsibility and the agency to create some new attitudes. At first, he sounded like a television special, all inspiration, but it became clear that he was gathering himself into a readiness to change. Although he continued to have some relapses into despondency, these were shorter-lived and more limited than they had been in his past. It looked like an explosion of change, but it was the result of many months of hard work.

"Why Do I Fall Back Into My Old Habits So Easily?"

This question identifies the very human potential to relapse. You can respond by building on what the client has stated already. "You just said it, your old ways are habits that will dominate your behavior unless you resist them. Eventually new habits will replace the old, and they will have the upper hand because they are more functional, but for awhile you will have to work hard at being different in the ways we have discussed and practiced."

"How Does This Change Thing Work, Anyway?

At some point in your work together, for your well-being and for your client's, it may be good to communicate that, even after the two of you understand the origins of a problem, work is required to change patterns and habits. Your theoretical viewpoint will guide your definition of the process of change. Some clinicians believe that greater self-awareness and corrective experiences can occur as your clients engage in behaviors that they have avoided or never thought of and, as a result, they come to see more possibilities. Reality testing leads to more corrective experiences, which you might call "working through" or "repeated exposure" depending on your theoretical beliefs. What a client needs to hear is that he is working on himself, and he is the agent who will shape his future. "Our focus is on you, on helping you better understand your strengths and areas for growth so that you can see the origins of your patterns and select from choices that will make the best use of your strengths."

Your theoretical beliefs will help guide you. For instance, if you take a cognitive approach, with the emphasis on changing thoughts and behaviors, you would evaluate change by considering the progress of your client's maladaptive and adaptive thought processes. More strictly behavioral approaches to client change, with their emphases on identifying and promoting positive actions, will watch for new, healthy activities as the indicator of change. Psychodynamic approaches, with their attention to intrapersonal and interpersonal relations, will look for change in diminished personal conflicts, resolution of painful experiences, and more satisfying personal undertakings. Humanistic or experiential approaches to psychotherapy expect to see change in increased understanding of feelings, more genuine encounters, and a stronger sense of personal identity.

Systemic-constructivist approaches to change emphasize resolution of rigid enmeshment within or, conversely, distant detachment from social systems and will anticipate improvement in those areas. Practitioners who integrate biological interventions with psychological strategies will likely have an eye toward changes in wellness strategies and improvements in mind-body awareness. Finally, multicultural and feminist practitioners will keep an eye on adaptive client strategies, particularly in the ways they relate to social forces, discrimination, and oppressive cultural norms and expectations.

Every once in awhile, you have an entirely different experience. Your client is eager and willing to change; she just doesn't know how.

Nancy Newton, Ph.D., professor at The Chicago School

Lilla was a 23-year-old client who came into therapy to overcome some of the limitations of an emotionally impoverished childhood. We had worked together for a couple of years when she asked me, apropos of nothing that I can remember, "How many bras do you own?" I was so startled, never having heard that question before, that my curiosity, rather than my technique, took over. I laughed and asked, "Where did that question come from?"

My reply led to a serious conversation about Lilla's uncertainty and lack of confidence in her own judgment about what was normal, even in the most ordinary way. She wondered, "How much underwear do women own?" "How many times do you wear a bra before washing it?" Her mother had never modeled feminine behaviors. Now, in her early twenties and on her own, she felt adrift. She assumed that there were shared feminine norms she was supposed to have learned as a child, and she was too ashamed to ask her friends for information.

We never got back to the question, but it made me wonder if I knew any more than she did about what was normal feminine behavior. This experience confirmed for me that our genuine curiosity about a client's questions can lead to meaningful dialogue.

FURTHER THOUGHTS

"The only person who is educated is the one who has learned how to learn and change."

—Carl Rogers

If you hail a cab in New York and say, "I want to go to the Empire State Building," you expect the driver to know the direction and get you there in relative safety. Many clients have similar expectations about psychological change. They assume that you will know the direction and guide their journey while they sit uncomfortably, maybe even white-knuckled, in the back seat, and they imagine they can arrive at their destination by just hanging on.

Change in therapy doesn't work like a New York cab ride, however, except for the occasional white-knuckle portions of the trip. Change isn't easy; you can't turn the driving over to someone else and sit back passively. There are too many streets and few signs, progress isn't a straight line, and potholes are unavoidable. Think about times when you have tried to change your own behaviors. How successful were you? What were the obstacles? It gives you an appreciation of the difficulty in making lasting change. Even with an advanced degree, you aren't the driver; some days you are the navigator, some days you are sitting alongside your clients, and on the other days, they leave you in the dust.

In this chapter, we provided examples of responses that we believe will further the process, but always, when you respond to questions about change, keep the specific client, problem, personality, and context in mind. We have stayed away from discussing change through only one theoretical lens. However, a general, transtheoretical model advocated by Prochaska and DiClemente discusses the general process of change as going through cyclical stages of precontemplation, contemplation, preparation, action, and maintenance. Your clients might find it useful to understand change as a skill they can develop and a process with different stages of readiness. Models like this can be best discussed in general terms and then made more specific for each client. With that focus, you may be able to provide a slightly different perspective with which to look at the situation, thereby freeing your clients from their old, repetitive ways of thinking.

Change takes courage because it involves some form of loss. One of therapy's best gifts is that clients become less afraid to change. They make change a part of their lives. After therapy ends, life will continue to require adaptation, for our clients and for us. The more we all get used to the fact that change is an inevitable aspect of life, the more we get friendlier with the idea and we fight against it less. Strangely,

without using all of that energy to prevent change, we have freed it up
and can apply it to guiding change and adapting well.

SUGGESTED READINGS

Glass, G. V., & Smith, M. L. (1977). Meta-analysis of psychotherapy outcome
studies. *American Psychologist, 32*, 752–760.

Hardy, G. E., Cahill, J., & Barkham, M. (2007). Models of the therapeutic relationship and prediction of outcome: A research perspective. In P. Gilbert &
R. L. Leahy (Eds.), *The therapeutic relationship in the cognitive behavioural psychotherapies* (pp. 24–42). London, England: Routledge.

Petrocelli, J. V. (2002). Processes and stages of change: Counseling with the
transtheoretical model of change. *Journal of Counseling & Development, 80*,
22–30.

Prochaska, J. O., DiClemente, C. C., & Norcross, J. C. (1992). In search of how
people change: Applications to addictive behaviors. *American Psychologist,
47*, 1102–1114.

Seligman, M. (1995). The effectiveness of psychotherapy. *American Psychologist,
50*, 965–974.

Wampold, B. E. (2001). *The great psychotherapy debate: Models, methods and find-
ings*. Mahwah, NJ: Erlbaum.

CHAPTER 5

Techniques

Clinical work is always a blend of art and science; we make some decisions based on the empathic connection we have with our client, and other decisions come from a cool assessment of information we have received.

All of the methods you decide to use to achieve some goal, whether it is insight or behavior change, are techniques. Your choice of techniques is based on your theoretical beliefs, your relationship with your client, the nature of your client's problem, your skills, and your client's needs. Used well and developed from your beliefs, techniques deepen the therapy, but tossed carelessly into a session, you have wasted time.

Linda

Writing this book has made me increasingly aware of the breadth of techniques that I believe in, but it hasn't protected me from slipping up on their usage. This week, I listened to a woman painfully describe the demon that lives inside her and that escapes periodically to go on lengthy, uncontrolled food rampages. She had gained eight pounds in the previous ten days. She was suffering greatly, was out of control and knew it, but she was unable to use any of her coping skills to get back to normal eating. In the session, we both worked hard and were able to connect the hungry demon to childhood accusations and adult rage.

At the conclusion of the session, I would have said that we made good progress. Then, as she stood up to leave, she asked, "Where is Chipotle? Isn't it near your office?" In my mind, the session had ended. Somewhere, I knew the session was continuing, but I didn't get the message to my head fast enough, so I answered, "It's down the street." She left and within a minute I wanted to scream at her to come back so that I could say, "I can't control your demon, but I'm not here to help her binge." My mistake was that I stopped being her therapist, stopped attending to the boundary, stopped watching my words, and stopped listening a few careless moments too soon.

The following week, I told her about my reaction and her response was, "There was nothing that you or anyone could say that would have stopped my demon. She rages until she's exhausted." She also said that she didn't look for food; she went directly home. I felt a bit better, but that doesn't turn my lack of attention into a good technique; it only means that the confrontation I imagined might have been ineffective.

Today, most clinicians agree that both the therapeutic relationship and techniques are essential in the change process and that they are inextricably intertwined. Debating the supremacy of one over the other is not a useful argument. Depending on your theoretical beliefs, relationship with a particular client, the point in treatment, and the problem to be addressed, you may emphasize one more than the other, but whether you believe that the relationship is primary or your techniques are primary, you will attend to both in every session.

Techniques include the relational elements of therapy, such as the establishment of clear boundaries, methods that are behavioral, such as cognitive-behavioral treatment, and other methods that clinicians rarely categorize as technique, such as dreamwork. Techniques can move treatment forward, but when they are misused, the alliance is damaged. When the alliance is damaged, clients balk at techniques and treatment suffers. In this chapter, we look at some questions that arise from use or misuse of a technique, and we examine the underlying dynamics and intentions.

QUESTIONS

With the exception of the first question in the following list, you may notice that these questions have a negative tone. That is because clients rarely ask questions when your interventions and techniques are working. When they are getting positive results, clients tend to focus on the outcome, but even when the questions are negative, your client is still demonstrating a desire to learn more or achieve different results. With that reframe, you will find it easier to respond without defensiveness. The following questions are answered in the Responses section:

"Do you use any standard techniques?"

"Why did you suggest that book/psychiatrist/behavior?"

"I didn't do that journal writing you wanted. Why are we doing this?"

"Why do you keep going back to bullying in middle school? I told you that I'm over it."

"Will you accept the fudge I baked? Is it wrong to bring you this stuff?"

"I thought that our sessions were longer. Why was last week's session an hour and today's is 45 minutes?"

"Why are you talking so much?" "Why are you silent?"

"Fine, I understand my problem. Don't you have any method of getting rid of it?"

RESPONSES

"Do You Use Any Standard Techniques?"

This question is most likely going to come up early in treatment. As such, it offers the opportunity to educate your client about the therapy process, and you can explain that your work is highly personalized for each person. "I don't think of it as standard techniques, but I always listen carefully for more information about how we can meet your goals and resolve the difficulties that you have brought in. As we find out more about your struggles and strengths, we identify specific ways to help you." or "I'm a firm believer in cognitive-behavioral therapy, and there are certainly techniques that I will guide you through." The two of you will figure out your goals and agree on specific procedures to follow because, to be effective, techniques require your client's involvement and investment in the process.

"Why Did You Suggest That Book/Psychiatrist/Behavior?"

Clinicians suggest books, people, and behaviors every day with varying degrees of acceptance and success, so let's first assume that the question is neutral. Think about the basis for your suggestion and disclose your reasoning, for example, "I am familiar with that *book/psychiatrist/behavior* and thought that it would help you with (your problem). It sounds like it didn't work for you." Next, we can assume that this question is more than a simple request for information. Perhaps it carries the implication, "Your suggestion was lousy. Do you know what you are doing?" Before you get insulted, it is still a good idea to disclose your reasoning and then ask for clarification. "You sound displeased. What happened?" There will be times when you make a suggestion because you are aware of your limitations in an area, and you can say, "I was hopeful that it (whatever it is) would be helpful." or "(That problem) is not my area of expertise. We needed to look to additional resources." or "If that didn't work, let's think about what will be a helpful addition to our work."

It is a commonly accepted technique to use adjunct material, and doing so can expand or deepen the work you are already doing. These additional resources allow you to transcend your own knowledge and tap into the wisdom of others. No clinician can be an expert in all areas of treatment. You are allowed to not know. In fact, you model curiosity and persistence by being open to other ideas. We all have limits and reach points where we don't possess a reliable answer, solution, or direction.

Let's look at another possible explanation for the question, "Why did you suggest that *book/psychiatrist/behavior?*" Your client may be complaining that your suggestion didn't help and you didn't help. That happens. Your potential mistake in this scenario is about intention—did you throw the technique at the client in desperation, without adequate consideration? That happens, too. Fight any impulses toward perfectionism, because it will hinder your ability to seek outside help or understand when to refer. Sometimes you will feel incompetent and unworthy as a therapist because of an action you suggested that didn't work. When that happens, you have misunderstood the nature of your work.

Charlie

Sometimes clients will ask me to recommend a book that they can buy to help them with their problem. I don't keep up with a lot of the self-help book literature. Instead, I suggest to clients that they indulge themselves by spending some time in the self-help/ psychology section of a local bookstore and browse through the books themselves to pick out one or two that really speak to them. I tell them that the $20 will be money well spent, and I also encourage them to bring their new learnings and observations from the books into our sessions so that we can talk about them. I believe most clients see this directive as being given permission to explore further, but some may see it as a cop-out from my sharing responsibility for their search.

"I Didn't Do That Journal Writing You Wanted. Why Are We Doing This?"

These types of questions are common reactions when you have suggested a behavioral technique. And, since we are responding to clients' queries, not constructing interventions, let's look at this question as an illustration of two interrelated dynamics that occur regularly, resistance and lack of client ownership.

Resistance in therapy is like weather; it exists on a daily basis. And like weather, you can get frustrated, be displeased, complain, rant, take it personally, and feel badly, but the snow and sun and wind go on. Sometimes you need to put on a raincoat. Resistance, like weather, is not a personal attack against you. Change is difficult; people are fearful and set in their ways, even when they are suffering. When you comment on your client's resistance to a technique, go easy. If a client feels assaulted, she will need to protect herself from you. If she feels understood, she will be able to remain open to your ideas. Start with, "You didn't like the journal writing. What happened?" although it could be a book, meditation, a referral, tracking a behavior, paying attention to dreams, exercising, or anything else. You can go further by saying, "I know that you want to feel better, but change is hard. Let's see if we can come up with a plan that you want to follow."

Be creative. Work with your client to customize techniques. "We planned the journal writing as a way for you to get your thoughts and feelings out of your head and on paper between our sessions, but if you don't write, it can't help. Let's talk about it further in terms of your goals. Then we can decide whether it is worthwhile for you to try it again or not." Another approach is to understand the resistance to journal writing or any other technique with, "It's obvious that you are having trouble with this idea. Tell me what happened when you considered writing in your journal. Then we can understand what works and what doesn't." or "I thought that you liked the idea when we talked about it. What happened when you tried to carry out our plan?" Techniques work when they make sense to clients, are grounded in the client's abilities, and the client is willing to participate. Otherwise, tossing journals, charts, exercises, and other techniques into therapy with the hope that one will stick is superficial at best and, at worst, has the potential to harm the relationship.

If your client doesn't buy into a technique, you are wasting your time if you pursue it without dealing with the underlying resistance. Your techniques need to come directly from your client's problem, build progressively on her strengths, be explained sufficiently so that she sees the benefits, and be accepted by your client or you are wasting effort. All of these requirements only work if they are in the context of a strong therapeutic relationship. Otherwise, they don't succeed. Also, it is easy to get comfortable with familiar techniques, but excellent new work is being done constantly, and we encourage you to stay up-to-date on new techniques for specific populations and problems.

"Why Do You Keep Going Back to Bullying in Middle School? I Told You That I'm Over It."

This client has a good point; we all want to put unpleasant experiences from the past behind us. Some additional explanation is in order regarding your persistence. "I don't go back to your middle school experiences to plague you. Those days were formative, and I see some behaviors/reactions in the present that we can probably trace to that period of your life." or "I know that you are over the middle-school experience, but I wonder if it has left some scars, for example (offer a present-day situation)." or "I'm not so sure it is in the past. I see behaviors/feelings today that may be left over from those days." When your client understands your intentions, you have a better chance of guiding the exploration in difficult directions.

Linda

During the early sessions of therapy, Tanya, age 28, explained to me that she quit working with her former therapist for two reasons. One, the other therapist continued to mispronounce her name, and two, he insisted that many of her problems stemmed from the guilt she experienced because she was the only daughter to avoid sexual molestation by her stepfather. She explained that being misnamed meant that he didn't know her and wasn't paying attention (I repeated her name in my head until I had it right), but the second complaint was more difficult. The guilt hypothesis had merit, but it was clearly unwelcome. It was difficult to be quiet about the abuse because Tanya was symptomatic and I didn't like seeing her suffer.

So for several months, we examined tangentially related material and I consoled myself with an old cliché that I've adapted to clinical work, "all roads lead to Rome." Sure enough, we reached the Roman suburbs several months later when she began to be in touch with her grief. She mourned for her sisters' suffering, then she felt anger at their lost childhoods, and finally she sobbed about her wrenching survivor's guilt. Tanya found her way in a circuitous route, but it made sense to her. Timing is everything, and interpretation is only useful if it is heard.

Experienced clinicians know how to listen so that they can figure out what technique will help, whether it turns out to be a behavioral plan, an interpretation, or one of the hundreds of possibilities in between. However, the implementation and follow-through can be difficult. Unyielding insistence on your part will result in your clients learning new forms of self-protection, including lying, aggression, avoidance, and like Tanya, quitting a former therapist. Always place yourself on the same side as your client—in a different role, but on the same side. If you join the opposing team, you will be met with unfriendliness rather than cooperation. This does not mean mindlessly agreeing with every pronouncement your client makes. You are always free, even obligated, to say generally, "I see it differently." or "I have an alternative view I would like to propose." Or specifically, if a client defends a problem (e.g., substance abuse), you can say "I'm worried about your heavy drinking even though you think that it is under control."

Depending on your theoretical beliefs, you will fall somewhere along the nondirective to directive continuum. Behaviorists have accused client-centered types of being afraid to exert control over clients and reluctant to use their power effectively. It is worth some personal exploration if this argument speaks to you. On the other side of the debate, client-centered clinicians believe that all dictators are bad, and they criticize those clinicians who have an excessive desire to control clients and exert undue power. It is good to be grounded in theoretical beliefs; that guides your work, but remain open to meet your client's needs.

"Will You Accept the Fudge I Baked? Is It Wrong to Bring You This Stuff?"

Your decision to accept or reject gifts is a classic boundary determination. In a twist, we want to use this question to note that setting and maintaining boundaries falls into the category of technique. It is such a basic technique that clinicians rarely discuss it as such, but we make these decisions all the time.

Some therapists refuse all gifts, although they are in the smallest minority. Most clinicians use caution when accepting a gift and seek to understand its meaning. "Thanks, I love fudge. Is there a special reason for this gift?" Regardless of your stance, it is beneficial to understand why your client is bringing you a gift. In our opinion, there is nothing wrong with accepting small tokens like fudge. Big offers pose a problem, whether they are stock tips or presents. "It's generous to offer me World Series tickets, but I have a policy of not accepting substantial gifts like this." Is the gift an attempt to impress you, thank you, buy your continued involvement, or something else? You don't know until the two of you discuss it. "This is a significant gift/offer. I think it might be helpful to understand your thinking."

The technique of setting and maintaining boundaries is the method by which we establish what is included in the treatment and what is not. And although there is much general agreement about boundaries, you consider what is appropriate to your client, at that time, in the context of your relationship. This guideline allows you to use your clinical judgment and accept or reject gifts and offers. Misuse of boundary management would be to either accept all gifts or reject all gifts without regard to context.

The situation changes with children and adolescents. For example, Joe, an adolescent client, presented a drawing to his therapist, who graciously accepted and talked about the importance of the picture. If Joe's therapist had been rigid and not accepted the drawing, they would never have had the discussion that culminated in Joe revealing that his parents viewed his passion for drawing as "a childhood obsession that will never get me anywhere." Acceptance of the picture demonstrated support of

Joe's interests and also gave Joe an opportunity to feel something other than shame, the emotion that followed each rejection by his parents. As therapy evolved, both Joe and his therapist came to recognize how much shame had dominated the young man's life. Offering his therapist this gift was a courageous, trusting move on Joe's part. This example demonstrates the therapist's flexibility and understanding. Here is the reverse.

Catherine Daley, Ph.D. (pseudonym)

A very skilled colleague told us this story: "When I first got out of school, I was ridiculously rigid. Instead of thinking about my professors' (who did little therapy on their own) instructions as guidelines, I followed all of their dictates as if they were carved in stone. For example, a client brought in cookies for me at the holidays, and I hounded her about the meaning until she was ashamed of herself for being thoughtful. Since then, I say, 'Thank you' for little things, maybe ask, 'Is there a reason for this gift?' and inquire more deeply if the behavior persists. Unfortunately, early on I took one legitimate technique so far that it became worthy of a *Saturday Night Live* skit.

Clients usually want to have something to offer their therapist, whether it is a joke, fudge, insight, personal change, or a more substantial gift. Everyone feels better about themselves when they have something of value that another person might desire or enjoy. When you say no, the dilemma becomes accepting the client while refusing the gift. Valuing this client and his offering represented an essential technique with this treatment. At the same time, boundaries are absolutely essential to treatment, and that's why we devote Chapter 9 to more questions that arise in this area.

"I Thought Our Sessions Were Longer. Why Was Last Week's Session an Hour and Today's Is 45 Minutes?"

Your client is wondering if your techniques change from week to week, and although some might, others do not. Respond truthfully, "That was a mistake. Sessions are 45 minutes, and I will be more careful in the future." This harmless question exemplifies only one reason why we maintain boundaries. In this example, your client feels less special during today's 45-minute session because you gave him the lengthy one last week. One reason to have rules about session length is so that both of you can depend on it and feel secure in the time frame. Limits provide security. Limits on time, space, or behavior inform you and your client what is in and what is out of bounds, an essential piece of information. You don't want to negotiate every session length, fee, and interaction as if each one is brand new and dependent on the client being entertaining or desperate. All boundaries, not just time, provide safety for both you and your clients. Too often, clinicians think about boundaries as only helpful to clients, but it is equally important as protection for clinicians so that you can depend on the limits and do your work freely. Understanding and using boundaries is one of the essential techniques of treatment.

"Why Are You Talking So Much?" "Why Are You Silent?"

Speech and silence are basic techniques. How much we talk, how little we talk, whether we ask questions, our style of language, our formality and informality, our tolerance of quiet, our management of tempo or revelation are all technical decisions that we make. Questions like this one bring your verbosity or silence into greater awareness. "Yes, I am aware of being silent because you are doing so well on your own that I want to stay out of your way." or "I didn't realize I was (talking so much/too quiet). I have to think about it. What do you make of it?" Speech, or lack thereof, ought to be used consciously rather than self-consciously. Many people, clients and therapists alike, have trouble with silence, in both directions.

Silence may cause you anxiety, so you fill the session with explanations, intellectualizations, too many questions, or tangential conversation. When you catch yourself, simply observe, "I am talking too much." or "This is becoming a Q&A. I think it is your turn." This issue seems extremely prevalent, with beginning therapists who worry excessively that there isn't enough to say and, in reaction, try to fill the time. If you hear yourself veering into chatter, just notice it and say, "I did go on a tangent. Let's get back to your story." or "Yes, the point I want to make is . . ."

We have also known clinicians who use silence to increase their client's anxiety and regression. In moderation, this comes from the analytic theories founded on legitimate rationale and respect, but when it is misused, it smacks of control or punishment. The same can be said about overtalking, which also has the potential to dominate the session and silence your client.

"Fine, I Understand My Problem. Don't You Have Any Method of Getting Rid of It?"

Maybe you do know a method for getting rid of the problem, maybe not. If you have a technique, you will use it; if not, you will try to find a helpful idea to implement. Either way, listen carefully to your clients. Technique is about creating conditions that will facilitate growth and change. Use them with intention. Know why you employ any technique, even as basic as listening. You choose the techniques, and there is always an interaction of your personal characteristics and style with your chosen technique that makes it your own. Go deeply enough into your techniques so that you can honestly, comfortably stand behind them. Sometimes, techniques go poorly; perhaps because the technique was incompatible with the client or the client was not ready, was resistant, or the technique was not understood or inadequately implemented. Some activities just don't turn out to be in harmony with your client's goals, expectations, or experiences.

FURTHER THOUGHTS

"If we can abandon our missionary zeal, we have less chance of being eaten by cannibals."

—Carl Whitaker

There is a wonderful scene in the iconic *Star Wars* movie *The Empire Strikes Back* in which Luke, the young Jedi warrior, is being trained by Yoda, the gnome-like therapist Jedi master. The contrast between the two of them is striking. Luke is young, impatient, and his powers are spotty. Yoda is the ageless, gentle master of the Force. In the dark swamp, Luke is drawn to a cave. "What's in there?" he asks his teacher. Yoda answers, "Only what you take with you." Luke begins to strap on his weapons. Yoda says, "Your weapons; you will not need them." Luke continues and enters the cave armed. Luke encounters the dark knight who he defeats, only to find his own reflection in the fallen soldier. Yoda's comment is wonderful as a serious psychological explanation of technique. Whatever you bring into the room, you will use, emotionally and technically. If you carry weapons, you will find a use for them. If you carry compassion, you will use it. If you are wedded to one technique, you will find that one necessary.

Techniques and methods can be used with skill or incompetence, they can be imprudently applied or chosen carefully, and they can become a one-size-fits-all application or designer crafted. Your techniques will only be as good as you are. There is a strength and clarity in being a person who works with one model, but you know that different problems may require different methods. Having a variety of strategies gives you confidence. Many strategies are sound and have solid research behind them. The danger in knowing many strategies is figuring out how they fit together and how you can use them comfortably in your treatment. Therapy is more than a collection of techniques; it is an art. If you could use techniques out of a box, self-help books would work better than they do.

Your techniques are most successful when they are consistent with your beliefs, when you have a good command of them, when you can choose to use them or not, and always when they are relevant to your clients' needs and best interests. This can be a great advantage. You may stay focused and get work done clearly and without distraction or you may be hiding from yourself and your client.

When you recognize that a technique has strained the therapeutic relationship, you need to repair it before the two of you will feel comfortable to move on. Ruptures in the therapeutic alliance occur if you (a) misuse techniques; (b) don't attend to the treatment relationship; (c) do something that your client didn't want; or (d) don't do something that your client actively wants. Resolution allows treatment to proceed in a deeper vein and helps clients develop skills to resolve conflicts with others.

When a technique doesn't work, don't be defensive. It is very tempting to turn away any questions or discussion that might cause you embarrassment or make you appear to be ineffective. To repair the break, acknowledge the problem, facilitate your client's expression of feelings, explore the rupture, accept responsibility for your part, or stop that particular behavior. The alliance destroyer is to be nonresponsive, dogmatic, ignore your client's point of view, rigidly adhere to your own perspective, or otherwise diminish the client's experience. You don't have to agree with the client's experience, but it helps enormously to understand it.

Professionalism, even expertise, is not about avoiding mistakes. We can guarantee that you will make mistakes, but it is about what you do after those mistakes occur. Mistakes make us sensitive to our vulnerabilities and imperfections. Try to remain open to examination; it is the behavior that models the best attitude for your client and, when a technique works, enjoy it!

SUGGESTED READINGS

Barber, J. P., Stratt, R., Halperin, G., & Connolly, M. B. (2001). Supportive techniques: Are they found in different therapies? *Journal of Psychotherapy Practice and Research, 10*, 165–172.

Erford, B., Eaves, S., Bryant, E., & Young, K. (2009). *Thirty-five techniques every counselor should know.* Upper Saddle River, NJ: Prentice Hall.

Goldfried, M. R., & Davila, J. (2005). The role of relationship and technique in therapeutic change. *Psychotherapy: Theory, Research, Practice, Training, 42*, 421–430.

Levitt, H., Butler, M., & Hill, T. (2006). What clients find helpful in psychotherapy: Developing principles for facilitating moment-to-moment change. *Journal of Counseling Psychology, 53*, 314–324.

Pope, K. S., & Keith-Spiegel, P. (2008). A practical approach to boundaries in psychotherapy: Making decisions, bypassing blunders, and mending fences. *Journal of Clinical Psychology: In Session, 64*, 638–652.

Yalom, I. D. (2002). *Gift of therapy: An open letter to a new generation of therapists and their patients.* New York, NY: Harper & Row.

CHAPTER

6

Professional
Role

When you assume your professional role as counselor or therapist, you combine deeply personal aspects of yourself with a set of skills and attitudes. A role is not a role-play, not superficial and not pretend. Your professional role means that you have specific responsibilities to carry out, greatly influenced by what you believe. As a result, your role as a therapist becomes integrated with deeper aspects of your identity. When considered in this light, your professional role develops forever.

Charlie

My client, Chuck, was a handsome, middle-aged, impeccably dressed, elected politician, winning awards at the national level for his amateur tennis accomplishments. He came to see me when his life was a mess and he was feeling fearful, enraged, and self-destructive. He had never learned that even when life included periods of mediocrity or setbacks, he was still the same man who won votes and tennis matches. Not surprisingly, as a child he was only prized by his parents when he was an exalted star at whatever activity he pursued. I believe that he needed me to be someone who accepted him equally whether he shone during personal highs or suffered during lows. In that way, he could experience a new way of being that did not involve becoming overwhelmed by disappointments nor over-identified with successes. I know that I need to be a good therapist in general and that particularly for him, I needed to demonstrate the ability to shrug off disappointment without being devastated and simply take any compliment in stride. As he came to value himself as a person, rather than as a recipient of public accolades or rebukes, he experienced himself more evenly and learned to meet his needs successfully without being plagued by the fear that if he wasn't the best at his work or play, he was worthless.

One graduate student told us, "We all read the article that talks about how therapists wear different hats, but knowing this doesn't really help." Excellent observation. The idea is like Harlow's wire monkey; technically interesting, mechanically functional, but with nothing to cling to. When you think about yourselves as wearing hats, you become a performer who plays the role of therapist. It is the opposite of what you long for—you want to feel present and authentic and instead you feel fake. When you start out in this field, you feel enough like an imposter without imagining yourself throwing your coach cap to the floor, grabbing your friendly pal hat only to replace that with your sophisticated teacher hat when confronted by a new situation. You can become confused and erratic.

As you can see from Charlie's example, you always remain yourself when you are in your professional role, and you are always recognizable, but depending on your assessment of your client's needs, you emphasize certain aspects of who you are and, in order to meet the needs of the client with whom you are working, you may call upon one set of skills or another.

Client's questions about your professional role are not especially complicated. They want to know what to expect and who you are. Your responses are actually far more intriguing than the questions. Just like you will try to respond to your clients' questions and their underlying concerns, we will try to attend, in the following answers, to all the questions in the room—particularly yours—about your role as a therapist and how it fits into your professional identity. In particular, we try to address developmental concerns, such as "Can I be myself?" "How much of myself is in the room?" "What happens when my professional role clashes with my personal identity?" and "Do I need to become a *Cirque du Soleil* contortionist to work with different clients?"

QUESTIONS

The following questions are answered in the Responses section:

> "Is therapy the same for everybody?"
> "Do you do the same thing with all your clients?"
> "Are you supposed to be like a medical doctor for me?"
> "What should I call you?"
> "You are going to talk to me, right?"
> "You're a counselor so you have to be nice to me, right?"
> "I tell my friends that you are like a coach for me, is that okay?"
> "Why don't we talk about you?"
> "We are not going to see each other for four weeks. How will I ever get by during this time?

RESPONSES

"Is Therapy the Same for Everybody?"

This question is reminiscent of the one-size-fits-all tag clipped onto garments that are flattering to nobody. Instead, think of therapy as designer or haute couture clothing. The question "Is therapy the same for everybody?" is too important to answer glibly with "Of course not; each relationship is unique." Although each relationship *is* unique, this response falls short of addressing your client's concerns. It is like asking, is marriage the same for everybody? Is sex the same for everybody? In your response to the question, remind your client that, "We create therapy together." or "We talk about your problems and develop ways of understanding your life." or "The way that you decide to live your life will be different from someone else's decisions. Our solutions have to be right for you." It is understandable and healthy that clients want to know what to expect from you. However, because you do create therapy together, each endeavor is unique for both of you.

Part of the assessment that experienced therapists undertake on a relatively automatic basis with each client is to consider where clients have deficits and what kind of therapeutic role addresses their deficiencies. Also, as you identify your clients' assets and resources, your attitude and skills can be directed to supporting them and furthering their development.

When you consider your response to the client who asks this question or similar ones, ask yourself what he needs in order to understand himself more honestly. When you have this answer, you will know how to relate to him better. You will also feel increasingly effective and comfortable with your language and the style you adopt. Understanding your role in relation to this client, you can answer honestly, "Therapy can never be the same for everybody. We have to figure out what helps you and then build on these discoveries."

Just like your clients show themselves differently to you than to others, you will respond uniquely to each person. You will reveal your sense of humor to some, be more open or guarded with others, stay quiet or be directive, or dread one session and look forward to the next. The common concerns of "Can I be myself?" and "How much of myself is in the room?" diminish in importance as you accept that, although clients will elicit different facets of you and evoke different emotions, you can only be yourself; any other approach will work poorly.

Your questions about being yourself, behaving in a role, or revealing selected aspects of yourself don't apply only to interactions with clients. Here is an example of a new clinician struggling with what to say and not say at the clinic.

Linda

In a consultation, I listened to a recent mental health graduate complain, "I am totally inauthentic in my new job. I don't tell my
(continued)

co-workers or my boss what I'm really thinking. I speak up in staff meetings with clinical ideas, but when they don't agree, I let it go." And then she groaned again, "I can't believe what an inauthentic fake I am." I knew that she was totally committed to her work, very hard-working, and passionate, but those high emotions made her slide toward extremes. "I have another way to think about your behavior," I said. "You are behaving in your professional role. That is not inauthentic. You know how you feel, but your agency is not the place for all of your raw thoughts and emotions."

"Do You Do the Same Thing With All Your Clients?"

This question hints at your client's fear of not being special. Nobody wants to feel like an interchangeable thingamajig rolling down the assembly line. Keep these implied concerns in mind as you decide how to answer. When a client wonders if he is interchangeable with others, there are implications for other aspects of his life, such as his sense of being special or genuine. We suggest that you file this hypothesis away for later work but, in your response, you can reflect on the relationship, for example, "I don't know what all therapists do. I do know that I'm different depending on the work that you and I are doing together, and that changes from session to session." or "I change somewhat with everybody just like you do. You aren't the same with your mother as you are with your best friend or boss." You could add, "Fundamentally I stay the same person, but luckily I think different things, and feel different things, depending on what goes on in here." Because you don't read to clients from textbooks, or even from our book, this answer gets close to describing your role, and you have probably advanced the empathic bond.

Becoming a clinician is like taking a lifetime membership in a strange club. Your awareness and analytical skills are quickly awakened, sometimes too often. You have probably noticed that you feel and behave differently with the variety of people in your life. Some people elicit one reaction from you and others pull different responses. You may be relaxed and free with one sibling and cautious with another. One friend evokes a bit of competition, another makes you feel safe, and a third is the person who receives your delicate confidences. Clients do the same things to you;

evoke compassion, sadness, anger, irritation, excitement, hopelessness, the desire to work hard with them, or the willingness to give up. You feel these emotions, but they do not completely dictate your eventual clinical decision about how to respond. For example, you may decide to be silent and let matters unfold, although you feel eager to speak out or rescue a client. You may need to confront a behavior that you would rather ignore. You may want to share advice when the client is better served by thinking it through without much of your input. Understanding each of these pulls and then being able to decide and act in ways that benefit your client are the professional, occasionally frustrating, parts of your professional role.

Linda

After I received my Ph.D., I worked in a community mental health center. One of my first clients was a distinguished older man, about my father's age. There could have been many difficult aspects in our work together since he suffered from paranoid schizophrenia, but the hardest part for me was asking him personal questions. In my head, I kept hearing my father's voice admonish me for being rude. "You have a big mouth" was really the phrase, and I was forced to remind myself over and over that I was not in a social situation, I was in a professional situation, and understanding this man's personal life was essential to our work.

"Are You Supposed to Be Like a Medical Doctor for Me?"

This question is one terrific illustration of the nature of the authority relationship that exists in all therapy, whatever your philosophical beliefs. The client comes to you for help, not the other way around. The client reveals problems to you, not the other way around. You are paid for your services. You have authority, granted to you by your training and experience and accepted by you, in varying degrees. Your client, particularly if he is unfamiliar with therapy, wants to be able to think about you in a familiar way, and one professional who conjures up the notion of help is a medical doctor. Your client has an internal picture of a counselor, often modeled on this recognizable figure. It is wise to keep the concept in mind as you compose your response, because you want to set up the relationship as more collaborative than that of a medical doctor with a patient. You can say, "No, this is going to be different. We work together; you tell me what bothers you and we discuss the problem and hopefully come up with ideas to improve the situation." or "No, our work is more like being on a team together. We have different jobs here, but we talk and figure out a plan together." Don't be falsely modest; you don't want to undermine your own credibility. You are a type of medical professional because of your knowledge, experience, and technical skills, but you depend on your client participating more fully than swallowing a pill twice a day for two weeks.

Charlie

Meg had been in therapy with me a couple different times, and the latest time in had been her longest stint, about two years. She always used therapy well to smooth out some very rough patches in her life. During one session she lamented: "Why can't I break out of therapy?" Knowing that she was a pharmacist, I answered: "For some people therapy is like antibiotics, for some people it is like insulin." We both knew that my role with her was to be the constant, available, healthy presence that she lacked in the family in which she grew up. She didn't need antibiotics—she didn't have that kind of ailment.

Teenagers have asked, "Where are the machines?" and "Don't you wear a white coat?" expecting to be passive participants in the process. Some adults also believe that they will be asked questions and then be given a diagnosis or label and told what to do. It's tempting, but if you intended to become a CSI agent, you have gone astray. In your role as a professional mental health practitioner, you will be called on to have receptivity, empathy, thoughtfulness, curiosity, restraint, self-reflection, sensitivity, open-mindedness, and much more. You had most of these traits before you entered the field. Your training is the method by which you discipline those qualities and learn to use yourself with intention.

The difficult moments occur when it feels like your personal self and professional self are colliding rather than cooperating. If you have to confront a client, you may need to experience yourself as tougher than usual. If a client cries or reveals a personal tragedy, you will be tempted to reassure her that everything will be okay, although that is a mistake because you don't know what the outcome will be. If a client is rude, aggressive, or demeaning and you want to say "get lost," you force yourself to sit and observe, interpret, or confront, and you feel constricted by your role. All of this is to be expected. Roles have boundaries that constrict you occasionally, but ultimately they provide the freedom needed to do your work, the work that is needed by the client.

When you work in a medical setting or with clients who are simultaneously receiving significant medical care, the relationship can easily tilt away from the collaboration we encourage but, as always, the requirements of treatment will dictate your responses.

"What Should I Call You?"

"Whatever you are comfortable with; Linda/Charlie is fine." Some clients have always called each of us doctor and probably will always address us that way. They may be more reserved; they may like the title, or they may come from cultures that require formality. Others have nicknames for us, like Dr. W. or Doc or, as one young teenager referred to Linda, "my lady." We live in a pretty informal society and using first names is common, but if you don't like that, introduce yourself the way you wish to be addressed. "Mr./Ms./Dr. Smith is fine." If you do that, you are setting a somewhat more formal tone, but it is important that you are comfortable.

Your clients will usually call you by any name that you request; you represent hope and skill to them. You, on the other hand, might need some time to get accustomed to your professional role and have to deal with whatever internal persona pops up that day, ranging from a confident healer to co-pilot to a fraudulent wannabe. When you are trying really hard to assume some imagined professional role, it's difficult to listen to your client. After all, your own voice is too loud and far too critical. When you try too hard to please, to be smart, to be helpful or useful, you set yourself up because, if you fail to demonstrate all of those qualities, you will disappoint yourself more than disappointing anyone else.

As always, your job is to listen and to understand the story. Even when you don't have anything brilliant to offer, listening is a gift and is well received. It's surprising how often clients put the pieces together and can come up with solutions just by speaking aloud to a good listener in a safe room. Don't rush to apply theory to your clients as if they needed a new coat of paint. Learn about them first and let the theoretical understandings fall into place. By the time that has happened, you will be fully engaged.

"You Are Going to Talk to Me, Right?"

This answer is easy: "Yes, of course." You may want to inquire, "Do you like me to be active in our conversations?" This question illustrates one of the mildest ways that your professional role can cause discomfort. Your client might need more verbal reassurance than you are used to providing. Techniques that you have learned, such as silence or following your client's train of thought, are important, but you always want to be responsive to the actual person sitting across from you. Some people don't want you to say much, especially in the beginning sessions, but they will not be the ones who ask if you are going to talk.

Your clinical judgment, and the feedback you get from each client, will guide you toward choosing your behavior. There may be sessions when silence, reassurance, confrontation, or interpretation is needed more than you would do in personal situations, but therapy is not a friendship. The role struggle can also happen if you were trained to be neutral, beige, or blank and it feels like the real, interesting person is disappearing behind a therapist persona that belongs to someone else.

Nontraditional settings may require higher levels of activity on your part but always in the service of your client's goals. Some therapists are more emotive, some more educational, and some are more interpersonal. Some clinicians like to lead and anticipate their clients; others prefer to track and highlight clients' statements. Some give homework, whereas others reinforce homework that clients assign themselves. What is best? A good-enough combination of the right responses with this client at this time. Good therapists meet their clients' needs, which can be discrepant from clients' wants. The difference between wants and needs is that clients may want you to be a certain way in order to fit into their life schema, but it isn't what they need. For instance, they may want you to be a stern taskmaster who holds their feet to the fire to accomplish tasks, when they need you to be tolerant and accepting of them regardless of their behaviors. Resist being pulled exclusively into their wants and remember their needs. You will feel your role shift and bend in order to provide clients with a corrective emotional experience.

"You're a Counselor So You Have to Be Nice to Me, Right?"

"I'm generally pretty nice. That doesn't mean I'm a fake. Where is this question coming from?" If you don't get a direct answer, listen for hints later in the session, perhaps in the form of a story about a hypocritical authority figure. Then, you have more information with which you can pursue the meaning of the question.

This question and others like, "You sound just like my mother. Why does everyone want to tell me what to do?" are transference comments. All relationships have some element of transference, that is, bringing old patterns, expectations, and behaviors into the present. In the previous examples, your client reveals expectations, whether it is anticipated phoniness or bossiness.

Repeating old patterns is normal in therapy, although you will have different reactions depending on your client's view of you. It feels a lot better when a client says, "You are the best therapist in the whole world" than when one snaps, "Thanks for making me feel like crap today." Clients will often attempt to move you into a role with which they are familiar. Answer empathically, especially when it is difficult. "It is hard when sessions temporarily make you feel worse instead of better." When these patterns are noticed, examined, and challenged, your client may have a new experience with you that may enlighten him about other available, novel possibilities.

"I Tell My Friends That You Are Like a Coach for Me, Is That Okay?"

"Sure. Is that the way you think about me or is it just the way you want to describe our work to other people?" This question and response can lead the two of you into a great discussion about your client's view of therapy and the relationship. Different clients would probably describe you in different ways, such as coach, friend, teacher, or guide, depending on their perceptions. With different clients, you might also describe your role in different ways, for example, mentor, advocate, guide, or companion.

Charlie

For as long as she could remember, Abbey's mother had been her buddy, but mom was not the person to consult for the problem that brought her into treatment with me. In her early thirties, she heard that her Irritable Bowel Syndrome could be linked to her early molestation by her uncle. She needed a mother figure to help guide her through the reclamation of her childhood and the sensitive release of her fury at her uncle. That was a role I took on with her. As we began to wind down our very successful work together, Abbey spontaneously laughed and announced: "You are my woman in a purple hat!" She asked if I knew the poem, which I did. She then blushed and asked sheepishly, "I think I just called you a woman, is that okay?" I was so touched and honored by her sentiment that I teared up in session and continue to do so when I recall the honor she gave me.

"Why Don't We Talk About You?"

You understand why the two of you are not talking about you. You have heard the rationale more times than you can probably bear to remember. Your client wasn't at those lectures, and for many people, it seems weird that you don't share information during the session. Clients often remark about it.

This question also has permutations that can sound like, "What do you look for in a romantic partner?" or "What are guys looking for (to a male counselor)?" or "Do guys ever change?" or "If you were my girl-friend, what would you have said/done?" The similarity in all of these questions is that clients are unwittingly attempting to change your role. In the original question, you are being invited to become an equal participant in the discussions; in the others, you have been cast as the expert in all matters, and your client wants to know your opinion, advice, or behavior. Your client no longer wants you to be therapist (as if that isn't challenging enough), but now wants you to be the spokesperson for an endless array of topics. It is flattering and tempting to expound, but it is not particularly useful for the client. Some mild disclosure can be helpful, such as "I wish I knew." or "I wonder about that, too." Maybe you can even state some fact that you know before returning to your client by asking, "What are your thoughts?"

There will be days when you want to answer, "Great idea, let's talk about me. I'm an interesting person with things to say." or "My ideal partner is evolved, likes walking in the rain, brews great coffee, and owns a private island," but you won't say these things. It isn't your hour.

"We Are Not Going to See Each Other for Four Weeks. How Will I Ever Get by During This Time?"

This kind of question can make you squirm with discomfort. You become important to your clients; you are trustworthy and they learn to depend on you. You need to be dependable in return. However, life doesn't stop because people are in therapy. There will be times when events in your life necessitate an extended absence, and some clients will be concerned, about you and about their own ability to cope. Your response needs to empathically acknowledge your client's concerns, even when you just want to deal with your own feelings (positive or negative) about the extended separation. "I know that you rely on our regular meetings, and I understand how difficult you expect this separation to be." After his expectations are revealed, the two of you can shift into a discussion about his strengths; you can identify available resources and come up with a plan, a goal, or a phrase that your client can emotionally hold on to until the two of you can continue.

FURTHER THOUGHTS

"If we can give up attachment to our roles as helpers, then maybe our clients can give up attachment to their roles as patients and we can meet as fellow souls on this incredible journey. We can fulfill the duties of our roles without being trapped by over-identification with them."

—Ram Dass

Your professional role is only one aspect of your identity, but it means that you emphasize certain elements of your personality and minimize others when you are working. It may feel awkward at first, like wearing someone else's clothes, but it gets comfortable and seeps securely into your identity. Your training has been about more than gaining information; it has transformed you.

The client walking through your door sees you as a professional and doesn't know if you have doubts about your role. On your side, you have agreed to be that person regardless of lack of sleep, other commitments, a bad day, a breakup, your own insecurities, a headache, or some other unsettling event. Your professional role may be uncomfortable or comfortable, make you proud or confound you, and be a source of possibility or restriction. Many factors have led you into this profession. Some of them you understand, but others are unknown. For example, you are probably a good listener, you are interested in people's stories, and you want to help. You have strengths that are useful to this work, so examine and sharpen them.

SUGGESTED READINGS

Arnkoff, D. B., Glass, C. R., & Shapiro, S. J. (2002). Expectations and preferences. in J. C. Norcross (Ed.), *Psychotherapy relationships that work: Therapist contributions and responsiveness to patients* (pp. 335–356). New York, NY: Oxford University Press.

Atkinson, D., Thompson, C., & Grant, S. (1993). A three-dimensional model for counseling racial/ethnic minorities. *The Counseling Psychologist, 21*, 257–277.

Bennett-Levy, J., & Thwaites, R. (2007). Self and self-reflection in the therapeutic relationship: A conceptual map and practical strategies for the training, supervision and self-supervision of interpersonal skills. In P. Gilbert & R. L. Leahy (Eds.), *The therapeutic relationship in cognitive behavioral psychotherapies* (pp. 255–281). New York, NY: Routledge.

Brooks-Harris, J. (2008). *Integrative multitheoretical psychotherapy*. Boston, MA: Houghton Mifflin.

Truscott, D. (2010). *Becoming an effective psychotherapist: Adopting a theory of psychotherapy that's right for you and your client*. Washington, DC: American Psychological Association.

Watkins, C. E. (2010). The hope, promise, and possibility of psychotherapy. *Journal of Contemporary Psychotherapy, 40*, 195–201.

CHAPTER

7

Money

Money is sometimes called the last taboo in psychotherapy, because clients seem to be more willing to talk about anything, even sex, rather than discuss money. Because clients pay for treatment, money is a topic that also exists between the two of you, not only in your clients' lives outside the session. The topic of money tends to have great meaning, even though clients are often unaware of their attitudes. These opinions are strong and formed in childhood, so when you have the opportunity, it is worth your time to examine your client's behaviors, attitudes, and emotions toward money.

Linda

Many years ago, in a brave and hostile moment, I suggested to my analyst that I pay for each session depending on how useful it was. If it helped me, I would pay full fee and if it didn't, we would discount the session accordingly. Interestingly, my analyst, who

(continued)

jumped on all comments that promised additional meaning, just laughed. Looking back, maybe we colluded in avoiding the underlying seriousness of my suggestion. In those days, being in therapy meant that I had to give up many other things because there wasn't enough money to do it all.

Even in therapy, where clients feel free to talk about so many personal concerns, money remains an odd subject. Talking about money is very intimate. Sure, clients complain that they don't have enough money, brag about having made a lot of money, regret losing or spending money, worry about running out of money, scheme to get more money, tell you about their partner's inability to handle money, or ask for fee reductions because they are having money problems, but rarely do we explore the meaning of money in their lives or in the therapy relationship. We suspect that most clinicians don't encourage clients to discuss money with the same zeal that they pursue these clients' relationships with friends, family, or work. Our reluctance to enter these conversations has the same result as avoidance of any topic: we learn less. In examining the following questions and formulating answers, we try to understand more about clients'—and clinicians'—general disinclination to talk about money.

When clients ask questions about money, you have the chance to respond and further the therapeutic process by understanding any additional symbolism. The meaning of money may, depending on your client, be related to security, saving, even hoarding, or feelings about power and acquisition.

Money can be a source of confusion, ignorance, incompetence, or conflict. Some clients avoid the topic because they don't want to deal with the feelings that may be aroused. If a client fumbles around, gets defensive, or shows hostility when money matters come up, you need more sensitivity, not less. Other clients are silenced by practical money matters. They lack basic personal finance skills and do not know how to make a budget, balance their checkbook, or access a credit report. Be careful not to shame them into further wordlessness.

The value and meaning of money is learned early. So is the way in which it is or is not talked about. When clients approach the subject, look for ideas that were formed in childhood and lessons learned from their mothers, fathers, and previous experiences. You can ask, "What did your parents teach you about money?", "What messages did you receive about money in the family in which you grew up?", "What did you learn from your first jobs?", "What are your fears about money?", or "Do you feel good about the way you handle finances?"

QUESTIONS

The following questions are answered in the Responses section:

"Do you have a sliding scale?"

"Can we negotiate our fee?" "May I have a discount?" "Will you lower my fee?"

"Why does psychotherapy cost so much?"

"Do you think I am getting my money's worth here?"

"Are you just in this for the money?"

"Did you charge me for that missed session?

"How much money do you make?"

"Does school cost a lot?"

"Isn't this like paying a prostitute? After all, how many people have to pay to have someone listen?"

"Can I pay for your services with a new set of tires I have?"

RESPONSES

If you are a student, clients probably assume that you are unpaid and are working to learn your craft, so they understand that their reduced fee or free session is in exchange for your gaining experience. If you work for an agency or hospital, you get a salary so clients can separate you from their payments. They forget that their fees are paying you. In private practice, the fees are your salary and the relationship to money, fee setting, negotiating, and collecting is direct. Keep these different settings in mind for the variety of answers that follow.

"Do You Have a Sliding Scale?"

If you are asked "Do you have a sliding scale?" on the phone, you may want to say, "My fee is $$$ but I do have a sliding scale. We can talk about that when you come in." A sliding scale is different than offering a set discount to special groups. Linda discounts significantly for full-time students but is more reluctant to provide the same reduction for working people, although when a client suffers monetary problems, Linda reduces the fee. In contrast, a sliding scale adjusts fees according to your client's income, so the amount goes up and down according to a financial formula. "Yes, the agency has a sliding scale according to your ability to pay" might be an appropriate response. At times, a variation on fee questions will be, "Do you charge for a first appointment?" which sounds like clients want a free test drive. We would answer, "Yes, I charge for all appointments."

If you are in training or worrying about money yourself, you may identify more strongly with clients' scarceness of money or lack of security. You may have a deep sense of empathy for clients who are struggling to meet their payments and understand their reluctance to pay the institution or agency. Coupled with guilt over whether you are worth the price, setting and collecting fees can become difficult.

Charlie

When I was in graduate school, a practicum teacher asked our class, "If you were in private practice right now, how much would you charge a client for an hour of psychotherapy with you?" Some students offered a specific amount. Others, practicing at clinics, stated the fees that were charged there. I kind of ducked the question and said, "Whatever the prevailing rate in this area is." Finally, one of the most thoughtful, experienced, and talented students among us, almost in a whisper, said "about 2 cents." Putting a value on what we do, what we offer, and what we are worth can be perplexing.

"Can We Negotiate Our Fee?" "May I Have a Discount?" "Will You Lower My Fee?"

If you work at an agency, there is often a staff member who negotiates and collects fees, usually after the intake. Fees are set depending on the client's ability to pay. It is not a good idea to completely separate fees from treatment. Even if you don't collect the money yourself, you need to know if your clients are paying or not, and you have to get comfortable speaking to them about fees, late payments, bounced checks, and whatever other money issues arise.

Be careful when you set fees, because your anxiety might lead you to quick decisions in order to get it over with. Similar to other topics, your clients pick up cues about how you feel about money and fees, so they will get impressions from your speech, bodily reactions, and your avoidance of the topic. You don't want to send the message "I don't talk about money," because this could be a significant issue that your client wants to eventually address.

Private practice clinicians generally have set fees and sometimes negotiate down, or sometimes not. You might answer, "My standard fee is $$ per session. It's a fair fee and I don't negotiate down very much." If new clients can't afford to pay for your services, then you can help them identify where they might get services that they can afford. You decide what criteria to use to set your fees and how to raise and lower them, but think it through ahead of time. If you set a reduced fee, consider your client's income and ability to pay, but also think about whether you will feel resentful if you lower the fee. You probably need to ask what your client earns to determine your final answer. We have each said, "I understand that you have lost your job and I'm glad to reduce my fee substantially for awhile so we can continue our work. When you are employed it will go back." or "This is a bad time for you to stop treatment, so I'm glad to reduce my fee while you get back on your feet."

When you work at a clinic with a sliding scale, money negotiations are equally important. A client's fee, whether it is $2.00 or full fee, represents his investment in your work together. It reinforces his commitment to the process and to showing up. Maybe most importantly, a fee reflects a mutual exchange of your professional service for an amount of money, and that exchange enhances professionalism and self-esteem.

"Why Does Psychotherapy Cost So Much?"

This question begs you to become defensive. You don't have a tangible product to sell; it can be awkward to explain your fees, especially if you are inexperienced. It is easy to forget that clients are paying for your time, education, and expertise as well as heating or cooling your office. Also, psychotherapy gains can be difficult to measure, so clients may express concern about the vagueness of the process and uncertainty about the outcome. If your client indicates a sincere curiosity, answer first, "My fees are in line with other therapists of my training." Some clients need to be educated, so you can say, "You are paying for my time, training, and expertise." or "Good mental health reduces or even prevents medical conditions. That makes our work quite practical and economical as you look ahead." You can follow with an inquiry, "Are you worried about money?"

Your client may not be worried about money but still want to hang on to every dollar. Money and payments may go against personality traits of obsessiveness and stinginess. Paying for help, whether it is an auto mechanic or medical treatment, can be difficult for many clients. This is important information to have for their treatment and, if that's the case, you will hear other comments that relate to independence, self-reliance, and need.

If, and it doesn't happen often, a client asks this question to intentionally demean therapy, try to recall the client's personality and consider the preceding comments in order to put the question in an appropriate context. If the previous discussion was about her insurance coverage or his shaky job status, that is different from the client who says, "Well, I guess you will be able to get away for a great vacation soon," as he writes your check. As always, the context helps clarify the meaning.

"Do You Think I Am Getting My Money's Worth Here?"

This question is another version of "Am I getting better?" and it is worthwhile to treat it as such, at least for starters. Begin by noting your client's specific gains, for example, "I have seen some changes in the way you manage your children." or "You seem to be more in control of your temper than when I first met you." or "Your attitude toward your elderly mother seems to be gaining compassion," and add, "To me, that's a real improvement. What do you think?" If, in your opinion, it is really a question about cost-effectiveness, you could provide some data and say, "Research has shown that people who attend to their psychological problems use fewer medical services, so they save money." Any answer you choose probably requires the traditional follow-up of, "Do *you* think you are getting your money's worth?" Whatever direction the discussion takes, stay attuned to disclosures about other techniques, topics, unexpressed goals, or styles that your client believes might be more effective for him.

Sometimes, this question, "Do you think I am getting my money's worth here?" marks the beginning of a retreat from therapy. To address any underlying concerns, you can inquire, "Do you think that we are working less effectively than we could be?" or "Are you saying that you want to end our work?" It is different when you work with couples. Any hint of money issues needs to be on the table, because it may have less to do with treatment and more to do with money as a source of conflict. When one member of the couple says therapy is "costing too much" or "We are not getting anywhere and it is expensive." or "We could be going out to dinner and talking," he may be demonstrating that he has different ideas about how to spend money. With couples, try saying, "Do you both feel this way?" and, once the topic is in the open, you will see whether it is a conflict between the two partners or between them and you.

Every once in awhile, you will also wonder if a client is showing improvement. Before you offer your opinion, ask, "What is your assessment of your progress?" Whatever the reason, some genuine exploration may be possible and could get you back on track. You probably already know the direction to take, for example, you might point out that, "There is a lot more going on for you that we have not talked about, such as (name an issue)." or "Although we talk about specific actions you want to take in your life, you seem reluctant to practice them outside this office. What's up with that?"

"Are You Just in This for the Money?"

It is very easy to take this question personally, but the query says more about the client than about you. It is a very unusual question and ought to be treated as the aggressive inquiry that it is. Responses such as, "Does it feel that way to you?" or "What gives you that idea?" will probably result in a response of, "I was kidding." Continue asking, "Kidding or not, it is quite a question. What has happened in here that made you ask it?" Whether this particular conversation proceeds in a useful direction, the comment still has significance about the way in which this client thinks about money, her own work, status, or self-worth, for example, whether you would be interested if you were not being paid to listen.

Perhaps the client also wonders if she will be cared about, or is therapy strictly a cash-and-carry deal, simply business.

"Did You Charge Me for That Missed Session?"

Most agencies and therapists in private practice have policies, verbal or written, that inform people: "Clients who do not cancel sessions without at least 24 hours' notice will be charged full fee/part fee for the session." Some offices adhere to this stated policy, but others ignore it. Most offices or clinicians who ignore this charge are likely doing so out of the goodness of their hearts, but it does send a message that policies are negotiable and questions the importance of attendance. It is preferable to think through a policy that you believe in, explain it early in treatment, and maintain it consistently. Otherwise, you unwittingly send the message that your rules don't matter.

"How Much Money Do You Make?"

Don't jump to conclusions. Respond, "Why are you asking?" A client might be motivated to ask this question because of envy, interest, curiosity, hostility, or aggression. You don't know until you ask. She might be trying to figure out your lifestyle, whether she can relate to you, or how many clients you are seeing. When you find out "What do you hope to know with that information?" you can reply, "I don't share that information with anyone but my accountant."

"Does School Cost a Lot?"

This question is very different if it comes from a high school student with dreams of becoming a therapist, an adult client who foresees a child's education expenses, or if it means something else entirely. Respond, "I don't mind discussing school, but I do have a question for you first. Why are you concerned about the cost of school?" and then you will be able to assess whether to respond with information, "Yes, school is very expensive these days." or treat the question as some other personal concern on the client's part.

"Isn't This Like Paying a Prostitute? After All, How Many People Have to Pay to Have Someone Listen?"

Focusing on payment removes some intimacy of therapy for your client because it is a reminder to both of you that you are being paid to help.

Intimacy and relational concerns about care and personal connection are just below the surface when you talk about money.

This question can feel hostile, and occasionally it will be, but usually it comes from clients who feel ashamed of being in therapy. Their needs and vulnerabilities make them uncomfortable. Simply reflect their concern, "This feels like a paid friendship to you." You can also suggest directly, "You seem to find it shameful to come to me for help." Depending on the client and your relationship, you may have an excellent opening to talk about shame and dependency, for example, "I know that this relationship is different from any other, but your question makes me wonder if you are generally uncomfortable asking for help/having needs/being dependent on others." Remember to value your time and effort, but keep in mind that you do not sell your love and care. Clients pay for your time, expertise, attention, and the holding environment of your office. Your love and care is not for sale, although it is a by-product of the work that you do.

"Can I Pay for Your Services With a New Set of Tires I Have?"

Bartering is tricky business, and serious boundary issues come into play with this question. Bartering is more common in rural areas than in urban regions. You will be tempted to say yes if you want your client to be able to continue in treatment, but think about this sort of exchange carefully before you answer. You don't want to regret your decision later. Many agencies have clear policies, so you may not have a choice. If you are making the decision, consider several points. Bartering is a bad idea when the client's offering does not have a set price. For example, a painting is different than a ticket to a ballgame, because a painting is subject to emotional attachment and monetary interpretation as opposed to the face value of a ticket.

The challenge of establishing a set price with which to barter becomes even more challenging with services rather than objects. Although you might agree that painting a room is worth X amount, you might be dissatisfied with the result and then what do you do? Time exchanges can also lead to resentment by either of you. Do you exchange an hour of therapy for an hour of leaf-raking? On the other hand, if you exchange an hour of therapy for six hours of leaf-raking, what does that say about the value of your client's labor?

It is never a good idea to have your clients do work in your home or office; it just crosses too many boundaries. So, an answer to this question might be, "That is an interesting idea. Why don't you find out the price of those new tires, and I will investigate what I would pay for new tires, and maybe we can work out an equitable exchange." or "I'm reluctant to barter. Let's see what other ideas we can come up with." Always consult the guidelines in your professional ethics code and state laws in these situations.

MONEY QUESTIONS UNRELATED TO THERAPY

Not all questions about money have to do with you or the fees for treatment. Next we present a few other questions about money, because your responses can help to turn these questions into more substantial topics for discussion. Because people learn the value and meaning of money at a young age, look for meanings communicated by clients' mothers, fathers, experiences, and culture. You can ask, "How did your parents handle money?" or "Let's talk about money and its meanings."

The following questions are answered in the Responses section:

"How can I talk to my parents/children/spouse about money?"
"How can I ask for a raise at work?"

RESPONSES

"How Can I Talk to My Parents/Children/Spouse About Money?"

"This is a wonderful question because it allows us to examine your feelings and attitudes toward money." In the ensuing discussion, you will learn more about the meaning of money in your client's life and his ability, or lack thereof, to broach delicate topics with family. As with other topics, you help him go from a place of silence and confusion to clarity.

"How Can I Ask for a Raise at Work?"

We would look at this broadly and wonder whether your client has problems with lack of confidence, passivity, or fear of authority, but first, he needs a response. "This is important and we can brainstorm possible ways of asking. But, before we go there, I am interested in the problems that surround your reluctance." After you have focused on work-related concerns, you can use the information to return to your client's general approach to life. "I think that there are implications for other areas of your life" is one way to talk more generally about self-value, considerations of others, possessions, and entitlement.

In thinking about all of these questions, don't forget that money is real. Don't skip that reality and instead look for some other meaning immediately.

FURTHER THOUGHTS

"For I don't care too much for money, for money can't buy me love."

—The Beatles

On the surface, discussions about money ought to be simple. Fees are a means of exchange—your knowledge and time in return for dollars. Of course, in reality it isn't a simple conversation, and money has psychological meaning to you and to your clients. For therapists, setting fees, feeling entitled to payment, and billing for your services is an emotion-filled responsibility, even though it is increasingly controlled by third-party payers. Don't let clients owe you lots of money. Deal with it and bring it up because they are also thinking about it. Be pragmatic as well as psychological, and clients will be relieved by your straightforwardness.

In the previous responses, we examined your client's relationship to money—what about you? It is a useful exercise to think about your own values and attitudes toward money. In this society, money is a mainstay, and everyone must have some relationship with it, whether that turns out to be love, hate, need, resentment, status, desire, or some combination. Begin with the lessons you learned from your parents, their attitudes toward spending, saving, and value, and move through your life and lessons learned from others who look at money differently from you. You probably have feelings about money and pride, power, ambition, independence, freedom, safety, security, or conflict. These attitudes will creep into your therapy sessions. Understanding your relationship, as well as your client's relationship, with money will be illuminating.

SUGGESTED READINGS

Feurerstein, C. W. (1971). Money as a value in psychotherapy. *Journal of Contemporary Psychotherapy*, 3, 99–104.

Field, R., & Hemmings, A. (2007). The role of money in the therapeutic exchange. In A. Hemmings & R. Field (Eds.), *Counselling and psychotherapy in contemporary private practice* (pp. 140–157). New York, NY: Routledge.

Groman, M. (2009). Lowering fees in hard times: The meaning behind the money. *Psychotherapy.net*. Retrieved March 8, 2010, from www.psychotherapy.net/article.

Lanza, M. L. (2001). Setting fees: The conscious and unconscious meanings of money. *Perspectives in Psychiatric Care*, 3, 69–72.

Levant, R., House, A., May, S., & Smith, R. (2006). Cost offset: Past, present, and future. *Psychological Services*, 3, 195–207.

Peck, J. S. (2008). *Money and meaning: New ways to have conversations about money with your clients. A guide for therapists, coaches, and other professionals.* Hoboken, NJ: Wiley.

Trachtman, R. (1999). The money taboo: Its effects in everyday life and in the practice of psychotherapy. *Clinical Social Work Journal*, 27, 275–288.

Tudor, K. (1998). Value for money? Issues of fees in counseling and psychotherapy. *British Journal of Guidance and Counselling*, 26, 477–493.

CHAPTER 8

Confidentiality

Confidentiality is the cornerstone of the therapy relationship. Every day, we hear secrets, pain, embarrassments, stories never before spoken, confusion, and confessions. If clients did not believe in our ability to keep their lives private, therapy might well be worthless. Confidentiality allows clients to trust us and feel that their lives are safely held.

Linda

There was one interaction when I totally blew it. I had treated Anne, a graduate student, for several months and had no understanding of why she was in therapy, what she was really like as a person, or how to be of help. It was an odd feeling. Anne was unfailingly polite and kept up a stream of talk but revealed little. At the university, I ran into one of her professors and without mentioning how I knew Anne, I said, obviously without thinking, "I know Anne Green is in your class. What's she like?" He answered, "Bright, seems nice." End of conversation.

(continued)

Anne walked in for the next session, sat down, and announced, "Before I quit, I want to tell you that you behaved in an unethical manner. I asked all my friends (*groan*) and they agree. You asked Professor Tattle about me. You broke my confidentiality. I quit." I sat there stunned and rightfully chastised. Quickly, I asked myself, "Why had I asked Professor Tattle about Anne?" and it suddenly, albeit late, became clear so I answered her. "I was wrong, probably not unethical because he had no idea how I knew you, but that doesn't matter. I was wrong. I think I wanted to know more about you. After all this time, I still don't feel like I know who you are."

Anne sat silently for awhile. The angry mood in the room evaporated and it was just the two of us, puzzled. "I think that's why I'm here," said Anne. "I don't think that I know me either." It was a breakthrough. She stayed in treatment and the work improved. I wish that I had used my confusion more constructively. I don't recommend fooling around with clients' rights in order to improve therapy, but it was another reminder that big mistakes can teach big lessons.

Clients can gossip with anyone and pour their hearts out to whomever they choose, but it is rare that they can count on their story remaining private, unshared, and unspoken. Think about it—when you tell a friend or family member about something you did, you will edit, shape, and adjust the story to suit your ends, whether that is avoiding embarrassment, looking good, reassuring the listener, eliciting sympathy, or hoping for another specific reaction or outcome. In therapy, although clients may shape events or even lie, there is no real purpose to doing so. We don't repeat their stories, we don't see them outside the office, we don't keep information as ammunition to punish or shame them, and we don't use the material except in ways that work to benefit their mental health. Unlike many other areas of life, in the therapy room, clients will not have vulnerabilities thrown back in an argument, used for manipulation, or announced in judgment. You provide safety when you provide confidentiality.

Unlike other topics where the suggested responses were guided by theory or by clinical judgment, the questions asked about confidentiality are explicit and pretty straightforward, so your answers can be direct as well.

Managing confidentiality is complex; answering questions is less so. Many of your answers will be guided by law and ethics and will not be based solely on your clinical judgment. States have mental health laws that govern confidentiality. For example, in Illinois, The Illinois Mental Health and Developmental Disabilities Confidentiality Act ("IMHDDCA" or "Act"), 740 ILCS 110/1, *et seq.* outlines extensive methods for handling mental health information and records. The IMHDDCA defines confidential communications, provides directions for access to and disclosure of mental health information, creates privileges, and provides for civil and criminal penalties for breach of its provisions. The underlying basis for the provisions of the IMHDDCA is found in the general statement: "All records and communications shall be confidential and shall not be disclosed except as provided in this Act." Your state has a similar law, and you can get a copy from your state government's website.

Understanding laws is important, but here we talk about responding to questions in ways that further treatment. Our job is to guarantee confidentiality even when our clients seem indifferent to this essential therapeutic element.

Linda

Every once in awhile, a friend or family member will preface a conversation with the phrase, "You can't tell anyone," and I've begun to respond, "You forget. I'm a professional secret keeper." The lessons learned in the office creep into the rest of your life, and you become aware of how precious and rare discretion is in today's world.

QUESTIONS

The following questions are answered in the Responses section:

"Is everything that I say confidential?
"Would you ever tell anyone what we say here?"

"I know that you can't talk about our sessions, but can I?"

"Who else knows about me? Who do you talk to?"

"Did you leave a message on my phone machine?"

"I think I saw a friend of mine leaving your office—does Joe come here too?"

"Do you take notes? May I see them?"

"What would you tell my parents if they call?" "My mother wants to call you. Will you talk to her?"

"If I bring my husband/mother/sister in here, will you tell them what we talk about?"

"Do any of your other clients talk about me?"

"I want my friend to come and see you. What if she talks about me?"

"If I tell you things, will you have to call the police/child custody/my parents?"

RESPONSES

"Is Everything That I Say Confidential?

Confidentiality may feel like a gift to clients, but it is your obligation, not your choice. Confidentiality is a standard of professional conduct that compels you not to discuss information with anyone except under certain circumstances, and it is spelled out in your field's ethics code and in specific state laws.

Everyone has taken an ethics class in graduate school, and it is essential to understand and live within the ethics code for your discipline. In replying to your client, it is important to provide answers that are factually correct, reflect your practice, and further the work of therapy. You can say, "You have confidentiality in here. That means that I will not discuss our work with anyone unless you give me permission. That said, there are a few mandated exceptions which include minor children, the threat of harm to yourself or others, and revelations of specific crimes." There are other instances when you are not mandated to report information but have a choice whether to take action.

There are specific ethics codes for all of the major mental health provider professions. Rules about confidentiality for psychology, social work, and counseling are similar, and you can find them at various websites, including:

www.socialworkers.org/pubs/code/default.asp for social workers

www.apa.org/ETHICS/code2002.html for psychologists

www.counseling.org/Resources/CodeOfEthics/TP/Home/CT2
.aspx for counselors

www.psych.org/MainMenu/PsychiatricPractice/Ethics.aspx for
psychiatrists

www.aamft.org/resources/LRM_Plan/Ethics/ethicscode2001.asp
for marriage and family therapists

"Would You Ever Tell Anyone What We Say Here?"

In all states, there are behaviors and thoughts that, without a client's consent, you *can* report, you *must* report, and you *cannot* report. Your state laws will tell you precisely what is included in each category. Clinically, however, in this question your clients may be asking about the law and ethics or may be expressing concerns about trust and confidentiality. Answer concretely first, and then you can explore their misgivings. "In certain circumstances, I am required to disclose information. For example, if you are suicidal or homicidal, I would move to protect you or others. I don't expect this to ever happen, but you did ask about my breaking confidentiality. Is there something that you are worrying about?"

Commonly, clients ask if you will send your notes to their insurance companies. "If you waive your rights to an insurance company or someone else, I have to respond." If your client is neither suicidal, homicidal, or abusing a child or elder, it is useful to inquire further, "I'm glad to tell you the laws and my own policy, but are you worrying about something in particular?" or "I wonder if you are worrying about the confidentiality in here. Are you deciding how much to trust me?" Or be even more direct when you add, "Do you have a secret in mind?" If you want to go broadly, you may consider asking, "Have you ever had a bad experience with someone who didn't keep your secrets?"

Confidentiality is both an ethical concept and a legal one, and it is recognized in courtrooms. There is disagreement on the exact parameters of confidentiality, but everyone seems to agree that clients have the absolute right to know its limits. It is always better to have this discussion early on, but you may have overlooked it or your client may have forgotten. Whenever it comes up, discuss it honestly and fully as it pertains to your specific situation.

When clients lie or distort an event, they are doing so because they want self-protection, not to protect anyone else. Your session is confidential, so the common excuse of protecting someone else's feelings doesn't apply very well. However, self-protection is a fierce inducement. When lies and distortions are later revealed, when protections are dropped, you will probably be faced with your client's shame or embarrassment. Ask about it: "Were you ashamed?" Learning to be honest in therapy sets the stage for being honest in the rest of their lives. This is one tremendous therapeutic by-product of privacy and confidentiality.

Charlie

Many sessions into my work with MaryBeth, she began to cry and held up her handkerchief to cover her face. When I observed, "I can't see you," she said, "Yes, I need this," and with that protection, she was able to talk about being molested at an early age. Despite all my previous assurances of confidentiality and MaryBeth believing me, she needed another layer of privacy. It didn't matter to me how she was able to talk; the important fact was that a little more physical privacy allowed her to say the words she had not voiced aloud for 30 years. Within a week or two of our session, she had a conversation with her sister about the abuse and learned that her parents had always believed her and had cut off relations with the offending relative. MaryBeth never knew. The information changed her view of a terrible period of her life. She could not change the molestation, but knowing that her parents believed her and acted for her made a great difference to her.

"I Know That You Can't Talk About Our Sessions, But Can I?"

"Yes, I am bound by confidentiality, but you are not. You can talk about our sessions to whomever you like, although therapy sessions can be difficult to describe and you might find yourself frustrated." A related answer is, "In therapy, you hold the privilege, which means that, without explicit permission from you, I cannot discuss our work with anyone—exceptions excluded, but yes, you can." More interestingly, you might follow up by asking, "Do you like to talk about our work with your friends or family?"

We don't want to inhibit you, but your clients will talk about you and therapy. They may describe insights or bits of conversations in ways that, if you overheard the depiction, you might not recognize as having occurred between the two of you. It happens. Be aware of what you disclose; it may get repeated and distorted.

"Who Else Knows About Me? Who Do You Talk To?"

"No one knows that you come here unless you tell them," or if the situation is otherwise, "There are other people covered by our confidential relationship, for example, I might seek consultation or supervision. I do sometimes ask a colleague when I feel the need of another opinion. I do/do not reveal your name in these consultations." or "In that case, my consultant will/will not know your name."

In agencies, there may be different policies and you can explain them simply by saying, "In this agency, we do consult with one another, but everything is kept in-house." or "I have a supervisor whose opinion I value, and I may ask her about different issues that come up." or "We strongly believe in collaboration, so we do share information at specific case conferences. Everything stays in the agency." or "There is no confidentiality among the therapists within this agency. We work together as a team." The team approach is used frequently in nontraditional settings, so you may need to clarify confidentiality more than once.

If you receive regular supervision, you need to reveal this information to clients. Sometimes you will feel like apologizing for this fact because you feel less experienced than you would like to be, but in our experience, clients appreciated knowing that a more senior clinician is available for consultation.

If a client is mandated by a court to be in treatment, you will be talking to other people, perhaps a lawyer or judge. Your client needs to know this and any other parameters that influence confidentiality.

There are other considerations that could prove useful. In the question, "Who else knows about me?" your client may be hopeful that you do talk about him or that he is interesting and worth talking about.

It appears often in adolescent self-centeredness, disguising the wish to be special or imagining that you only have this particular client about whom to think. Any and all of these considerations could be contained in the question and, if you think that your client is motivated by those wishes, you can ask, "Would you like me to talk about you?"

"Did You Leave a Message on My Phone Machine?"

It is probably useful, when a client first gives you a phone number, to ask whether it is a private one and whether you can leave a message on it. Phone machines, office voice-mails, shared messages of all kinds, including e-mail if you communicate that way, are not as private as we would like to believe. It is best to keep your message simple and unrevealing. On office machines and home voice-mails in particular, we leave messages without using formal titles or organizational references, just in case someone else picks it up. The simplest answer to this particular question is either "yes" or "no," but that doesn't elicit the client's concern, so ask, "Yes, I did/No, I did not leave a message. Is there a problem with that number?" It may be helpful to also clarify, "Yes, you left that number for me. I only gave my name, no information. How would you like me to communicate with you?

"I Think I Saw a Friend of Mine Leaving Your Office—Does Joe Come Here Too?"

Whether Joe or Jen or anyone else comes in, it doesn't matter. We smile and say casually, "You know that I don't talk about who might be a client." No elaboration is needed. This response not only answers the question, it also provides reassurance that, if anyone asks about this client, your answer will be the same. A similar question, "Do I know your other clients?" can be answered with, "Everybody who comes in here has confidentiality. That means that I don't reveal if they come here, who comes here, or what they say—you included." This answer is generally met with relief. After all, if you aren't going to gossip about other clients, you won't reveal this client's secrets either.

"Do You Take Notes? May I See Them?"

Do you keep notes? Most people in agencies and in private practice take some sort of notes. Some people keep detailed records in accord with an outline and others just sketch rough reminders. Legally and ethically, it is a very good idea to keep records up to date. Clients do have the right to see their records, but we don't encourage it. "Yes (or no), I do (do not) take notes. I like to keep certain aspects of our work together fresh for me." If there is a need, you can continue, "You do have the legal right to request your record, but I'm not keeping any secrets from you. I'm happy to discuss any ideas with you. What do you want to know?"

If your client is a minor or has a legal guardian, there are very specific laws about what you are required to reveal. Confidentiality is not identical for adults and children or teenagers under certain ages. It is wise to discuss the legal versus clinical differences and implications with the parents and with the child, assuring parents that, "If I see any cause for concern, I will be in touch with you immediately. I understand that you are worried." If it comes up, you might add, "Despite the laws that say you have the right to read any records that I keep about your child, I can tell you that therapy proceeds better when your child retains the right to speak confidentially." or "Your son is a teenager, and I would like to respect his desire to have a place to talk freely."

"What Would You Tell My Parents if They Call?" "My Mother Wants to Call You. Will You Talk to Her?"

If you treat children, you already know that parents hold a lot of power. They bring your clients in and can pull them out or make it impossible for their son or daughter to continue. Even if that was not the case, always treat parents with respect. Most of them are well meaning and terribly worried about the child, adolescent, or young adult whom they have entrusted to your care. The answer to these questions and the ensuing discussion can be very helpful to treatment and can model manners and boundaries for young people. So, to the underage child, we might say, "Of course I would talk to your parents if they called. They are concerned and that's a good thing. However, I will tell you about it, and I am always careful what I share with parents or anyone else." If you suspect that the question has come up because the parents may be in touch, you can return to the specifics of this client's life with, "We have talked about a lot of things; let's go through them and decide what can be shared and what remains confidential." You may want to ask, "Why would your parents call?" or "What do you want me to say? Let's compare your ideas with what I believe will be helpful for them."

In this question, the age of your client matters greatly. Children and early adolescents don't expect confidentiality; they think that the grown-ups always talk about them, but older adolescents have increased needs for individuation, ownership of their minds and bodies, and therefore, they will prize their privacy more highly.

You will also get this question from young adults whose parents want to call. Confidentiality is clear in these instances, and it gives you a chance to discuss, "Why would your mother call?" or "Do you want to involve your family in treatment?" You will learn a lot about family dynamics.

You may work with severely impaired people of all ages who have guardians. Be sure you know the rights of all these people. With your client, the work is to keep them apprised of communications and maintain trust.

"If I Bring My Husband/Mother/Sister in Here, Will You Tell Them What We Talk About?"

The first thing to think about is why your client wants to bring other people into the session. Often, it is a good idea. Different theoretical perspectives have specific things to say about the usefulness and about the techniques to use. As a privacy or confidentiality question, we assume that some discussion has already taken place and the two of you have agreed to include others. "Before you bring anyone in here, the two of us will discuss what we do and do not want to talk about. We will also discuss what you want me to convey to them and what I think is important to tell them."

"Do Any of Your Other Clients Talk About Me?"

"That's a fascinating question. Where does it come from?" We would be wondering if the reverse is true, meaning that this client is curious and wants to talk about others. Explore your client's concern for his image. The concern that you or others are talking about him could mean many things, including some paranoia or entitlement that is worth discussing.

"I Want My Friend to Come See You. What if She Talks About Me?"

It is never a great idea to see very close friends and certainly not family members. If, in your opinion, this is a legitimate referral, some discussion is needed. "How would you feel about me seeing your friend, even if she never talks about you? Are you comfortable with it?" Even if the client is okay with it, you have to think about the potential problems. For example, will both clients now be restricted in the material they choose to share? Will they, even unknowingly, enter into a competition to become your favorite? You might say, "It is very flattering that you would put your friend in my hands" and then finish the sentence by either saying: "go ahead and have her call," or "but there are lots of good therapists to whom we could refer your friend and avoid the chance of any confusion."

"If I Tell You Things, Will You Have to Call the Police/Child Custody/My Parents?"

Again, laws are very clear about what information must be revealed to police, parents/guardians, and the authorities. In some instances, you have a choice, but other times you do not. Depending on the scope of your practice, be familiar with the laws about child abuse and neglect and the abuse of disabled persons and elders. Clearly state: "If you are in danger, I will work to protect you." Next, observe, "It seems that there is something you ought to be telling me now," and be sure to follow up.

FURTHER THOUGHTS

> "Everyone is like a moon, and has a dark side which he never shows to anybody."
>
> —Mark Twain

By entering this field, you have agreed to become a secret keeper. You will learn about the dark side of people's lives, and that information must remain confidential. Broken confidentiality is broken trust and will not be easily repaired. We seem to live in a society that places little value on confidentiality and great value on gossipy revelations. Information, true or false, travels with greater speed than ever before. Such free and easy access to shared knowledge, innuendo, or fantasy makes our work even more special. Years ago, a friend of ours read an article written by her therapist, recognized the client described, and lost trust in the treatment, eventually ending therapy without ever explaining the reasons to her therapist.

Vanity, hidden in sharing, is a real danger for clinicians. It is easy to carelessly reveal "I know so and so" to a friend. Casual in-the-office comments can also be revealing, even if your hope was to teach or model a solution. For example, "I have a client who was injured playing a sport but was able to become a coach" may reveal too much or cause your client to wonder if you also speak about him to others. Be careful. Even if you are convinced that you are being altruistic or educative in your casual disclosure, you can divulge too much. When you are confused, consult with a colleague. One of the ironies of doing clinical work is that, although you meet and talk with people all day, your work is often isolating.

Linda

When my older daughter was in middle school, she often asked me to tell her about my clients and any unusual situations I had come across that day. She was young and curious, and I imagine that my stories would have been even better than sixth-grade gossip or a television show. Certainly, she had been at friends' homes and heard delicious stories from parents who were in other fields of work. Each time, when I explained that I couldn't talk about my work, I felt cranky, not virtuous. I wanted to be the mom with the entertaining story, but instead I was the mom with rules about confidentiality.

SUGGESTED READINGS

Fisher, C. B., & Oransky, M. (2008). Informed consent to psychotherapy: Protecting the dignity and respecting the autonomy of patients. *Journal of Clinical Psychology: In Session, 64,* 576–588.

Fisher, M. A. (2008). Protecting confidentiality rights: The need for an ethical practice model. *American Psychologist, 63,* 1–13.

Pomerantz, A. M. (2005). Increasingly informed consent: Discussing distinct aspects of psychotherapy at different points in time. *Ethics & Behavior, 15,* 351–360.

Younggren, J. N., & Harris, E. A. (2008). Can you keep a secret? Confidentiality in psychotherapy. *Journal of Clinical Psychology: In Session, 64,* 589–600.

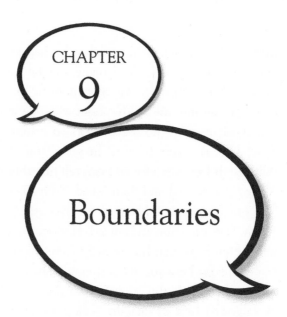

CHAPTER

9

Boundaries

The work of boundaries is in every decision you make and in every session you conduct. Like the purpose of skin on your body, boundaries keep in what needs to be in the therapeutic relationship and keep out what needs to be out. And like skin, you don't think about them very deliberately until you have a problem. However, the placement of boundaries and the ideas about what behaviors constitute boundary crossings are subject to much discussion. We present an entire chapter on boundaries because, when mistakes happen, it is often here.

Linda

I treated a 28-year-old man named Bill. At least, I thought that was his name. He paid weekly and he paid in cash. He was in treatment because he had been fired from a job in Miami and returned home in disgrace. He had wanted the earliest appointment in the morning so that he would not run into anyone else. Several weeks

(continued)

into treatment, Bill confessed that he had given me a fake name. He wouldn't tell me his real name, but he was too honest to continue with the charade. Another morning, it occurred to him that he might run into me on the street when he was not alone. "Would you speak to me?" he asked. "Do you want me to?" I wondered aloud. "I've thought about it," he said. "You can say hello to me but that's all. If I'm with a friend I can tell him that you know my sister." "Okay," I answered and then asked, "Why would it be so horrible?" "No one knows that I come here. No one knows about therapy." "Okay," I assured him and guided our discussion to his shame. Shame was the problem that had brought him in, and shame produced his fear of anyone knowing about therapy. The time and space boundary of my office made the conversation possible. The clear boundaries also allowed him to imagine seeing me elsewhere in an inadvertent boundary crossing and opened up our subsequent conversation. The discussion that followed these questions and answers provided another way to deepen our understanding of his tormenting shame.

Therapeutic boundaries demarcate what is appropriate, professional, and ethical conduct versus what is therapist conduct that goes against the professional commitment to nonmaleficence. Clear and appropriate boundaries allow clients to reveal their important experiences and disclose their feelings because they believe that they are safe and will be treated properly.

By design, therapy suspends typical social interactions so that you can create a setting that temporarily insulates your clients. One reason that they can allow themselves to be exposed is because they decide what information remains inside the room and what information leaves with them. But please do not think that boundaries are exclusively for your clients. You need boundaries to maintain your sense of safety, comfort, and your ability to attend to work without distraction or conflicting agendas. Additionally, when you feel comfortable with the boundaries you have established, you are better able to respond professionally to a client who presses for overly intimate self-disclosure, repulses you with unwelcome physical contact, threatens physical harm, or brings inappropriate gifts. This might mean explicitly explaining the nature of boundaries to your client. You will work with many people who have spent a lifetime in situations with poor boundaries and recurring violations. Your clarity communicates the importance of the work being done and helps your clients feel connected, safe, and secure while they experience and develop their own healthy boundaries.

As you may have noticed in other chapters, many questions that you receive compel you to think about some aspect of boundary management, and the answers are directed that way, although not always explicitly. The other chapters that touch most directly on boundaries are Chapter 8, Confidentiality; Chapter 10, Personal Questions; Chapter 20, Out of the Office; and Chapter 21, Keeping in Touch.

The following questions occur regularly and rarely lead to significant boundary violations. If you find yourself in these situations on a consistent basis, get a good consultation about your boundaries and also examine this topic in your own therapy.

QUESTIONS

The following questions are answered in the Responses section:

"I know that you belong to this group I want to join. Would that be a problem for you?"

"I gave your name to a friend who wants a therapist. Will you see her?"

"How could you agree to see my roommate/co-worker/hairstylist?"

"How could you let me run into so-and-so in your waiting room?"

"Rather than pay you for my next three sessions, can I paint your garage/mow your lawn instead?"

"I met your son/friend and he said that you drink too much/punished him/fought with your kids/had a bad temper/got divorced. Did you?"

"Sorry I am late. Can we have extra time?"

> "Maybe this is weird, but can you hold my hands while I tell you about this painful experience?"
>
> "Would you like to have some cupcakes from the batch I made this morning?"
>
> "I know that your birthday was yesterday. Can I give you this card?"
>
> "Why didn't you give me a sympathy card when everyone else did?"
>
> "Will you take my friend as a client?"
>
> "This movie says a lot about me. Can I loan it to you to watch?
>
> "Do you have an extra $3 so I can take the bus home?"
>
> "Can I borrow that book on your shelf?"

We also discuss certain boundary slips by therapists:

> "What do you mean you booked someone else into my appointment time?"
>
> "How could you lock me out?"
>
> "How could you not have been here for our appointment?"

RESPONSES

Some considerations of boundaries are easy. You maintain clients' confidentiality, you don't have sex with your clients, you don't go into business or get stock tips from them, and, as Linda once had to explain to a student, you don't fix them up on a date with your friend, even if treatment is coming to a close. However, boundaries are not laws. They are guidelines that grew out of client care and responsible practice and are not absolute.

Not all boundary crossings are violations. A boundary *crossing* refers to any deviation from the strict professional role or from the traditional forms of therapy but is probably not exploitative of the client (e.g., minor self-disclosure, the exchange of small gifts or greeting cards, nonsexual touch, incidental encounters outside the office, and home visits). A boundary *violation* occurs when a therapist crosses the line of integrity or misuses her power in a way that could exploit or harm a client. Ideally, your alertness to boundaries becomes second nature, and you give them as much consideration as decisions regarding clinical interventions. When you face complex ethical, clinical, or legal considerations about a boundary concern, get a consultation with an appropriate expert.

We have clustered the questions in this chapter into five categories: overlapping relationships, time, touch, gift giving and receiving, and material exchanges. Overlapping relationships is the theme of this first set of questions. There will be times when you unavoidably wind up in a dual relationship with a client. You might attend the same church, have kids at the same school, or be invited to the same party. This is awkward but not unethical. Sometimes you can alter the situation, and other times you cannot, but you can always discuss it together.

"I know that you belong to this group I want to join. Would that be a problem for you?" "I gave your name to a friend who wants a therapist. Will you see her?" "How could you agree to see my roommate/co-worker/ hairstylist?" "How could you let me run into so-and-so in your waiting room?" "Rather than pay you for my next three sessions, can I paint your garage/mow your lawn instead?" "I met your son/friend and he said that you drink too much/punished him/fought with your kids/had a bad temper/got divorced. Did you?"

"I Know That You Belong to This Group I Want to Join. Would That Be a Problem for You?"

When a client asks you ahead of time, you are fortunate because you can talk about the issues and complications, and the two of you can decide on a comfortable course of action. In fact, there is much to learn that will increase your alliance and add to your client's understanding of herself. If there is only one school, everybody's children will attend and you will run into each other. In small communities, if you are gay or lesbian, you may have to attend the only local pride group.

We suggest responding initially to this question with, "I'm glad you brought that up. Let's look at what that would be like for each of us." The second sentence is a reminder that you, the therapist, also matter in the discussion. Having your client's best interest in mind does not mean that you simply accede to every request or ignore your own interests. Your assertion of appropriate boundaries may be the best lesson she can experience. "Yes, we can both belong, and now let's talk about how we will manage when we run into each other." or "No, I don't think it is in either of our interests to have this additional contact, because it could compromise both our experiences here as well as in the other group." As always, there needs to be a discussion of the implications of either action.

"I Gave Your Name to a Friend Who Wants a Therapist. Will You See Her?"

"Do you want me to see her, or do you want me to help her find someone else?" Clients usually pause at this question, but they need to think about whether they are comfortable sharing their therapist. We have found that many clients have a small "A-ha!" moment, and they realize that what seemed like a simple request is more complicated. They often reply, "Oh, maybe I don't want you to see her. Are you willing to help her find someone?"

"How Could You Agree to See My Roommate/Co-Worker/ Hairstylist?"

This question provides a twist on boundary management in overlapping relationships. If you are asked this question, it means that you have already agreed to see the roommate, co-worker, or hairstylist. You may or may not have known about the social connection. When you knowingly accept clients who are closely associated to one another, be aware of your own needs to gather referrals, see more clients, or desire to help everyone instead of referring out. An appropriate response to this question could be: "You know that I can't talk about another client with you, but I am very interested to hear about what is going on with you in this regard." After the discussion, you will be in a better position to protect everyone's rights.

"How Could You Let Me Run Into So-and-So in Your Waiting Room?"

The previous questions illustrated situations over which you had some control. In this example, you may not have had much to do with the client's experience. For most clients, your waiting room is an extension of your protected environment, and they are rattled by the perceived intrusion. Explore this concern, even when it means that you can expect hostility. "I certainly didn't intend to set you up for this experience, but

I can see that you are upset. Can you tell me more about how running into so-and-so affects you?" As emotions are reviewed, more reasoned considerations can be addressed, and accommodations can be discussed, if needed. Your office is a safe place but not a perfect place.

"Rather Than Pay You for My Next Three Sessions, Can I Paint Your Garage/Mow Your Lawn Instead?"

We have included this question in the overlapping relationships section because trading services with your client creates a secondary business association and becomes a dual relationship. In Chapter 7, Money, we went into more detail about bartering your therapy time for goods that have a firm and objective dollar value versus services that involve complicated, subjective factors. Here, we want to point out that overlapping relationships have a potential to harm treatment. What if the painting or mowing is substandard? A gentle, and resolute, rejection of this offer is in order: "Although your service could solve one problem because it would pay for your sessions, it also brings up other factors that can really mess up our relationship. Let's explore other ways to help continue our work."

"I Met Your Son/Friend and He Said That You Drink Too Much/Punished Him/Fought With Your Kids/Had a Bad Temper/Got Divorced. Did You?"

This final question about overlapping relationships is the most complicated. This question and its variations is another reminder of the lack of control we have over our personal worlds. Although it may present a real challenge to do so, your job hasn't changed. Focus on your client, don't make this personal, don't get defensive, and deal with your anger at your son/friend/former friend later. Now is the time to observe, join, and explore with this client: "Wow, what an interesting observation. Certainly you have become privy to details, perhaps true or not, of my life. I am really curious what these revelations mean to you and to our work together." Whether or not you decide to address the substance of the information, your client's reaction is the work of therapy.

"Sorry I Am Late. Do We Have Extra Time?"

The second category of boundary questions to examine regards the time parameters of therapy. You are the time keeper for the session. Your appointments commit you to a definite start and end time. It helps to create the structure for your work and dramatically distinguish therapy from other relationships. Time provides one form of container for you and your clients so that they can depend on a regular length of session and your availability. That said, time boundaries are not sacrosanct, and minor shifts—for instance, if a client is 5 minutes early and both of you are ready to begin—are reasonable. Generally, reliability about time is a gift to you both.

With clear boundaries of time, you know when you have deviated, intentionally or unintentionally, from them. Whether your client is asking for something additional, "Do we have extra time?" or wants to know if you value her, "I have so much more to talk about. Can we go a little longer today?" be careful because you may not be able to honor these requests again. Clarity helps. "Yes, today it works for me and we do have an extra 10 minutes." or "Sorry, I don't have extra time today." or "Let's figure out the best way to use the time that we do have today." If this client needs more time, an additional session might be in order. If requests for additional time become a regular part of therapy, give some serious thought to whatever factors are creating the request.

There will be some sessions when you have to be flexible with time; for example, when clients need to compose themselves after difficult conversations, when you have allowed them to continue with a thought or story, or when you have started your session late. In each of these situations, stretching the time frame may contribute to the therapeutic alliance and it makes sense. You also might need to communicate possible future limitations, for example, "Are you okay to leave? Do you need a moment to get yourself together?" or "Yes, I do have an extra 10 minutes before I need to end." or "Finish your thought before we end." Don't give away time and then resent your client for the decision you made. If you must start a session late, or answer an emergency phone call during a session, be sure to ask your client if she can stay for an extra few minutes to make up the time, rather than assuming that she can do so.

"Maybe This Is Weird, But Can You Hold My Hands While I Tell You About This Painful Experience?"

The third category is touch. There has always been serious debate about the place of touch in treatment. We want you to be comfortable sorting out the gentle touch on your client's arm that communicates empathy from touches that may become flirtatious. Simple actions like high fives and handshakes are common and represent the usual amount of touching. Not surprisingly, the major concern is that nonsexual touch may be perceived of as sexual or may lead to sexual touch and the exploitation of clients. For example, a high five becomes hand-holding, becomes a back massage, becomes a boundary violation.

Our major focus in how to respond to requests for touch is to consider the degree to which touch is appropriate. Consider your client's personality, history (especially any sexual inappropriateness), age, culture, gender, and relationship to you; what you believe about touch; your client's problems and level of functioning, and your comfort level. These factors are critical and will guide you. Think about age, for example, in working with children, touching is always initiated by them, not you. The other variables are equally important in order to understand the meaning of touch.

Certainly, refusing to shake a client's outstretched hand at an initial meeting or after an important session would be strange. However, Linda used to treat a young man who insisted on shaking hands after each session so that he could use that touch and subsequent fantasies in order to masturbate later. His insistence became a pattern, and that made it available to examine. Usually, inappropriate requests for touch become obvious, if not immediately, then over time.

Still, touching gets complicated. With some clients, the occasional hug will seem natural and probably will happen without a lot of questions or delayed personal recriminations. However, if you are uncomfortable or have any concerns that physical contact will be troublesome later on, consider saying, "I can really tell that this has been emotionally draining for you. However, hugs are not usually part of the therapy that we do here." Use your judgment, but, when it comes to touch, we suggest a conservative response until you know your client, whether a child or adult. With an established client, you know that your relationship rests on a history of respect for boundaries, and you have learned about your client's history of relations with others, so you may have more latitude.

In the previous question, your client is telling you very specifically that she is looking for comfort while she tells you about her painful experience. Although this client is asking for a more intimate contact than the previous client example, it probably makes sense in the context of your existing therapy relationship and might seem very natural to reach over and take her hand.

In addition to the personal context, touch has cultural meanings. Some clients, and some therapists, think little about a pat on the back, quick hug, or other casual touch. For other clients and therapists, any form of touch can cross boundaries of distance, formality, respect, or sexuality. This element of your relationship, like others, develops uniquely with each client and requires you to look closely at the individual meaning.

"Would You Like to Have Some Cupcakes From the Batch I Made This Morning?"

Gift giving and receiving is the fourth category to examine. "Would you like to have some cupcakes from the batch I made this morning?" "I know that your birthday was yesterday. Can I give you this card?" "Why didn't you give me a sympathy card, when everyone else did?" "Will you take my friend as a client?"

These are all questions that we use to illustrate the major concerns about gift giving and receiving. In a nonrandom sample of our colleagues, we did not find one person who had received a wildly inappropriate gift. A few said that they had to pleasantly refuse an overenthusiastic gift, but no one received disturbing gifts. So, you can relax and think about understanding the ideas behind gifts and how to handle these interchanges respectfully and therapeutically.

This could be cupcakes, homemade jam, apples from the garden, a poem, or a book. There is a lot of sharing in therapy, although not usually of material items. You give time, attention, emotion, expertise, and careful professional treatment planning. Clients share their time, effort, trust, and energy. Payments are usually money or, in training clinics, clients also give the training therapists needed chances to learn and improve their skills.

Because gifts represent departures from your standard procedures, you have to think about whether they are excessive or disruptive. Excessive compensation alters the relationship and raises questions of its influence on the process. There are good reasons why we are paid fees and do not work on commissions or get a percentage of our clients' successes.

Mostly, you simply say, "What a thoughtful gesture, thank you." Because gift giving isn't a regular aspect of sessions, you might ask, "Is it a special occasion?" or "Is there a special reason for the cupcakes?" In our experience, holiday gifts are often presented without much thought, especially to therapists who work with children. You are on the list with teachers and other helpful people in the child's life. Students can also get gifts, because clients know that you are not being paid. Some gifts are ways of saying, "I know you, too," and recognize your tastes, like a certain book, or postcard depicting an artist, a piece of special chocolate, or an article about tennis. Other gifts are about the clients, and they are sharing aspects of their lives with you, like a book of photos from their home state. Still other gifts contain requests for you to get to know them better (e.g., a book about depression or a movie depicting a certain culture). In these latter instances, be sure to ask about the meaning.

A good example of an inexperienced therapist struggling to figure out his comfortable boundaries follows.

Charlie

A male therapist at our in-house training clinic was seeing Barb, a client who developed an erotic transference to him. Barb wanted an out-of-the-office relationship with her therapist and regularly told him so. He, under the guidance of a supervisor, spent a great deal of their therapy time reminding her of his boundaries and his desire to have an ethical in-the-office-only relationship. When they were ending, with two more sessions scheduled, Barb brought her therapist a gift. She had painted a tree and included a poem that acknowledged how the tree had grown and prospered because of the life-enhancing care it received. He did not know how to react to this gift. After all, he had felt intruded upon during much of treatment, but here was an appropriate parting remembrance and an acknowledgment of her growth. Uncertain about what to do, he said he would hold onto it while he thought about the gift and that they could talk about it again at their next session. In supervision, he weighed what was in his client's best interest as well as his own
(*continued*)

and, the next week at their final session, he thanked his client and told her that he was pleased to accept the painting and planned to hang it in the clinic.

This example is less about the gift and all about boundaries. The therapist felt intruded upon by the gift and interpreted it as the client's desire to infiltrate his personal life. Boundaries had been a continuing problem and had been a regular topic between this client and therapist. From another client, this handcrafted expression of growth would have been highly valued. Because of the nature of this therapy relationship, the meaning was less clear, and a satisfactory response was arrived at with consultation.

"I Know That Your Birthday Was Yesterday. Can I Give You This Card?"

Gestures by clients can send the message that says you are being thought of outside the therapy sessions. If you reject her effort, you are embarrassing her and dismissing the consideration behind the card or small gift. You would need a very substantial reason to reject a gift at this level. Likewise, excessive exploration and discussion of naturally flowing gifts tells your client that you see her only as a set of problems and not as a whole person. In this case, you would probably say, "You knew about my birthday! May I open it now?" If there is something to be processed, you will recognize it. If, and this would be a rare occurrence, there is seductive, excessive, hostile, or confusing content in the card, you can address the material, "This is a confusing/strange birthday wish. We need to understand the message you are trying to send."

Linda

In the midst of my analysis, I brought my analyst—a man—a Mother's Day card. It was a picture of a tolerant mother watching her messy child throw spaghetti around the kitchen to create a Jackson Pollack–type pasta painting. Inside it said "Happy Mother's Day." It was very intentional. I wanted to thank him for being a supportive and encouraging mother to me. He laughed and enjoyed it, but then he noticed something I had completely missed. He asked, "Are you the child?" I had concentrated on him being the mother, but of course, I was the child, trying awkwardly to be creative and free. It was embarrassing to be caught off-guard, but his question was a useful and on-the-mark interpretation that set me thinking.

"Why Didn't You Give Me a Sympathy Card When Everyone Else Did?"

This question exemplifies the reverse of the previous questions. Rather than gratitude, your client is angry about the gift not given. This client has a point if you are normally in the habit of sending cards, but we don't know of any therapists who make this a common practice. You might need to disclose your thinking and guide her to explore her experience with this issue. "That isn't my normal practice. I knew that I would see you and we would be able to talk about your loss in here. At the same time, I can see that you have some strong feelings in this regard. Can we talk more about them?"

"Will You Take My Friend as a Client?"

The final type of gift to discuss is a referral. Clients offer your expertise to their friends and family, and that makes you the gift. They send referrals to you because they believe in you, and the referred person is a gift to you. We discussed referrals in the questions about overlapping relationships and previously in Chapter 8, Confidentiality, but you can see how referrals can also have other meanings.

If you haven't yet seen the potential client, you can check with your present client to be sure that you are not compromising his treatment. If you have already met with your new client, confidentiality prevents you from commenting and you can acknowledge that restriction.

If an existing client says that she is referring someone to you, it is important to point out potential compromises to confidentiality and objectivity. After reflecting on the decision, clients often do mind sharing their therapist, and once you have established the new client relationship, you will not want to end it. If a roommate or friend is sent to you accidentally through another source, and you discover it later, you have to talk to whoever is aware of the dilemma. When you treat people who are related or close friends, be aware that one may conceal certain information in these situations, lobby for your support, badmouth the other, compete with each other, fill you up with information, or try to coax you into a strange alliance. In these instances, you will often feel that your work with one or the other client is compromised. We suggest that you pursue understanding before making any decisions and explore with the client by asking questions such as: "Could you foresee this complicating our relationship?" or "Could my seeing her make you cautious about the things you tell me?" As a general practice, we do not accept new clients who have close, existing relationships with present clients. To try to avoid these conflicts, when we get referrals, we ask how they found us.

"This Movie Says a Lot About Me. Can I Loan It to You to Watch?"

The fifth category of questions illustrates material exchanges. "This movie says a lot about me. Can I loan it to you to watch?" "Do you have an extra $3 so I can take the bus home?" "Can I borrow that book on your shelf?"

This question is different because it is a loan, not a gift. Your client has something personal and meaningful to share. Watching the movie will mean setting aside several hours to view the film, but you will learn a lot. Whether or not you intend to take the movie, your reception is important. "How considerate of you to bring this for me. Can you tell me what you think this movie says about you?" If you do not intend to take it, you might say, "Let's talk about the movie, because I have no time this week to give it the attention it deserves, but I want to understand the film's importance."

If you plan to watch, you might pursue the movie's meaning after you watch it. Clinicians read books and articles in order to understand their clients; a movie might be more enjoyable. Always be respectful if you turn down your client's request. He is engaged in your work together and trying hard to communicate his world to you.

"Do You Have an Extra $3 So I Can Take the Bus Home?"

This is a rare question and usually a one-time, emergency request, as is, "Can I borrow a couple of quarters for the parking meter?" Still, consider your client's presenting concerns, age, socioeconomic status, therapeutic setting, focus of therapy, and agency policy before you reach into your pocket or purse to pull out $3 for the bus. If this becomes a regular practice, or if you begin to feel scammed, the request changes and so does your response.

"Can I Borrow That Book on Your Shelf?"

Borrowing books is a common request, and most therapists we know would simply honor this request unless they have some reason to think that the client will never return the book or believe that the client's needs have become excessive. We always wonder aloud, "What do you hope to get from this book?" Good intentions aside, your book may not be returned, so if it is important to you, explain that and suggest the library.

BOUNDARY SLIPS

> "What do you mean you booked someone else into my appointment time?"
> "How could you lock me out?"
> "How could you not have been here for our appointment?"

These questions bring us back to the fact that no one is omniscient. You will make mistakes and, when you do, they will often be in the realm of boundary slip-ups. When your fallibility intrudes on your clients, you have a temporary rupture in the alliance and need to address it without becoming defensive. Take responsibility clearly. By doing so, you validate your client's view of reality and give him permission to have an emotional response free of shame. "I am sorry. Yes, I did make a mistake, and I know that it caused a problem for you." You will work with many people who have never received an apology that was not followed by blame; you will work with people who are unsure of their rights because they haven't had any; and you will work with people who don't trust their own reality because someone else has trampled on their experiences. Modeling mistakes and repair is a remarkable step in healing.

FURTHER THOUGHTS

"It's a slippery slope, Carrie. Without boundaries you never know what might happen."

—Miranda, from *Sex and the City*

The concept of boundaries is similar to that of having a good budget. A budget reminds you of the limits of your resources, but what people often overlook is that, within those parameters, they are free to spend. With boundaries, you know where you cannot go and what you cannot do, and within these clear limits, you can feel free to act. Boundaries are not just for protecting your client—they also guide and safeguard you so that you can remain effective. That security permits clients to be vulnerable, whereas poor boundaries create tentative, superficial treatment. Therapy is difficult work for both of you; to be able to accomplish therapeutic goals, you both need to be protected by strong, consistent boundaries. When clinicians make ethical mistakes, it is often in the area of boundaries. For a clear list of principles to guide you through ethical decision making, read Ken Pope's list at http://kspope.com/memory/ethics.php.

More than other topics—more than technique, more than theory— the topic of boundaries, because it is so basic, is about you as a person. You have daily experiences with boundaries from the time of infancy, so many beliefs and practices are ingrained. In graduate school, you read the ethics books, but you really learn about boundary crossings, maintenance, and violation through your work, supervision, and reflection. If boundary issues such as client lateness, lack of payment, excessive flirtation, or other acting out occur very often, look at yourself instead of focusing solely on your clients. You may be unwittingly colluding in these crossings or violations. Something in your own past may be at work, and you can figure it out with your therapist or consultant. Finally, don't only think about boundary issues as horrible mistakes to be avoided. Instead, remind yourself that boundaries demarcate a protected territory of time, space, place, and behavior that, like most protected spaces, can encourage growth.

SUGGESTED READINGS

Borys, D. S. (1994). Marinating therapeutic boundaries: The motive is therapeutic effectiveness, not defensive practice. *Ethics and Behavior, 4,* 267–273.

Horton, J. A., Clance, P. R., Sterk-Elifson, C., & Emshoff, J. (1995). Touch in psychotherapy: A survey of patients' experiences. *Psychotherapy, 32,* 443–457.

Pope, K. S., & Keith-Spiegel, P. (2008). A practical approach to boundaries in psychotherapy: Making decisions, bypassing blunders, and mending fences. *Journal of Clinical Psychology: In Session, 64,* 638–652.

Willer, J. (2009). *The beginning psychotherapist's companion.* Lanham, MD: Rowman & Littlefield.

Zur, O. (2007). *Boundaries in psychotherapy: Ethical and clinical explorations.* Washington, DC: American Psychological Association.

CHAPTER

10

Personal
Questions

All of the questions in *What Do I Say?* are personal, but in this chapter, we address questions that feel particularly intimate. Ninety-five percent of the graduate students who responded to our survey commented on their apprehension about being asked personal questions. We want you to be comfortable during sessions and feel open to your clients. Therefore, we've created responses that prepare you for commonly asked personal questions as well as the rare, but dreaded, intrusive queries.

Melissa Perrin, Psy.D.

Dave, a newly divorced client, was frustrated and unsuccessful in his recent dating life, leaving him feeling desperately unconnected both sexually and emotionally. I responded by naming the issue, connection, so he asked me, while looking at my jewelry-free left hand, "You're single, right? How do you get those needs met." I paused, briefly, and said, "It's really uncomfortable for you to talk about how lonely you feel. This need is a core human need and we should brainstorm about how you can meet it without getting into a relationship too soon."

We asked Melissa to contrast this session with what she would have done years ago, when she was just starting out.

Years ago, I would have worn a ring with a stone on my left hand just for this client; I would have blushed furiously and felt help-less; I would have fumbled about; I would have stopped the session to talk, in detail, about the boundaries of our relationship, talking about whether or not we could date or touch (thus colluding in his avoidance, increasing his sense of alienation, and proving that women are unattainable and unfeeling bitches); or I would have changed the subject.

As I became more seasoned, I would have smiled knowingly and made a joke, for example, "My mentors would tell me that answering your question or following up in any way will distract us. I just can't let them down!" (I admit that I still use this response for some questions.)

Today, I understand that I must be willing to let my client be uncomfortable, even when he wants to distract us, or pull me into his pain, or swiftly tilt the discussion toward intellectualization. Our contract is that I help him navigate through painful experi-ences. If I respond directly or become as caught up in foggy material as he is, I break my side of the bargain. We both have to be okay with his anger, pain, loneliness, and alienation in order for him to learn how to manage these feelings and his behaviors.

Personal questions seem to evoke the highest levels of anxiety because everyone is vulnerable to being questioned about one topic or another, whether it is your age, experience, sexual behavior, religion, relation-ships, drugs, or trauma. Personal questions request more than factual information as a reply; they call for self-disclosure. Predictably, as your discomfort increases, you become uncertain about whether to answer and how much to disclose, particularly if the question threatens to redefine the boundary of your professional relationship. As you will see in the following responses, your clinical judgment dictates most of your answers.

Therefore, in addition to providing practical answers to questions, we emphasize and examine the reasons that prompt you to self-disclose or not. In the responses, we offer answers that have two aims: (1) keeping the focus on your client and (2) maintaining an appropriate—not too much or too little—level of freedom between the two of you. Disclosure can be a powerful tool in therapy, and as such, is accepted by all theoretical viewpoints. What varies are the names by which it is called, the degrees to which it is used, and the reasons justifying its use.

Strategies for dealing with personal questions have changed over the years, but the basic reasons for answering or not remain consistent. The following questions provide examples in many areas and, as we progress down the list, range from minor to intrusive.

QUESTIONS

The following questions are answered in the Responses section:

> "Are you a counselor, a therapist, a social worker, or a psychologist?"
> "Where do you live?" "Do you live nearby?"
> "Where are you going on vacation?"
> "Did you have a good time on vacation/at the wedding/visiting family?"
> "Where are you from?" "Where did you grow up?"
> "What do you do for fun?"
> "Do you have children? How many, how old?"
> "Are you in a relationship?"
> "Did you fight with your parents?"
> "Is school hard?"
> "What is your family like?"
> "How did you do in school? Did you get good grades?"
> "How do you deal with your kids/partner/parents/supervisor?"
> "Why did you get divorced?"
> "Do you get along with your ex-husband?"
> "Do you keep in touch with your ex?"
> "Do you drink/smoke/do drugs?"
> "Do you know what it's like to lose a child/parent/pregnancy/ sibling/partner/have an addiction/suffer from a mental illness?"

"Are you in AA? Have you tried oxycontin/weed/ecstasy? My
      AA sponsor answers my questions. Why don't you?"
"Have you ever had an affair?"
"Have you ever been raped/molested/abused?"
"Were either of your parents alcoholic/abusive/absent/crazy?"
"Do you think I'm hot?"

You will also be asked personal questions about the therapy relationship:

"If I wasn't your client, would we be friends?"
"Am I your favorite client?"
"Do you like me? Do you like working with me?"
"Do you think I'm a good person?"
"Do you think that I work hard in therapy?"

As you read, think of this chapter as having the subtitle, "It's Not About You." Although difficult to keep in mind, this phrase can help you respond to personal questions. When your client is asking about some of the most intimate aspects of your life, it is difficult to imagine that your sexuality, drug use, failures, or losses could be about anyone other than you. Trust us, to be a successful therapist, you never forget that this work is always primarily about the client. This doesn't diminish your hard work, your psychological well-being, or the essential significance of the therapeutic relationship. Repeating "It's not about you" as a mantra reminds all of us that there are impersonal elements to this most intimate process.

RESPONSES

For each response, your decision will be based on your knowledge of your client's history and personality, theory, the therapeutic alliance, the context and timing of the question, the content of what you propose to disclose, the potential effectiveness or harm in disclosing, and your own motivation for making a self-disclosure. It's an impossible amount of material to think about in the several seconds available before you open your mouth to respond, but with practice, these factors become second nature to you. In the meantime, we hope to bolster your confidence with illustrations of answers that represent the angels and the devils of self-disclosure.

"Are You a Counselor, a Therapist, a Social Worker, or a Psychologist?"

Personal questions exist on a continuum from mild to invasive, and we have clustered them as such based on the degree to which the questions ask for material pertinent to treatment versus those that emphasize your private life. The questions in each cluster may be dissimilar in content but call for comparable responses with regard to the level of appropriate disclosure and provide good illustrations of the concerns to think about before you answer. For example, the first question, "Are you a counselor, a therapist, a social worker, or a psychologist?" and others that are similar such as, "What are the differences between all you therapists?" and "What did you study in school?" or "What's your degree in?" are personal questions, but they are related to the work being done in the room. Your answers are dictated by the rules of informed consent. Your clients are entitled to have answers to questions that ask about credentials or for professional information. There is little clinical judgment involved. Many more questions of this type are covered in Chapter 1, The Early Sessions, and Chapter 8, Confidentiality. We mention these questions primarily for contrast with others that fall further along on the continuum.

Most personal questions fall in between the extremes of always being answered and never (or rarely and only under unusual circumstances) being answered. In the clusters of questions that follow, we offer some guidelines to help you think through your decision of how to answer, how much to say, and at what level to answer.

"Where Do You Live?" "Do You Live Nearby?" "Where Are You Going on Vacation?" "Did You Have a Good Time on Vacation/at the Wedding/Visiting Family?" "Where Are You From?" "Where Did You Grow Up?"

This set of questions is mild. Why wouldn't you answer them? Linda would respond with facts, "I live in southeast Evanston." or "I grew up in New Jersey." and then inquire, "Why do you ask?" This could lead to, and often has, "I thought I heard an East Coast accent. I've vacationed in Jersey." This bit of common ground may be a small step toward trust and understanding, something we work to achieve. Perhaps it will further therapy and, unless a client has a hardcore dislike of therapists who grew up in New Jersey, it certainly does not impede the progress.

The answers contained simple facts, "southeast Evanston" rather than extensive content, "in a condo on the second floor; the building with the sinking front walkway" or whining, "I still miss the ocean; the Midwest is soooo flat." In your decision to self-disclose, even though it is minor, consider the type of information that you plan to reveal and whether it is clinically appropriate and responsible. As you will see later on, other answers can do double duty and provide strategies, insight, support, or challenge as well as factual information. When you respond to minor questions about vacations or visits to family, use common sense and stay away from any inappropriate content, including jokes such as, "I'm off to California. Weed is practically legal there." or "I hate visiting my family but mostly I'm drunk so it doesn't matter." In addition to overwhelming your client, you have just provided information that the client doesn't need to hear, you have managed to sound unpleasant, and, if that wasn't enough, it is inappropriate.

We said that this chapter is subtitled, "It's not about you." It's also not about your vacation, your money or lack thereof, your parents or your bad relationships, or your headaches. Answer in ways that serve the best interest of your client. Experienced clinicians have a mental tattoo that reads, "What is in the best interest of my client now?" Even if your client can tolerate hearing about your mother's coldness, your obnoxious sister, or your eating disorder, when you talk at length about details of your life without a clinically based reason to do so, then the focus of the session has shifted to you, and that goes against your goals for treatment.

We can only think of a couple of reasons *not* to answer the mild questions at all. If you are working with an intrusive client, "I live in the city." or "I'm local" is sufficient disclosure. If your client is potentially dangerous, you model strict boundaries and share no personal information.

Linda

When you answer, pay attention to what happens next. In treating a very bright, but self-conscious, image-conscious, highly critical graduate student, I revealed almost nothing about myself in any obvious way. It seemed natural. She wasn't interested and I saw no

(continued)

point in disclosure. Then, well into treatment, after she had been frustrated by the dissertation committee process, I intentionally shared a mild story about my own grad school days. She looked at me with horror and I had no idea why. Later she admitted that she was rattled to think that I'd ever had a run-in with a committee member. She wanted to protect my image as well as her own. The result was good. After we talked about it, she became more honest and less guarded about her persona.

This set of mild questions about addresses, family, and vacations is probably asked out of clients' desires to know more about you and compare your activities to theirs. Generally, whether you majored in biology and adore scuba diving isn't going to have much of an impact on the therapy, even if your client is a philosopher who hates water and climbs mountains. That said, ask yourself, does this question tell me anything helpful about my client (e.g., is she worried about a vacation, uncertain about school, feeling deficient in her social life, or distressed about a family visit?). If there is some aspect in the question that is pertinent to your client's life, answer briefly and return the focus to her.

"What Do You Do for Fun?"

You can usefully answer, "I'm learning how to cross-country ski. It reminds me that we never talk about your activities and your social life." In addition to sharing simple facts, the response to this type of question can promote client reflection.

The next cluster of questions is commonly asked and speaks to relationship issues—yours.

"Are You in a Relationship?" "Have You Ever Had a Bad Breakup/Divorce?"

Other similar queries such as, "Do you have a boyfriend/girlfriend?" or "Are you married?" or "What is your husband's/wife's name?" present you with the choice of whether or not to answer. Either way, these questions are worth looking at in more detail, because we can use them to illustrate helpful guidelines to keep in mind as you make your decision.

Consider your client's particular personality, history, and probable motivation for making the inquiry. Note the context of the question and how it fits into your ongoing discussions. If you decide to answer, have an appropriate reason for self-disclosing that is consistent with existing boundaries and your treatment objectives. And, always know that it is not necessary for you to answer in any way that makes you feel uncomfortable.

Your answers to these relationship questions can remain general and skim the surface or you can go deeper, depending on what you believe will be helpful. When clients ask about your relationships, they may be looking for commonalities and reflect a normal wish to be understood and share similarities.

Charlie

Clarissa, age 36, came in for therapy because she hoped to clarify her thoughts and feelings about a marriage in which she saw little future. During the course of treatment, we talked about her whole life, including her management of her type-1 diabetes condition, and the limits that this placed on her. In one session she asked, "How do you know so much about diabetes?" I thought, "What a legitimate question." She didn't know that it was a personal question. For all she knew, my knowledge could be from a training rotation I had at some point in my career. Thinking briefly about the level of disclosure I wanted to make, and trusting that this was not going to be a pattern with her—considering that this was the first real moment she asked me to disclose any personal information in our months of working together—I answered honestly, personally, and specifically, "I have a 15-year-old stepdaughter who was first diagnosed as having type-1 diabetes at the age of 4½." She said, "Yes, I guess you would learn a lot," and then went on addressing her own issues. Initially, Clarissa had no idea that my knowledge about diabetes was learned at home, and I could have answered with a less intimate disclosure, but based on our relationship, her personality, and the treatment, I chose to tell her about my stepdaughter.

"Do You Have Children?" "How Many, How Old?" "Are You in a Relationship?"

Your client is probably wondering about the presence or absence of significant relationships in your life because she is curious about how you live your life outside the office, how it compares to her life, and who else claims your time and attention. You cannot predict the impact of your answers. They have the potential to evoke a range of emotional reactions, such as jealousy, anger, admiration, pride, closeness, or satisfaction, depending on your client's unique personal circumstances. Therefore, remain mindful of your client's uniqueness and consider the strength of the therapeutic alliance so that you disclose at the appropriate level of intimacy. An overly intimate disclosure, "I never wanted children," may frighten or overburden the client with excessive information, whereas an overly impersonal response, such as ignoring the question, may lead the client to perceive you as cold, rejecting, or inaccessible. The appropriate level of intimacy lies between these two polarities and is one that understands the client's experience, demonstrates your empathy and humanness, benefits your client, and adheres to ethical boundaries.

Your client may be motivated by the hope that you will understand the complexities of marriage, the absorption of parenting, or the heartbreak of loss. And even when clients share similar motivations, your responses may differ. For example, a question like, "Are you divorced?" is different if it follows revelations that your client is an unhappy husband experiencing marital difficulties and feeling a great deal of guilt for being "a failure when all my friends have successful marriages" than if your client is a teenager who says, "My parents' divorce is ruining my life." Both clients want to know your experience with marriage and breakups. A general response might be, "Yes, marriage can be difficult and all breakups are sad," but then go back to their unique situations, "Can you tell me more?" In this way, you support the client's experience, disclose without providing excessive details, and you return the focus to the client.

Clients aren't the only people in the office with motivations. Therapists can be motivated to disclose because they want to let their clients know that their understanding emanates from having undergone a comparable event. Sometimes, having similar experiences may provide your client with a sense of being understood, such as, "Great, if you have a spouse or kids, maybe you'll understand that there are days when I want to run away and start a new life somewhere else." On the other hand, your marriage or children could stimulate the fear, "Oh, you probably have the perfect marriage and kids and you will never understand my mess."

Strong bonds are not forged by having had similar or identical experiences with clients. Bonds are created and strengthened through understanding, empathy, and hard work. Keep this in mind when your revelation highlights a difference between you and your client. Your response, "No, I have not been married." or "No, I don't have children," can make you unnecessarily fearful that you have driven a wedge between yourself and your client. Don't get preoccupied with differences. Find words that are honest and convey understanding. "Although I haven't been married, I do know about relationships, and am learning from you that . . ." or "I have not raised my own children, but I can understand the powerful experience you are having with . . ." If a client balks at how different you are from her, you can empathize with her concern and potentially suggest that, "one advantage of us having different experiences is that I will definitely not impose my way of handling situations on you." At the same time, if a client is looking for a reason to avoid treatment, any reason will do.

Finally, relationship questions also raise the conundrum of values. We are never blank screens, and we are always revealing ourselves, but we don't want to come on so strong with our values that we inhibit our clients from disclosing theirs. For example, when a client asks about your children or a partner, he may be testing the water to see if it is okay to say that he doesn't want marriage or children or religion or heterosexuality or some other conventional value. Be careful that your enthusiasm for any of those relationships doesn't restrict your client.

Questions that ask about your marital status may indicate a desire to be understood, but they may also conceal the fear that you are either gung-ho for divorce or violently opposed, so if you provide an answer, you may need to include, "Just because I'm divorced, that doesn't mean that I don't respect marriage." or the reverse, "Just because I'm married, that doesn't mean that I can't understand the need to divorce." It is impossible to be value-free, just be value-sensitive.

There are different implications for therapist self-disclosure when a child client asks questions. Children, particularly young children, tend to conceptualize and communicate more concretely than adults. Therefore, answers that are abstract or impersonal may baffle and frustrate them, impeding an alliance. The questions that a child asks you about your schooling and your parents are likely to be genuine requests for information rather than attempts to distract from or resist the therapy process. These also tend to be issues that child clients are *currently* struggling with, and thus their requests for information on these topics tend to be congruent with their presenting problem and relevant to the therapeutic process. When an 11-year-old girl asks, "Did you get good grades?" a developmentally appropriate answer might be, "Mostly I did, but I had a hard time with math. Are there any subjects in school that are hard for you too?" This answer uses simple, concrete language that the child can understand, it demonstrates to the girl that it's okay to talk about difficulties in school, and it returns the focus to the child's exploration of her own experiences.

With children, the focus of therapy is more geared toward the creation of a new therapeutic relationship that provides a corrective emotional experience. Therefore, the benefits of self-disclosure include engaging the child in therapy through creating a bond; modeling identification and exploration of feelings; and promoting the child's self-esteem through modeling realistic rather then perfectionistic self-standards. For example, in the scenario of the 11-year-old client, the therapist self-disclosed that she received mostly good grades but that she had trouble in math. In doing so, the therapist modeled and normalized a realistic self-image. We hope that this would encourage the child to accept her own imperfections and flaws.

Charlie

The client with whom I have probably done the most self-disclosure was Mary, a 40-year-old only child who had lost both her parents. She was struggling as a single parent to raise her teenage sons. She felt alone in her world, and her shame at what she saw as poor parenting led her to withdraw from others and feel further isolated. Whenever I self-disclosed, my goal was to help Mary see her struggles as severe, but not aberrant or shameful, and I wanted her to believe that she was better off sharing her experiences with others who could understand and support her rather than cloistering herself at home. During treatment, Mary read parenting books and asked questions about how my family was raising our teens, and together we found some solutions for her, helped her normalize her experience, and increased her ability to reach out to other adults to help her make the best of her situation.

"Did You Fight With Your Parents?" "Is School Hard?" "What Is Your Family Like?" "How Did You Do in School?" "Did You Get Good Grades?" "How Do You Deal With Your Kids/Partner/Parents/Supervisor?"

These questions are further along on the continuum because they are personal in a more specific way than previous queries. These questions ask how you managed in certain circumstances or how you solved a particular problem. As such, these questions provide clues that could guide the session. It seems reasonable to answer honestly but generally, such as, "I was a rough teenager." "School is hard but I really like the clinical courses." "I like my family; they are warm/fun/a bit nutty." "I'm not very proud of my grades." "What issues are you referring to about my kids/partner/parents/supervisor?" These are quick, preliminary responses before you turn it back to your client. "Have you been fighting with your parents?" "Are you thinking about going to school?" "Do you like your family?" After all, it is your client's life that remains to be understood.

If the discussion moves to a specific focus, you may decide to model a method of dealing with the particular problem. Your responses can shine a light onto a previously unexamined idea. "I think my rough teenage years kept me from experiencing any of the good parts of high school." or "My first boss and I didn't get along until an old-timer suggested that I concentrate on learning from her expertise and try to ignore the rest." Self-disclosure can be used specifically to model solutions or collaborate on management of problems. You can also use self-disclosure as a way to suggest a means of being effective, such as, "Before I left my job, I made sure that my resume was ready to go." Obviously, that suggestion could be made without the disclosure, but inserting your own experience makes it a shared dilemma.

Before you get overly enthusiastic about revealing your solutions, consider the likelihood that your client has already received an abundance of recommendations. In fact, advice from friends, colleagues, and family is usually plentiful, if not endless. Keep disclosures to a minimum because, after your clients have been overwhelmed by other people's good intentions, they don't want to feel inadequate by comparing your good solutions to their rotten ones. They need you more than ever to help them unscramble their thoughts and feelings in order to come to a decision.

"Why Did You Get Divorced?" "Do You Keep in Touch With Your Ex?" "Do You Drink/Smoke/Do Drugs?"

These questions are rare and illustrate the type of queries that are increasingly uncomfortable because they strain the boundaries of your professional relationship, bring into question the appropriate level of disclosure, and put you right in the spotlight. You don't have to answer any of these questions, and at the end of this chapter we provide a dozen ways of saying that you have limits.

These questions make us think that your client is looking for something from you, perhaps permission, understanding, or something else. We wouldn't answer any of the questions directly without a better sense of exactly what is going on in the room. Instead, we would reflect on the content of the session leading up to the question, then attempt to tie the question to previously discussed material. In this way, when and if you decide to answer directly, you will have thought about the interpersonal and individual contextual factors that have shaped the discussion.

In any case, say, "I need to understand where this question is coming from." After the client explains his struggle with his spouse or ex or drugs or cigarettes, the two of you have probably moved on and the question about your life becomes moot. Let it go. If the client returns to it, then decide if you want to provide a brief answer, such as, "I was divorced a long time ago." or "Getting along with an ex is even harder than getting along with a partner." or "Drugs was never my thing, but I can see how it has plagued you." or "I quit smoking after a bunch of tries. It was rough." If you decide not to answer, that is also fine and you can say, "I don't want to complicate this discussion with my life, but I certainly understand that you are in a difficult situation."

Even if you decide to refuse to answer, you still use your life experiences in order to understand your clients. When you have had similar reactions or experiences to those described by your client and worked through them, you remember those feelings or events and may be able to better understand others because of your past. You may find it easier to formulate their problems or think about a diagnosis. Being able to use your experiences, understandings, and feelings is considered a cherished tool among many therapists, whether you disclose or not.

Linda

Without answering directly, we still use our experiences. We reach inside to locate an identical or similar experience in order to try to get a sense of the client's feelings. I work with many clients who have experienced losses. When Jane's mother died of a stroke, I thought back to the deaths of my own parents years ago—one slow and agonizing, and the other shockingly unexpected in the middle of the night. I did this in order to imagine what Jane might feel. I can't know until she tells me, but I can use my life to imagine some of the parameters of her experience. I don't share this information, but I recall the aloneness and the awful sense of finality when I lost the two people who had always been in my corner. These memories and recollection of feelings may shape the material I look for, such as whether the death was expected and what the living relationship was like. Often, the universal elements of mourning are shared but are like the color wheel—three primary colors can make an unlimited variety of hues. The danger was that I would only understand myself, not Jane, overlay my reactions on hers, and not hear her describe her mother and her loss.

With these questions and any other personal questions, there are significant self-disclosure problems to address. If you disclose, no doubt clients will be momentarily reassured that you also reunited with your ex too many times, set his clothes on fire, or reacted in some other strange ways. They may be amused that you have three ex-wives or had credit card debt. They may be reassured that they are not the only people who have screamed at a child or cheated on a partner. But, clients are not ultimately looking for buddies who are equally out of control; they are looking for counselors who can listen, not judge, and help them find better ways of managing their lives. The possibility of turning therapy into a gab session always exists.

When your experiences are still raw or unworked, it becomes easier to be pulled into disclosing impulsively. The next question provides an opportunity to examine that dilemma.

"Do You Know What It's Like to Lose a Child/Parent/Pregnancy/Sibling/Partner/Have an Addiction/Suffer From a Mental Illness?"

These are examples of very intimate inquiries. The answer may still be your secret or have been previously disclosed only to close friends, family, or your own therapist. This response would mean a deep level of disclosure, and you could feel very vulnerable. We are very cautious about answering these types of questions directly and rarely do so. You may have any number of reactions to being asked such intimate questions. You could react with disgust, you might shut down, you might get angry, or you might have a rarely discussed type of response: an eagerness to answer. Until now, we have been talking mostly about reluctance or apprehension, but that is not your only possible reaction to personal queries. Sometimes, and it probably happens more or less to every therapist, you feel the urge to tell your client about some personal experience. Examine the impulse, but don't act out. Perhaps you want to bond, "Yes, I also went through that experceince; you are not alone." or to show that you understand. You may want to show off, to rescue, to combat your own helpless feelings, to overcome your isolation, to demonstrate a happy outcome, or to share their pain. You will never get used to seeing people in pain, particularly when you can closely relate to their experience, but be very cautious when you feel strong urges to divulge your life. Discuss your reactions with colleagues, your own therapist, supervisors, and consultants, but not with your clients.

Here is one way that disclosure impedes treatment. Let's imagine that you answer a loaded, personal question with a direct, honest response, "Yes, I was molested by a family friend when I was seven." or "Yes, my mother died from alcoholism." or "No, I'm strongly opposed to drugs/

abortion or keeping in touch with ex-anybodies." Your goal may be to convey understanding and demonstrate personal knowledge, but is that what your clients have heard? You may cause them anxiety because now they have to worry about your mental health. They now have additional emotional baggage—yours—to haul around. Has it done them any good? Does it further therapy? Do they now have to worry about you? You've let them know that you've been there, but that information alone doesn't promote therapeutic gains; otherwise, everyone with a tragic past would be licensed and successfully practicing therapy. Answer honestly, "That's a question about me and we want to learn about you."

"Are You in AA? Have You Tried Oxycontin/ Weed/Ecstasy? My AA Sponsor Answers My Questions. Why Don't You?"

These questions are included because they are fairly common and, more importantly, they introduce other models of treatment. Some clients who you treat will have attended, or be simultaneously attending, a 12-step program in which the relationship between the sponsor and member is quite different from that of therapist and client. This can be confusing. In AA, SA, NA, and OA, everyone shares their experiences as part of the treatment.

We asked our colleague, Abbey Prujan, M.A., a certified addictions specialist, to comment on this question. She replied that it is a very uncomfortable dialogue to sit through, but in her experience, few clients ask directly. For those who do, she understands it as a vulnerability issue, a trust issue, typically coming from a place of shame. If the therapist can be identified as flawed, then the client can feel better about himself.

Abbey Prujan, M.A.

When confronted, I answer, "In therapy, you will talk about yourself, but I will not talk about myself. Whether or not I have experience with this drug or that drug is not the reason that you've come

(continued)

to see me today—it's your experience that is our focus." Then, with clients who really pursue the question, I reiterate, "That is not a question I ever answer." In an effort to generalize that it is not just that client I won't tell, sometimes I list other personal topics that I won't answer: "I won't talk about my sex life or how I was raised, or how I pay my bills either!"

Most clients know that therapy is different from AA if they've spent any time at AA. Sponsors are not therapists, and they are only qualified to address the program and how they go about the business of sobriety. There's a saying in AA about sponsorship, "no romance, no finance," meaning sponsors should stay out of the lives of their clients and refrain from giving advice about anything that is not about staying sober. That doesn't always happen, but it is a good guideline. Sponsors are supposed to *only* talk about themselves, which is radically different from therapists, who *rarely* talk about themselves. Sponsors only address their programs, advise about how they handled situations without drinking or using, and guide their sponsees through the 12 steps. Therapists should address their clients' programs and stay away from the 12 steps unless they know what they're talking about. Sometimes, clients really only want to know, "Do you know what I'm talking about?" or "Will we speak the same language?"

What you answer, how you do or do not answer, and how you conduct yourself when answering or not answering is all observed by the client. Many of your clients, not just those who have substance abuse problems, will have suffered from years of poor boundaries. In therapy, they are relearning where to draw the line. When you calmly, kindly say "no," it often gives them courage to establish boundaries of their own. Chapter 9 is devoted to the essential topic of Boundaries.

Shortcuts are often a problem with disclosures. Everybody likes a shortcut. On the road, you save miles. In conversation, you save words. A direct answer to a personal question is a problematic shortcut because it often eliminates the client's explanation. And therapy is all about explaining, talking, and organizing thoughts, feelings, and understandings into a unique personal story. Healing happens while we do the work, not afterward when we cross some imaginary finish line as if mental health is some externally awarded prize. If you answer, "Yes, my divorce was the longest, nastiest on record," you are telling your client that you understand what divorce can become, you are implying that the two of you are similar in important ways, and you may free your client to speak up, but the danger is that you may also be telling your client that she doesn't have to fully tell her story.

When a client knows that you have experienced a divorce, it can provide false reassurance. The client makes assumptions when, in fact, your experience with rotten relationships or drugs or abuse may be similar to hers in name only; the reality may have been quite different. The two of you have missed an important element of the therapeutic process, that of the client searching for her own understanding. Particularly if your divorce/drug history/abuse was similar to her incidents, it reduces the amount of listening that you will do, because you will unintentionally fill in the blanks with your life rather than searching for the answers in your client's life.

This final set of questions may at first stun you, but they are the easiest ones to answer—once you catch your breath.

> **"Have you ever had an affair?"**
> **"Have you ever been raped/molested/abused?"**
> **"Were either of your parents alcoholic/abusive/absent/crazy?"**
> **"Do you think I'm hot?"**

The answers are all comparable. We have provided several possible responses, all of which are variations on the answer, "No way, we are not going there!"

> "I'm not going into details, but I certainly understand love loss/grief/abuse/addictions."
> "This is a question that I'm not comfortable answering."
> "Some of my experiences are similar to yours and others are different, but whichever, I am trying to understand your life, not my own."

"This is the wrong time to turn our attention to my life/ experience."

"I always pass on questions like that from all my clients."

"Are you concerned that I can't understand your drug use/ molestation/family?"

"I'm not sure why it matters if I've had the same experience. Our work here is about our ability to understand you."

"Are you worried about being understood?

"Are you worried about being judged?"

"This session is about you."

"Sorry, I do not disclose about this topic."

These replies are included so that you can hold onto them and allay your anxiety about knowing what to say. The questions are, in our opinion, under ordinary circumstances, not to be answered. They cross too many boundaries, take the focus off the client and put it on you, and disclosures in these areas can unnecessarily burden your client.

QUESTIONS ABOUT THE THERAPY RELATIONSHIP

You will also be asked personal questions about the therapy relationship:

"If I wasn't your client, would we be friends?"

"Am I your favorite client?"

"Do you like me? Do you like working with me?"

"Do you think I'm a good person?"

"Do you think that I work hard in therapy?"

Clients are allowed to wonder, to ask, and to be curious about the potential for a different relationship with you. You are also allowed to have favorite clients, dislike others, and know that there are people who could be your friends—under other circumstances. Answer questions honestly, maybe not with every thought that you have, but honestly and then inquire, "What brought this question up?"

"If I Wasn't Your Client, Would We Be Friends?"

"Maybe, but it would have evolved so differently. We are lucky that we have created this relationship so well."

"Am I Your Favorite Client?"

Only a favorite client would dare to ask this one. Just laugh and acknowledge his or her specialness. "You are my most (whatever is true: open, hardworking, creative) client, and I think that you are terrific."

"Do You Like Me? Do You Like Working With Me?"

Answer honestly: Either "I find you difficult to work with. You are angry a lot of the time and you seem to hang onto it so tightly." or "Yes, I like working with you. You already knew that, didn't you?"

"Do You Think I'm a Good Person?"

"What are you worried about?" After you have an answer, you can continue if needed. "I'm surprised to hear you ask that question. I thought you felt pretty good about yourself." or "I know that you are a good person, imperfect like the rest of us, maybe (whatever is true) but good." or "Yes, I do." or mention specific good qualities.

"Do You Think That I Work Hard in Therapy?"

Again, say whatever is true. "Some days you are very hard-working. Lately, you seem distracted." or "You work hard when we talk about . . . but move away from discussions about . . ." or "Yes, you are hard-working here."

Therapy is a unique, peculiar, but very real relationship. The trend, even in analytic circles, is toward judicious self-disclosure. In proposed answers to the previous questions, we are not saying that "anything goes" or "if it feels right, go for it," but rather that there is a definite place for answering questions with self-disclosure, especially about the experiences that you have had together—your therapeutic interactions. There is also a place for withholding information that is meant to be private. Too much anonymity on your part is extreme, nontherapeutic for the client, and too restrictive for you. Too much disclosure can derail psychological treatment in ways that never allow it to return.

FURTHER THOUGHTS

"Don't be afraid to take a big step if one is indicated. You can't cross a chasm in two small jumps."

—David Lloyd George

Personal questions are the most awkward because they bring our lives into the room, often in ways that we would prefer to remain outside. These questions raise the issues of the place your private life and experience has in your work. Because personally revealing responses to client questions can be among their most memorable experiences, using self-disclosure in a disciplined, intentional way that accounts for the client's experience of the disclosure makes it a therapeutic technique rather than a casual conversation.

When we hear that a therapist is continually asked personal questions by many clients, we wonder if she may have set a tone of social conversation. As with everything that goes on in the sessions, you are a participant in the development.

Your life is always there to guide you and occasionally to trip you up. The better you know yourself, the easier it is to entertain and respond to personal questions. Again, we make the case for personal therapy. Imagine the difference in your responses when a client asks about an emotional issue that you have previously considered and worked through in your own therapy versus your response to an issue that blindsides you. Maybe you will choose to answer directly, maybe not, but you will be able to identify—not overidentify—with the core issues and move the discussion forward.

SUGGESTED READINGS

Geller, J. D. (2003). Self-disclosure in psychoanalytic-existential therapy. *Journal of Clinical Psychology in Session*, *59*, 541–554.

Knox, S., & Hill, C. (2003). Therapist self-disclosure: Research-based suggestions for practitioners. *Journal of Clinical Psychology in Session*, *59*, 529–539.

McCarthy, P. R., & Betz, N. E. (1978). Differential effects of self-disclosing versus self-involving counselor statements. *Journal of Counseling Psychology*, *25*, 251–256.

Wachtel, P. L. (1993). Therapist self-disclosure: Prospects and pitfalls. In P. L. Wachtel, *Therapeutic communication: Knowing what to say when* (pp. 206–234). New York, NY: Guilford Press.

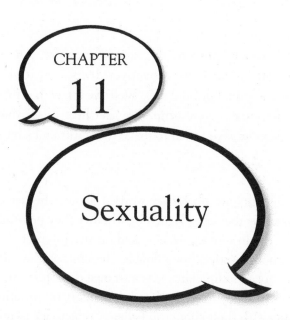

CHAPTER

11

Sexuality

We live in a culture that has progressively transformed sexuality from a private act between two people into a hugely successful commercial enterprise. As a result, most people are bombarded by simplistic, perfectionistic, airbrushed discussions, popular articles, movies, and television shows. Simultaneously, we engage in little serious, comfortable, honest dialogue. Your office may be one of the few places where reasonable, nonjudgmental discussions about sexuality can take place. However, if you are ill at ease talking about sexual matters, your clients will oblige you and avoid this significant area of their lives. If you can stay comfortable, you can handle sexual questions. The following vignette was a sophisticated answer by a relatively new clinician who took a bit of a risk and coupled her answer with a mild interpretation.

Diane (pseudonym), a second-year counseling student

A male client my own age (late twenties) said, "My girlfriend is afraid that you will fall in love with me." I asked him, "Do you
(continued)

have any idea why she would have those worries?" "I told her that I find you sexually attractive." It took me a while to begin breathing again, but I did say, "Well, we know that this is a close, but professional, relationship. She isn't here to see that. It does make me wonder if you tried to make your girlfriend a bit jealous."

Clients are no longer worried about whether or not to have sex as much as they are plagued by whether they perform as well as the people on TV, in movies, videos, and on the Internet. Because this is real life, without a script, body double, director, and award-winning writer, they do not. As clinicians, it is a strange dichotomy to read professional articles that describe therapists' discomfort in initiating discussions of sexuality with their clients and clients' reluctance to talk about sexuality, and then to pick up a magazine, turn on the television, or go to the movies and be deluged by sexual activity.

In this chapter, we attempt to at least touch on the myriad of questions and underlying concerns that are attached to discussions of sexuality. We want to include two different types of questions. First, there are questions that clients ask about their own sexuality, and second, there are questions like the previous example, which draw you personally into the sexual issues. In thinking about these questions and your potential responses, we urge you to consider the layers of unspoken concerns that lie beneath the questions, such as "Am I desirable?" "Am I normal?" "What is wrong with me?" "How do I know what I want or expect?" and "How do I handle myself?" These concerns and others will deeply affect your answers. As always, your personal relationship to each of these issues, to your client, and to your own sexuality will exert a strong—and often unconscious—influence on your work with your clients.

QUESTIONS

The following questions are answered in the Responses section:

"**Do we have to talk about sex?**"
"**Why is sex so important?**"

"Why is sex so difficult?"

"Is it weird that I'm still a virgin/have a different lover every month? Do you think that I'm a freak?"

"Is it normal that I want more/less/different sex?"

"When are we going to talk about sex?"

"Am I mean to be angry when my partner says no?"

"Will you think that I'm crazy if I tell you what I like/think about/did sexually?"

"Why doesn't he/she like sex as much as I do?" "How can I change him/her?" "My girlfriend is unadventurous; don't you agree that she has a big problem?" "How can I make him more adventurous?"

"I'm feeling better but maybe there are other things to talk about. What do you think?"

RESPONSES

Our clinical experience suggests that these questions do not differ much whether you and/or your client is gay or straight, old or young, male or female. And, no matter what the questions are, your answers are best when they convey an attitude, style, and language that encourages a comfortable discussion appropriate to the relationship. Clients will take their cues from you; if you are unsettled, they will shift topics, edit, or reveal less information. You may find that to respond effectively, you must first work through some of your own issues with sexuality. The best place to do this is in therapy with your own therapist rather than unconsciously with your clients. Becoming comfortable with conversations about sexuality, as well as the sometimes stimulating nature of these discussions, can go a long way toward creating productive conversations.

"Do We Have to Talk About Sex?"

Many clients are resistant to talking about sex, even though it may rank high on the list of problems that brought them into treatment. It is important to try to understand the client's reluctance while you normalize his anxiety and make your office a safe place. "I get the impression that you would be happier if we never talked about anything sexual." You can add, "It is an aspect of life whether you are having sex, not having sex, like it, or don't like it." or "What is your reluctance to talk?" If your client's reticence seems to be cultural or mannered, be reassuring: "I know it's awkward, but that's why we keep it confidential." If a client is tired of the discussion or wants to move on to other things, shift directions, but keep in mind that sex is being avoided, the same way that you would keep it in mind if drinking or family problems were being avoided. You can always return to it at a later time with a casual remark, "Did we finish with our earlier/last week's discussion of . . .?"

Sexuality can be an awkward topic to discuss. If people talk about sex at all, it is with friends, and in these conversations, there is generally a secondary agenda of validation, boastfulness, or reassurance. Therapy is different. Conversations are for examination and understanding. If needed, you could say, "Many people find sexuality awkward to talk about at first, but it gets more comfortable." or educate your client by saying, "Sex occurs in private, so there are no real role models to learn from. There is an abundance of information about sex in the popular media, but little elsewhere." or "Sex is a strange topic; sometimes it seems like everyone is talking about it and other times, real discussions are taboo." or "Sex is personal, but the nice thing about being here is that we can simply try to understand rather than judge." As with all your clinical conversations, when you create a climate of comfort in the room, your clients come to understand that no matter what the topic is, you are willing to engage in judgment-free discussion and work toward their well-being.

Charlie

June was a delightful, energetic first-grade teacher who was several years into marriage to a man she had dated since they were both in high school. She described her marriage as "lousy," but she was worried about her future because the couple had just separated. After a few sessions, June said, "My husband used to say that our relationship stinks because our sex life stinks, and he blamed me." After exploring a bit more, I commented, "Could it be that your sex life stinks because your relationship stinks?" June thought about this and talked a bit more, and then said, "Well, how would you know what causes what?" I replied, "I guess if you got into a good relationship and the sex was better, then you would know for sure." Months later, June started to have fun dating another man. Then, she came into a session beaming and reported that she discovered that sex could be loving and fun with the right person.

"Why Is Sex So Important?"

Sex becomes a more important topic in therapy when it is going poorly, but whenever it is broached, you want to encourage your client. "Sex and intimacy are significant in people's lives." or "People seek sexuality, physical closeness, and intimacy. If it goes badly, they are hurt." Depending on the context, you might say, "Sex has so many different meanings—it can be fun, intimate, powerful, healing, abusive, or harmful. I don't know what it means in your life." You probably also want to inquire, "Do you think that sex is important?" Many of the questions that clients ask about sex have underlying concerns about desirability, performance, normalcy, and adequacy. Reassure your clients that there is great variety about sexual desire, likes and dislikes, and behaviors. People worry about adequacy, how to measure themselves, and who to measure themselves against.

"Why Is Sex So Difficult?"

First, clarify what your client means by the terms "sex" and "difficult," but the implication in this question is that everyone ought to be able to have sex easily, with everyone else, any time, any place, uncomplicated by physical or emotional reactions. It is strange that intelligent people who would not expect to speak French when they are first exposed to it, or to immediately play tennis well, or to know what is required in a new job, somehow believe that they ought to be comfortable, knowledgeable, and relaxed with any partner from the very beginning of the relationship. Keep those ideas in mind while you ask, "Could you be more specific for me? What aspects of sex are you finding difficult?" Then you can talk about the relationship and the physical or emotional aspects of sexuality.

Sex occurs in private, so it isn't easy to learn about. Many clients want to think through their beliefs, desires, and sexual practices, and your office may be the safest place to get started.

"Is It Weird That I'm Still a Virgin/Have a Different Lover Every Month? Do You Think I'm a Freak?"

In a culture that believes more is better, remaining a virgin can be a big deal for clients. On the other hand, having too many sexual partners—an unknown but clearly felt number—can also carry with it a freakish quality. Whether virginity is by choice or accidental, it puts some clients at odds with the behaviors of their contemporaries. So, too, casual sex can also put clients at odds with others. You don't dictate people's behaviors, but you can help clients to clarify their choices and become comfortable and confident with their sexual decisions. "No, I don't think that you are strange, but I am interested in understanding your decisions, how you arrived at them, how you feel about them, and whether they present any problems for you." This response can be used for both ends of the spectrum.

Don't make assumptions about promiscuity or abstinence; ask questions and listen to the answers. You can also provide basic information or referrals to books or physicians when needed. If the question had been, "I'm sick of being a virgin. It's making me feel weird, and I want to get rid of it. What do you think about that?" you could respond, "I think that we are all bombarded with TV and movie sex so it makes most people feel freaky if they are not in the imaginary mainstream of sex." You can also be more directive, "Let's talk about whether you really want to have sex or you just want to stop feeling strange." Or take ownership of your feelings about the topic, "I wouldn't want your first experience to be unsafe or awful. Can we talk about these plans of yours?"

Linda

Several years ago, an undergraduate woman sat across from me and described the previous Friday evening. She finished her schoolwork, took a nap, and went out late to a nearby party that was hosted by other undergrads who lived in an off-campus apartment. She then steadily and seriously drank until she was trashed, hooked up with a guy she knew, and thinks she had intercourse. "I was very drunk; I'm not sure." I thought that I understood her distress until she asked, "If I don't remember, does it count?" She had an idea that certain amounts of casual sex were too much, but she seemed to have little idea of everything else connected to her behaviors and values about being a sexual person.

"Is It Normal That I Want More/Less/Different Sex?"

This may be one of those important times to remind your client that, "people are very different with regard to their desires, needs, enjoyments, and attitudes about sex." Then, you can get more specific and see what your client is really talking about. "What do you and your partner disagree about?" Normalcy is a big issue when it comes to sex or other behaviors that people are uncertain about. "We are not talking in order to pass judgment; we are talking in order to understand you better and figure out what is right for you." When you respond, keep in mind that talking about sex is similar to talking about alcohol and drug use. You need clarification. "I drink a little, or party, like everyone else" can mean occasional drinking and recreational drugs or serious engagement. Be precise and ask, "What would be more agreeable to you each week or month?" just like you would ask, "What kind of drugs?" or "How many drinks in an evening?"

"When Are We Going to Talk About Sex?"

"Have you been waiting for me to bring up the topic? Okay, let's talk." or "Yes, I also realized that we've talked about a lot of topics but not sex." This client may have been taking cues from the clinician. Therapists who do not feel comfortable talking about sex will ignore or avoid the topic. Therapists who fear being seen as voyeuristic or seductive will also be reluctant to talk about sex. On the other hand, some clinicians are titillated by sexual discussions and look for opportunities. As in all topics, don't avoid your client's needs, don't make your needs predominant, and don't be defensive. If you do not have knowledge or experience with the sexual practices that clients bring up, you may be tempted to back away from the conversation, which, in turn, communicates to the client that the discussion is wrong, shameful, or does not belong in the therapy session. Ask, be interested, and you will be better able to understand your client's experiences.

"Am I Mean to Be Angry When My Partner Says No?"

"Everybody is vulnerable and exposed when it comes to sex. Differences in desire easily cause a feeling of rejection. Perhaps that is what makes you angry." or "Tell me what exactly makes you angry." or "Give me a typical scenario so I can get an idea of how the situation evolves." If he has trouble with that question, you can prompt with, "Is it frustration, rejection, regret that you initiated sex, or something else that makes you angry?" You are talking about thoughts and feelings, the same as you do during most sessions on most days. Underneath the anger may be questions about, "Are my demands unreasonable?" or "Am I desirable?" and these are also questions to explore.

"Will You Think That I'm Crazy if I Tell You What I Like/Think About/Did Sexually?"

"I doubt it. Why don't you tell me?" or "I don't think that you are crazy, so I doubt that your sexual behaviors will change my mind." This is generally followed by your client's description of same-sex sex, drunk sex, casual sex, rough sex, an unusual sexual practice, or an unlikely attraction. Occasionally you will hear violent stories. Your client is afraid of shocking you and of being judged negatively. You might ask, "Are you worried about my reaction?" but it seems more useful to stay with the client's desire to discuss sex, not talk about you. Stay focused on your client. Does he worry that his behavior is strange? Your client may be asking, "Will you accept who I am?" or "Will I accept who I am?" or "I'm not sure that I'm normal sexually," so if you have reason to believe those questions lay beneath the discussion, notice it aloud.

"Why Doesn't He/she Like Sex As Much As I Do?" "How Can I Change Him/Her?" "My Girlfriend Is Unadventurous; Don't You Agree That She Has a Big Problem? How Can I Make Him More Adventurous?"

These are all questions in which you are being asked to validate your client's concerns and help him fix his perceived inadequate partner. These are common examples of questions that draw you into a discussion of whether the partner is sexually hopeless and/or your client has the right to be disappointed, confused, or angry. And don't get caught in gender stereotypes. Both men and women voice this complaint—and often—so get used to talking about it.

In these examples, your client has two underlying questions: (1) "Don't you agree that she is wrong?" and (2) "Will you help me get her to see the light?" You can respond with "I can see how frustrating this has become for you," to show your understanding and reflect your client's experience, whether it is frustration, anger, hurt, or disappointment. Second, when talking about sexuality and changing the nonclient, it is a good idea to keep in mind that it is a complex dance and the partner who is not in the room might tell a very different story. Get specifics of the situation and avoid making assumptions.

All questions that draw you into a discussion of the partner shift the focus from your client to someone outside the office. It is better to begin with your client, her wants, desires, feelings, and then, if you want to solve the problem together, you can introduce possible strategies for changing the relationship. Certainly you can commiserate that it is a rough situation to negotiate. It is tempting to engage in fixing a third party's behavior, but this approach is rarely successful. Maybe a referral to couples therapy is an answer.

If you work with couples, expect to talk about their sex lives. Clients sometimes need to be reminded that sex is not all about technique. It is a part of the relational dynamics, whether it is present or absent, good or bad, conventional or adventuresome, and often reflects other patterns that exist between them. Change takes time, but increased understanding and compassion makes the outcome more promising.

"I'm Feeling Better, But Maybe There Are Other Things to Talk About. What Do You Think?"

Clients probably would like to talk about sex more than therapists allow. There are few places where they can discuss their practices, fears, and desires without judgment and without it being thrown back at them after a couple of drinks or during an argument. However, this is not an easy topic to bring up, so be alert to oblique references and veiled statements.

Clients often test the waters with more distant statements such as the one above or comments on, "My friend did . . ." or "I heard about . . ." The distance provides protection if the subject matter is rejected. Your answers need to have an invitation, such as "Of course I want to hear about other personal aspects of your life. What sorts of things come to mind?" Your client may need some help. If other topics come to mind, and sex might be one of them, note it, "Well, now that you mention it, we hardly ever talk about sex (or your father, money, or whatever topic has been notably absent)."

Every once in awhile, a client talks explicitly about sexual topics from the first session. It is unusual, unless you are doing sex therapy, and this says something about him, whether it means unregulated anxiety, a personality disorder, or self-esteem issues. In the beginning, the direction is unclear, but as you continue it will make sense. Whenever a client leads with an unusual introduction, you have received information that will ultimately help you to understand him.

Linda

In the first session with Bruce, a middle-aged businessman, he offered information about his successes, his importance, and the fact that he had been faithful to his wife. I noted it only because people don't usually start off with out-of-context protestations of fidelity. About eight months later, when he was much more comfortable, he told me that his morning office routine consisted of arriving at the office at 9 a.m. and getting fellated by his secretary. He kept talking, and it was awhile before I collected my wits to observe, "Don't I remember you telling me that you were faithful to your wife?" "I never touch my secretary," he answered sincerely. His problems were less sexual than ethical, and his morning routine illustrated the direction for our therapeutic work.

QUESTIONS THAT INVOLVE THE THERAPIST

These questions are rare but uncomfortable. You will be able to attend to your client if you are prepared, so we include them.

> "Do you find me sexually attractive?" "Do you think I'm hot?" "Would you go out with me if I wasn't your client?"
> "I saw you at GayBar last weekend. Why do I always wind up with guys like Ed? What does it take to date a guy like you?"

RESPONSES

"Do You Find Me Sexually Attractive?" "Do You Think I'm Hot?" "Would You Go Out With Me If I Wasn't Your Client?"

Whether you are straight or gay, man or woman, these questions require consideration of their underlying significance before you respond. Your client wants to know more than your level of arousal. In the context of the specific transference and countertransference relationship, your client may wonder if he or she is valued and worthwhile.

If your client is a woman, we would first wonder if she appraises her own value based on her physical features and expects you to do the same. Your sexual attraction to her might be the expected response based on her past relationships, or she may have learned that sexuality is her power, and she intends to play it out with you. Again, with regard to the transference and countertransference dynamic, if your client is a man, the questions may be flirtatious or even aggressive, designed to deemphasize your professional role and emphasize the potential for a romantic relationship. He may have learned that there is power in a strong sexual come-on.

In your response to either men or women, we suggest that you show your understanding of the explicit and implicit aspects of this communication, as well as curiosity about what it means for the client. For example, "You're wondering if I find you physically attractive, and I get the impression that this question has some unspoken significance for you. What are your hopes or expectations about what I might say?" If you have been seeing this client for awhile and have an idea about the existing motivations, you can gently confront him, for example,

"You seem to think that the best way to relate to women is with a sexual come-on. There are other ways, like talking, and you can practice that in here." You cannot control your client's fantasies about you; it is just one aspect of treatment, but you can control how you present yourself.

These questions may indicate an erotic transference, which means that your client's reaction to you is positive and includes sexual fantasies that are understood to be unrealistic. If that is the case, you will be able to continue to work with your client and the fantasies will not interfere as therapy progresses. In contrast with the erotic transference described previously, the following questions illustrate the beginning of an eroticized transference.

Questions like, "Do you know what really sweaty sex is like?" or a male client who brought in a silky piece of lingerie and asked, "Would you hold it up against yourself so I can see if I like it for my girlfriend?" or "Do you know that you are my fantasy?" make us think about aggression, psychosis, or a severe personality disorder. Variations of these questions occur when your client is not talking directly about you but resorting to graphic talk about sexual partners, hoping to stimulate, titillate, intimidate, or get another strong response from you.

In an eroticized transference, your client is stuck in an intense, irrational preoccupation with you. The work of therapy will be bypassed in favor of repeated attempts to get love and sexual gratification from you. In these situations, get strong, regular supervision in order to assess whether therapy is possible and how to proceed.

Joe may have more severe problems than anxiety and anger, but Jen is receiving good supervision and handling the sessions well, even if she feels miserable.

Jen (pseudonym), Psy.D. student in California

I've been working with Joe, an undereducated, unemployed bartender. He is financially dependent on his girlfriend. He is anxious, angry, and vulnerable. A couple of weeks ago, he cried when he talked about how bad he feels about himself. Since then, I feel like therapy has stopped. It feels more like I'm in a bar and some nasty guy won't go away. He makes suggestive comments about the colors of my clothes, about my ankles, and even winked at me. At first, I kept trying to direct the session back to his concerns, but I was pretty ineffective. I began to feel sick to my stomach. Finally, my supervisor suggested that I treat this as a management issue rather than continuing to try to work it therapeutically. I now stick to variations of, "Joe, you are here to talk about your problems, not my appearance. You need to stick to that." Once when he would not stop, I said, "Joe, you are going off the tracks again. We will have to stop for today if you cannot get focused."

There may be gender differences in how male and female therapists respond to questions of a sexual nature. The younger female therapists interviewed for this book almost universally reported feeling "deskilled" and/or "devalued" when male clients asked them sexually provocative questions. They often felt that these questions were attempts to sexualize the therapeutic relationship, as if the men felt that their female therapists had nothing better to offer them. Common countertransference responses on the part of the women clinicians included shame, self-doubt, and anger at themselves and their clients. Some women admitted that they dread the day or hour when they have to see certain male clients. One woman admitted that she "lumps all male clients into one day" to get it over with. Another said that she tried "to reschedule some clients so the men who are sexually aggressive aren't my last clients of the evening. I get afraid to walk to the el."

These reactions show that, despite being bright and well-trained, the women clinicians feel diminished. Over time, they will learn to use their own reactions as an aid to diagnose and treat clients. Until then, good supervision is essential to processing reactions and planning strategy. Newer clinicians may fear talking to supervisors about the sexual nature of sessions, but they need advice and support about appropriate confrontation and containment. Every clinician wants to be taken seriously, especially when you are just beginning.

Men, by contrast, did not seem to feel deskilled, ashamed, vulnerable, or angered by clients' sexual questions. The idea that their clients might be sexually attracted to them was more likely to flatter them than to insult their clinical skills. The different responses of men and women clinicians to sexual questions may reflect more generally on a cultural phenomena in which men experience their sexuality as more compatible with their professional selves, whereas women experience their sexual selves as incompatible with their professional selves. Many men may feel that their sexuality is consistent with their ideal of being a successful professional. Some women, by contrast, may feel that their sexuality is inconsistent with their ideal of being a legitimate, respected professional. It may be important for women to show to themselves and the world that their professional accomplishments are related to skill and hard work, rather than to their capacity to sleep and seduce their way up the professional ladder. Therefore, some of the sexual questions may feel particularly aggressive to women clinicians.

The following anecdote is another example of the harmful effects of aggressive sexual comments.

Kelly (pseudonym), 24-year-old M.S.W. student in St. Louis

I've had continuing unpleasant experiences this year with Micky, a 50-year-old client. In the latest interchange, he said, "I was walking to Dunkin' Donuts on my coffee break and saw a woman ahead of me. I thought, 'What a great ass she has. I wish my therapist had an ass like that.' And who do you think it turned out to be?" I knew this wasn't any sort of real question and certainly didn't require a legitimate answer, but I think that he was intentionally devaluing me as a professional and turning me into a sexual object. I've become very self-conscious wondering if my shirt, heels, or skirt are provocative. It's hurting my self-confidence at work.

"I Saw You at GayBar Last Weekend. Why Do I Always Wind up With Guys Like Ed? What Does It Take to Date a Guy Like You?"

This is an opportunity for the therapist and client to explore the client's ideas about his own self-worth and about what it would mean for him to end up with someone like the therapist, whatever that means to the client. Responding to this question doesn't matter if the therapist is gay or straight. You can direct the discussion to an inquiry primarily about the client, "What do you think keeps you from dating someone you admire?" or interpersonally, "Guys like me—what kind of qualities are you looking for?"

For this topic of sexuality, two immediate treatment concerns appear for therapists who are gay or lesbian. One is the reality of living in a smaller community where you and your client may have friends in common and even know each other's former dates or lovers. That is an awkward fact of life. Second is the question of self-disclosure. It can be argued that to remain closeted with gay clients is to reinforce shame. This is your very personal clinical judgment.

FURTHER THOUGHTS

"Sex is the only game we play in the dark."

—Leonore Tiefer

Discussions about sexuality illustrate the difficulties in surmounting cultural, religious, social, and interpersonal differences in order to talk openly. Many people need explanations as to why it may be important or relevant to talk about sex, and some clients may require permission to do so. Clients will discuss sexual matters on different levels. Some will never talk about sex, others will hesitantly move to the topic, and the minority, usually younger clients, will talk openly. We doubt that sexuality was treated with the same attention in your training as other topics received.

How clients feel about themselves sexually is part of their sense of self and development. Most people have a normal desire for connection or yearning for love. Their partners may be the only people with whom they talk about sexual matters, and sometimes even that doesn't occur, so always appreciate that you are being permitted to enter a very private personal space.

Just like discussions about abuse can make you angry, discussions about sex have the greatest potential to become intertwined with sexual feelings, in either the therapist, the client, or both. At different times and with different people, you may feel voyeuristic, uncomfortable, stimulated, intrigued, pleased, intimate, or occasionally repelled. This work has an important component of feelings—yours—so don't be dismayed or surprised when you have physical or emotional reactions. The art lies in figuring out how to talk about sex comfortably, for both of you. You want to create an atmosphere where the two of you can talk freely but not so warmly that one or both of you gets confused about whether the conversation will shift into action.

Your own experiences, history, comfort, problems, and attitudes are always with you in the room and will affect how you handle this topic. Your readiness to discuss sex probably dictates when, how, and whether the topic will come up. Of course, all areas of clinical work require your self-reflection. Somehow, when the topic is sexuality, it can feel more dangerous than other topics. With regard to the topic of sex, you might think about the messages you received in your own family about sexuality and the experiences that have influenced your attitudes.

SUGGESTED READINGS

Gochros, H. L. (1986). Overcoming client resistances to talking about sex. In J. Gripton & M. Valentich (Eds.), Social work practice in sexual problems (pp. 7–15). Philadelphia, PA: Haworth Press.

Levine, S. (1989). Sex is not simple. Cleveland: Ohio Psychological Publishing Company.

Timm, T. M. (2009). Do I really have to talk about sex? Encouraging beginning therapists to integrate sexuality into couple's therapy. Journal of Couple and Relationship Therapy, 8, 15–33.

van Lankveld, J. (2009). Self-help therapies for sexual dysfunction. Journal of Sex Research, 46, 143–155.

Wincze, J. P., Bach, A. K., & Barlow, D. H. (2008). Sexual dysfunction. In D. H. Barlow (Ed.), Clinical handbook of psychological disorders: A step-by-step treatment manual (pp. 615–661). New York, NY: Guilford Press.

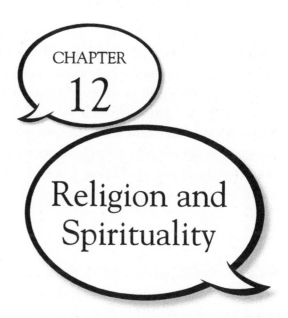

CHAPTER

12

Religion and
Spirituality

A common misconception is that if we share a religion, we have a great deal in common, and if we differ in religious beliefs, we vary sharply and dangerously. Few topics will strike clients' core sensitivities as much as a discussion of religious and spiritual values. The fear is about discrimination, intense discomfort, or pressure to disavow beliefs. Our therapeutic task, once again, is to provide a safe place for reflective thought and productive exploration, not to impose rights or wrongs.

Linda

Years ago, when I first interviewed Mary Lou and asked how she found me (a question that I often ask), she answered, "I was looking for a Jewish therapist and your name sounded Jewish. Are you?" I got lucky. She was willing to be honest, so I asked her, "Why are you looking for a Jewish therapist?" Quite remarkably, she said, "Because my boyfriend is Jewish, I'm not, and I thought that you
(continued)

could help me to be a better girlfriend if you are Jewish." To make a long therapy short, once she got some confidence back and realized that her life's goal of pleasing demanding men was doomed, the boyfriend was jettisoned, and we could get to work on building her identity and self-esteem. Despite the initial questions and answers, this did not turn out to be about religion. It did, however, like many questions, open up an essential door to understanding and helping Mary Lou.

For some clients, having a Jewish therapist is important because they are Orthodox Jews, their parents had been Holocaust survivors, or they had a problem related to being Jewish that they imagined a Jewish therapist would understand more easily than would a non-Jewish therapist. Again, the search for a Jewish, Lutheran, Episcopal, Wiccan, or atheist therapist is less about religion than about being understood, having something in common, or looking for certain real or imagined beliefs. Religion can be a difficult topic, even in therapy, for many reasons. Many clients shy away from discussions about religion because they have no idea how their beliefs will be received. Some therapists are also reluctant because psychology thinks of itself as a secular field, making conversations about spiritual matters or religion seem less clear than other topics.

Questions about religion invite us into important issues of individual differences and cultural considerations that, if initiated by us, might raise defensive reactions. And, because we live in a competitive culture that is loaded with delicate sensitivities and political correctness around discussing very personal beliefs—think about the admonition to "never talk about religion or politics in public"—these questions can provide an opportunity to demonstrate that therapy is a place where anything and everything can be neutrally discussed without censoring. In fact, in our experience, questions like the ones that follow are relatively rare, because clients seem to have gotten the same admonition to not discuss religion. So, when these do come up, work them; they can be fruitful and have great importance for your client.

QUESTIONS

The following questions are answered in the Responses section:

"What religion are you?"
"Should I pray about my problems?"
"Should I go to church/synagogue/mosque?"
"Are you religious?"
"Is it sinful to date out of my religion?"
"How are you different from my priest/rabbi/shaman?"
"Does God think I'm a sinner because I swore/am gay/cheated
    on an exam/had an affair/hate my father/had sex before
    I got married (on and on, sin after sin)?"
"What do I do about my anger with God?"
"Are you saved?" "Do you accept Jesus as your savior?"
"How do you really feel about Jews/Muslims?"
"Are you observant?"
"Should I leave things in God's hands?"
"What do you know about Catholicism/Judaism/Hinduism/
    Mormonism/Lutheranism?"
"Do you consider yourself to be spiritual?"

RESPONSES

Religion encompasses both the personal practices, beliefs, and world-view of an individual and the group practices that are endorsed by a shared, organized faith. Each religion has a set of beliefs, traditions, writings, holidays, rituals, a history, prayers, practices, and myths. At the core, having a religion often means having a belief, a relationship with, or commitment to a supreme being. Using these parameters, we can ask ourselves, as we do in all clinical encounters, "What is my client trying to tell me?"

The underlying issues are more important than creating meticulous answers to selected questions. There are no perfect answers, only answers that help or hinder the process of therapy. We also know that for many counselors, it helps to have some ready ideas that allay your anxiety and allow you to listen more freely.

"What Religion Are You?"

This question is usually veiled as, "Do you celebrate Christmas?" or something similarly phrased. What does your client want to know? Does he really care what you believe about an ultimate supernatural force (or Santa Claus)? Other related issues would probably be more therapeutic to explore. You might simply answer the question and then inquire, "What does it mean that I am Christian/Jewish/Muslim?" Our usual answer to a direct inquiry of "What religion are you?" is to return with the question, "I'm glad to answer, but I am curious—in what ways does my religion matter to you?" And then we listen very carefully. We listen for the hopes, fears, statements, and questions that were not asked directly but lay beneath other queries.

You will see that this question and others that follow often mask additional unspoken concerns, such as: "Will you share my beliefs and values? Will you understand my faith? Will you be judgmental? Do you know about my faith or beliefs? Will you dismiss my concerns? Can you possibly identify with my problems? Will I be able to talk freely? Will you mock me? Will you try to convert me? How will you react to my love or hate of my religion? Can I use religious shorthand with you rather than explaining everything?" This is a long list, especially since the original question seemed simple, but you can see that "What religion are you?" is not really about you. Here is a good example of fruitful questioning.

Charlie

Steve was a client in late adolescence who was depressed. He was endlessly angry at almost everyone and everything in his world. His favorite movie was *Fight Club*, which I rented and watched to really understand him. Steve relished his role as linebacker on his high school football team, and he was known as a hard hitter despite constant neck and shoulder pain. To our sessions, Steve brought fantasy stories about death and destruction that he had written and, after hearing each one, I worried about his potential to harm himself or others.

In our eighth session together, out of the blue, Steve stated, "You wear a cross." I do, so I responded, "Yes, I do." Steve then asked, "What does that mean to you?" Steve had probably seen the cross at each of our prior sessions and hadn't asked about it until now. He also had never really talked about faith or religion in our therapy except to say that his mother, whom he saw as naïve and out of touch with his life, was quite religious and tried to get the rest of the family to go to church with her. I asked, "Well, before I share some of my experiences with you, can you tell me what that might mean to you?" I expected to get another angry rant, this time about Christianity and its shortcomings. I was pleasantly surprised.

The quick reply that surged out of Steve indicated that he had given this previous thought. "Well, it tells me that, even though you see and hear all kinds of awful and horrible things in your work, you still have faith. I think that really says something." I savored his revealing statement for several moments before responding, "Well, it really seems to have said something to you," which began a brand-new exploration of Steve's desire to develop a faith in himself, others, the world, and perhaps a higher being. In our subsequent work together, we gave voice and power to convictions that he perceived as being alive in another person (accurately or not, as we never really talked about my feelings about the cross) whom he supposed, like him, also saw much in the world about which to be sorrowful. Steve's reaction was a welcome surprise and reinforces our belief that we cannot possibly know in what directions clients' minds will travel.

"Should I Pray About My Problems?"

Thinking that your client is asking permission or validation to pray, you might respond with a quick, reflexive, "Sure." or "That is up to you." Those answers are probably consistent with most therapy guidelines, and even sound respectful of your client's autonomy. But before you answer, consider that you don't know what praying does for your client. It could be harmless, helpful and restorative, or an instrument of self-flagellation. An alternative response would be: "That's an important question. Tell me about your prayer life and what role that serves for you?"

If your client has never thought critically about the place of prayer in his life, and he looks at you with a blank gaze when you inquire, prompt him by adding, "I am asking what this experience is like for you because some people find that prayer is comforting, while others find it more of a punitive and upsetting experience. What about you?" Your initial attempts to get clients to reflect on religion may be experienced as criticism or moral judgment. Issues of faith are steeped in family-of-origin and cultural identifications. Whatever questions you have, ask them with interest and neutrality; these questions are delicate. Your client's trust and your therapeutic alliance can be damaged with one sentence that makes you sound like too much of "an other." Therefore, try to communicate that it is critical that the two of you focus on your client's view.

With this question and all those that follow, you have the opportunity to help your client articulate his thoughts about religion, for example, "I'm here to help you figure out where, if anywhere, prayer, God, and religion belong in your life." You can also add any of the following, "For instance, the last time you prayed/attended church/practiced your faith, what was this like for you?" or "What has happened for you in the past when you prayed about your problems? or "Do you find comfort in prayer/ church?" or "Tell me more about how you feel about prayer." Try, "What happens when you pray? What might happen if you don't?" or "Has prayer helped you in the past?" or "What would it mean if your prayers were/ weren't answered in the way that you desire?" From the ensuing discussion, you will both learn whether prayer is about belonging, confession, absolution, following rules, comfort, or inviting punishment.

"Should I Go to Church/Synagogue/Meeting Hall/ Shambala Center/Mosque?"

This question is often asked in desperation because nothing else has worked. You can see immediately how it is weighed down by a moralistic tone of what *should* I do. Shoulds comes from a real or imagined external authority. As such, the question is seductive and urges you to join your client in passing judgment or deciding right from wrong. This is the last place that you want to be with a client, because being judgmental lures you away from being a therapist and toward donning the robes of the morality magistrate. You understand your job—to examine your client's thoughts, feelings, and conflicts. Consider responding, "What do you imagine yourself gaining from such an experience?" or "Would you find comfort there?" or "Was this an experience that you had as a child?" or "Tell me about your church/synagogue/meeting hall/shambala center/mosque/sangha." If the topic remains open, you can examine both sides of the should question and wonder who the client is trying to please. Inquire, "Are you trying to please God/your parents/your partner/the church/the community?" Then, "What happens if you don't please them"? You may find that your client expects ostracism, disappointment, or being struck by lightning bolts. Is this question about worship or autonomy?

"Are You Religious?"

We don't know if, or in what ways, your religion might be a problem or bonus for your client. If you try to guess whether religiosity is a plus or minus, you might miss out on an essential piece of information about your client's interactions in her world, so we suggest responding with, "In what ways is that important to you?" or "I'm fine answering, but first, let's talk about religion in your life." or "I'm glad to answer, but I wonder, what if I am and what if I am not religious?" or "What impact does that have on our work together?" You can still answer directly, but in this way, the focus remains on the client and the importance of religion to her.

It may help to acknowledge the cultural context for the question: "We both know that discussing religion is not done very often because it can be such a hot topic. But for us, it is useful to explore your personal experiences." It takes courage for many clients to talk seriously about religion in their lives, and when the two of you achieve that open discussion, you will have created intimacy and trust between you. Furthermore, the tone of the discussion models very powerful behaviors that clients can duplicate in their other relationships.

"Is It Sinful to Date Out of My Religion?"

In discussing religion, there is always the possibility that your clients will incorrectly assume that your expertise on psychological matters extends into spiritual realms. As such, they can end up asking specific questions related to religious doctrine—questions that, unless you have specialized training *and* have an agreement with the client that this will be part of your work together, need to be directed to an expert in the area of religious doctrine. You can say, "We can talk about your thoughts and feelings about dating out of your religion, but I can't imagine that we will reach conclusions about sin." or "I don't know about the sinfulness of dating out of your religion, but this is an important topic to talk about as you try to make good decisions about the way that you live your life." Determinations about sin is somebody else's job.

Religious counseling is done by people who are specifically trained in religious or pastoral counseling. Pastoral counselors espouse a particular religious point of view, and their practice is informed by, and often based on, these beliefs. If they are practicing ethically, they also are transparent about their beliefs and affiliations so that clients can make informed choices about their psychological care.

Charlie

When I presented a poster session about answering client questions about religion and spirituality, a psychologist stopped by and gave me a wonderful example about using professional consultation. He told me about a client whom he was seeing in psychotherapy because of her trauma due to losing her brother to suicide. Several weeks into therapy, through her tears, this Catholic woman asked, "Is it true that I'll never see my brother in heaven because he took his own life?" Quite appropriately, the therapist responded, "I think that might be a question best asked of your priest." "I did ask him" was her response. "And what did he tell you?" asked the therapist. "He said I should ask my therapist." When my colleague told me this story, I laughed, and he said that is exactly what both he and his client did as well. Although the laughter helped bring them closer together, this question and the hot potato answers demonstrate the delicacy of discussions about religion.

"How Are You Different From My Priest/Rabbi/Shaman?"

Unlike the previous description of pastoral counseling, your psychological expertise is in a variety of theories and techniques and does not have a basis in religious doctrine. Perhaps that is what your client wants to know. Clarify your position as, "I'm trained in psychological theory, in people's growth and development. That is very different expertise than your religious leader." Having a religion of your own does not make you a pastoral counselor any more than having pots and pans makes you a chef or taking medication makes you a physician. Your responses as a psychotherapist are different from those of a religious counselor. For example, Matt comes in, excited that he has met Jessica, an interesting woman, *but*, he wants to know, is it sinful to date her? Jessica may be, for example, Catholic, Seventh-Day Adventist, Jewish, atheist, Muslim, Animist, or born-again. A pastoral counselor may say to Matt that the church frowns upon dating out of the fold. The pastoral counselor may bring up aspects of Jessica's faith that differ from Matt's—issues that could pose potential problems for them as a couple or family.

In contrast, as a therapist, your job is to explore the client's concerns, issues, and conflicts around dating someone different. "Tell me about your reservations dating Jessica?" or "Why would you think that this is sinful?" or "How do you feel about dating a Wiccan/Muslim/Buddhist/pagan/Free Mason?" It has been our experience that clients who want the religious explanation go to their priests and rabbis; they come to us when they fear ostracism from those institutions because of the questions they pose. If clients do have specific questions about particular doctrine, we suggest a consultation with an expert in these areas.

"Does God Think I'm a Sinner Because I Swore/Am Gay/ Cheated on an Exam/Had an Affair/Hate My Father/Had Sex Before I Got Married (On and On, Sin After Sin)?"

Neither one of us has ever heard all of those supposed sins in one question, but we do hear crushing experiences of guilt, negative emotions, regretted behaviors, unpleasant thoughts, or lapses in personal responsibility every day. You don't have to be religious, or even believe in God, to understand how thoughts, feelings, and behaviors destroy lives. Don't fall back on the reflective stance of "What do you think? Do *you* think that God is angry?" Not only do these responses repeat the moralistic tone your client invites, but they sound like you have memorized standard phrases from the imaginary counselor's manual. These issues torment people and need to be discussed fully and sensitively. You can begin with, "Tell me about contracting herpes/having an affair/not going to your mother's funeral . . . and we can try to sort through it together."

These client concerns demonstrate the power of religion to feel punitive to some people; they fear additional punishment. This issue is important to discuss. You cannot know in advance where the dialogue will go, maybe toward guilt, fear, shame, regrets, or personal responsibility, but you have signed on for the emotional ride to explore the thoughts, actions, and feelings along with your client. The destination will certainly be a healthier place than the stepping-on point.

"What Do I Do About My Anger With God?"

Clients don't only talk about their fear of God. They talk about their anger toward God. Anger is anger, rarely comfortable and often confusing. We don't know a better response than a sincere invitation to your client, such as "Let's talk about the anger." or "Let's sort it out."

It isn't always anger or confusion about God's view of your client's behavior. Questions like, "How do I tell my parents that I'm not going to church with them on Easter?" has more to do with relationships with parents than with religion. The same problem happens when people who were raised in a fundamentalist doctrine want to live freely in a same-sex relationship or with a partner before marriage. Sometimes, your clients are simply seeking confirmation that they are not terrible people.

"Are You Saved?" "Do You Accept Jesus as Your Savior?"

Our colleague, Melissa Britt Perrin, Psy.D., offered an insightful comment on these questions.

Melissa Perrin, Psy.D.

To be frank, when a client asks these two questions, I first reply, "What does this mean to you?" because the questions are often coded inquiries as to whether the therapist is the same type of Christian as the client. Generally, this question expresses a belief in salvation that can only be found through acceptance of Christ's teachings. If I answer that I am saved, I identify myself as safe to interact with. If I answer that I have not been saved, I am perceived as someone who has missed out on the Answer, someone who is missing a crucial piece of wisdom, information, and thus different from my client.

You are equal to the questioner (if you are both saved) or you are a lost soul who may not be aware of the devil's care. Magical thinking is in play here as well as polarity. After hearing their answer, I respond honestly. These questions are often deal breakers if they are actually asked. If clients need a saved or Christian therapist, 99% of the time they will ask for a referral to a Christian counselor. If they have made it into my office and ask the question, any hedging I might do to try to maintain the therapeutic alliance will be marred by my hedging. It is better that I answer truthfully and build credibility based on being forthright, even at the risk of losing the client.

"How Do You Really Feel About Jews/Muslims?"

This is a clear invitation to join in disliking one group or another. One answer is to comment, "You seem to have some strong feelings about them yourself, so let's start there." It can be achingly tempting to lecture on social justice, but we don't think that lecturing is the way to approach it with this question. We do comment when a client espouses religious hatred, and then we observe the feelings expressed, "You really hate Jews, why?"

"Are You Observant?"

"If you can explain the feelings or behaviors that *observant* includes, I will try to answer." But, as we have stated often, your real interest lies in how being observant, or not, will matter in your work together. Some clinicians assert that people's sense of religion and God parallels their image of their mother or father. It is an interesting idea. If that is true, tread carefully in both areas. Never dismiss or talk glibly about a client's parents or their deity. These discussions require the same sensitivity, because there are elements of all religious beliefs that are irrational and archaic.

Linda brought up the topic of religion in a psychology writing group, a small cadre of creative psychologists with whom she writes. One friend's reaction to religious discussions with clients was plain, simple, and unmistakable: "Ugh." She dreads the topic and hates hearing biases. Another one lit up with excitement. She sees engagement. Questions like the ones posed previously bring out the biases that underlie our responses to a client's religious life. We all have biases. We know some of them and are oblivious to others. Take a moment and think, what are yours? How will your personal beliefs interfere with your ability to view your client's religious world objectively?

You will find that, over time, you will further develop your ability to discuss religious issues sensitively and nonjudgmentally as you practice doing so. Getting to that point, however, does take intentional review, or you will find yourself consciously or unconsciously avoiding the topic, just like some of our supervisors used to do. In your years of practice, you may also find yourself working in consultation and coordination of care with culturally based healers, religious leaders, and care providers.

"Should I Leave Things in God's Hands?"

There is an old story about two young boys running to school. They are on the verge of being late. Tired and panting, one says, "I'm going to sit down and pray that we will get to school on time." The other boy looks at his friend and says, "I'm going to pray and run at the same time."

Religion, like other resources in life, can facilitate personal action and responsibility or encourage passivity. Clients who have been enculturated to turn things over to God may take less responsibility for their lives and become inactive. You will hear phrases such as, "It's in God's hands," "My reward will come in heaven," or "This must be God's plan." This attitude discourages additional open dialogue because, when answers have already been found, exploration is unnecessary. Leaving one's life in God's hands can run counter to psychotherapy's goal of empowering clients to take personal responsibility for expanding knowledge about themselves and implementing change where possible.

If a client seems to be outsourcing certain aspects of her life, you can try to discover where her sense of personal responsibility lies as she continues to live in an existing situation. Reassuring statements can also be helpful, such as "For some people, discussing religion is important because it clarifies and focuses their concerns. They gain wonderful assistance in changing their lives. For others, religion diminishes the personal responsibility they take for their life and instead makes a higher power responsible for their well-being. Let's figure out what part of this problem is in your hands."

Conversely, there are situations where mental health is promoted by accepting one's powerlessness or relinquishing control in favor of stepping back or disengaging. Sometimes there is nothing we can do but work for acceptance. Who, if anyone, has control, and how much control, extends far beyond a discussion of religion or religious questions and will arise in every type of problem as clients wrestle with decisions.

When the question of powerlessness comes up in the context of religion questions, you can comment, "Your question certainly gets to the heart of an issue that is important throughout life. Some days, we need to accept that we have little power over some situations. On other occasions we do have power and responsibility to activate changes in our lives. When that happens, I believe that we have a responsibility to reflect on whether or not we want to take action to bring about change. What are we talking about here?"

"What Do You Know About Catholicism/Judaism/Hinduism/Mormonism/Lutheranism?"

It's okay not to know, to be an interested student, and to ask about the finer points of someone's religion if it is important to her, just like you would ask about a relationship or job responsibilities. Just say, "Not as much as I would like to." or "I want to hear more." Clients are pleased to explain their religion if it is important to them and they want you along as a fellow explorer. We are trained to listen, discuss, explore, understand, and solve problems. Even when there is no solution to a problem, the discussion, examination, and understanding helps a great deal. Psychotherapy is one of the fields where the genuine engagement and attempt can be as healing as a clear solution. You can't say that about auto mechanics or orthopedic surgeons.

Every topic is embedded in a cultural context, but religious institutions are certainly some of the strongest forces that you and your clients will encounter. Whether your clients espouse loyalty to a specific religious doctrine, it does not negate the social and cultural component of religion in the United States. For many people, their religious home serves as a primary social outlet and interpersonal resource. Religious affiliation serves as a needed source of personal esteem and may be the foundation for charitable work. Some of our clients have found their partners, jobs, babysitters, social activities, car repair, and career education through their synagogues or churches. Rituals, rites of passage and belonging, such as first communion, serving as altar boy/girl, confirmation, adult baptism, bar and bat mitzvahs, weddings, and funerals all take place in the house of worship and bind people to tradition, if not always to the religious doctrine. For others, religion offers opportunities to be involved across generations, supports biological families, or allows them to create found families. The sense of community cannot be overlooked as a resource for helping many clients improve their mental health.

"Do You Consider Yourself to Be Spiritual?"

We have treated clients who have felt pushed out of organized religion or cannot abide religion because of personal trauma. They may still consider themselves spiritual because of deep, satisfying beliefs that continue to exist outside of religion. Answer honestly and, perhaps, if you are also searching, you can admit, "I think I am, although I'm not sure of what spiritual means to others. What about you?"

There is increasing diversity in religion, and many people identify themselves as spiritual. We have found that many clients who cannot continue in the religion of their childhoods still consider themselves spiritual, exploring alternatives. Spirituality concerns itself with nature and the meaning of our lives. Spirituality also relates to matters of sanity and of psychological health, matters with which we are extremely concerned. We raise these matters because mental health professionals need to be able to touch on both sets of issues, religion and spirituality, to be of use to clients.

One client said that he does not envision religion as welcoming him because, as a teenager, his church helped his parents engage a "conversion therapist" when he acknowledged emerging sexual thoughts about a same-sex friend. Another client was distressed about her church's laws and asked, "What would God say?" about her same-sex relationship. A Catholic client implored her husband to attend her church, but it brought back too many negative experiences of having been humiliated and having his head pushed into the blackboard by the nuns at his parochial school. Some clients are struggling to not feel guilty when they have feelings contrary to church teachings, like anger, lust, or jealousy. Don't be surprised when you also have strong reactions to the stories you hear and to the problems that cause pain to your clients.

At the worst extreme, there are people who were abused by clergy who cannot return to church. These clients and others, whose experiences, beliefs, or lifestyles run counter to church policy, see themselves as unwelcome if they are authentic, so they often find other ways to live spiritually rich lives.

FURTHER THOUGHTS

"We have just enough religion to make us hate, but not enough to make us love one another."

—Jonathan Swift

We have introduced previous topics with the phrase, "outside of therapy, people don't get to talk about . . . ," and it is true every time. There are many reasons that therapy is special; one is that clients can talk about the beliefs, behaviors, and feelings about which they are normally inhibited in other settings. Religion is near the top of the list of those topics. Generally, people talk about religion with others who are clearly like-minded, so there is little danger. However, clients don't know your views, so they take a risk when they discuss their religion and what it means to them. More often, they don't take the chance.

Your respect for your client's beliefs is not enough to bring religious topics into the room. Often you have to draw people out to talk about their faith. You can do so by letting them know that their thoughts, feelings, and behaviors are legitimate topics for therapy, even when your counsel is not focused directly on their religious identity.

Religion can be a hot topic when you are comfortable with it and a searing one when you are not. Be aware of your own beliefs. You will have reactions to clients' religious ideas and practices, so be careful not to pollute their examination of the topic. Many discussions have no clear answers, religious topics being one, but it doesn't make the conversation less significant. Whether clients are religious, questioning, spiritual, or atheistic, religion evokes people's concerns about belonging, being understood, being loved, and the serious existential issues of finding one's meaningful place in an often isolating world.

SUGGESTED READINGS

Bartoli, E. (2007). Religious and spiritual issues in psychotherapy practice: Training the trainer. *Psychotherapy: Theory, Research, Practice, Training, 44,* 54–65.

Genia, V. (2000). Religious issues in secularly based psychotherapy. *Counseling and Values, 44,* 213–221.

Hathaway, W. L., Scott, S. Y., & Garver, S. A. (2004). Assessing religious/spiritual functioning: A neglected domain in clinical practice? *Professional Psychology: Research and Practice, 35,* 97–104.

Miller, W. (Ed.). (1999). *Integrating spirituality into treatment: Resources for practitioners.* Washington, DC: American Psychological Association.

Plante, T. G. (2007). Integrating spirituality and psychotherapy: Ethical issues and principles to consider. *Journal of Clinical Psychology, 63,* 891–902.

Richards, P. S., & Bergin, A. E. (2000). *Handbook of psychotherapy and religious diversity.* Washington, DC: American Psychological Association.

Zinnbauer, B. J., & Pargament, K. I. (2000). Working with the sacred: Four approaches to religious and spiritual issues in counseling. *Journal of Counseling and Development, 78,* 162–171.

CHAPTER

13

Prejudice

Prejudice is a great teacher of tolerance. Listening to clients utter prejudicial statements during the therapy hour is difficult, but it isn't your time. You may get angry at them, but try to put your own emotions aside long enough to understand your client's point of view, what it means, and what response would be helpful. It is always your decision whether to respond directly to prejudicial comments. In this chapter and the one that follows, Chapter 14, Stigma, we present various possibilities.

Charlie

In three sessions, 55-year-old Seth had revealed two significant personal challenges. First, he had moved his family to Ohio, where they were all having adjustment troubles, and second, he struggled with two adolescent daughters who had grown distant from

(continued)

him and who were "recruited by his wife to side with her" in their failing marriage. Toward the end of the third session, Seth stated that all his problems would disappear if he returned to Phoenix to work in a firm that he had established. He was reluctant to do so, because it meant that his family would have extended contact with his sister, who was a lesbian, "and I don't want my daughters to be exposed to that lifestyle." He believed that his sister would try to "recruit" his daughters.

This was a fork in the therapy road. I had several potential directions; the most interesting would have been a gentle interpretation that he seemed to fear "recruitment by the other side," whether that enemy was his wife or sister, and that he stood to lose his daughters in the process. I was less certain about confronting him with his prejudice; it was early in treatment and he wasn't particularly open. He decided for us by asking, "Are gays and lesbians born that way or created by bad experiences they have while growing up?"

An awful thought flashed through my mind: Could he have been one of those "bad experiences" that his sister may have had while she was growing up, or had someone tried to "recruit" him? Instead of following any of these ideas, I fumbled a reply that attempted to give a middle-of-the-road answer. I explained that there is a sexual map in which people come to their adult behaviors based on genetic predisposition toward either heterosexuality or homosexuality at either end of a wide continuum and personal developmental experiences being in the middle. Seth said something about this being "interesting" and that he would think more about it.

Before his next session he cancelled his appointment with me and did not return. Looking back, I ought to have saved the education about sexuality and said, "I don't know if you realize, but several times now we have almost talked about your daughters being recruited into different viewpoints. I think that you will feel better if we discuss that idea directly."

In this chapter, we deal with client questions that reveal a negatively biased view of other people or groups of people. We examine the challenge of attempting to tolerate, without agreeing with, intolerance. We all find it easier to tolerate prejudice when it is an academic exercise or a free speech issue. However, when you are caught off guard by a client who expresses prejudicial hatred, you may feel a strong reaction.

QUESTIONS

The following questions are answered in the Responses section:

> **"Are you like all those other liberals who believe gay people have equal rights?"**
>
> **"Our company changed the work titles for most of the women we employ, so we are able to pay them less and save money. Pretty smart management, don't you think?"**
>
> **"That guy wouldn't have been promoted if he wasn't Black. You've seen people get ahead just because they represent a minority group, haven't you?"**
>
> **"We could spend our money on schools if we didn't have to worry about those militant Muslims blowing up buildings. What psychological term would you use to explain their terrorist ways?"**
>
> **"Will you think I'm terrible if I tell you about my prejudice?"**

There are many instances when clients express statements that make an unmistakable reference to an -ism: sexism, racism, ageism, ableism, classism, or some other prejudicial belief, such as, "I didn't get placed on that influential committee because they were looking for more minority representation." or "I should never go shopping on a Tuesday. It's double-coupon day for seniors at our grocery store, and I don't have the time to waste wading through that group." With each comment, you must decide whether to file this information away for a later time, explore the reactions, attempt to examine any underlying meaning or feelings, place the comment in the context of your client's present clinical concerns, or advocate against prejudice. In the questions discussed as follows, we have used examples that are not veiled, probably do not indicate a passing frustration, and often require a more immediate response because they invite you to join in the vitriol.

RESPONSES

"Are You Like All Those Other Liberals Who Believe Gay People Have Equal Rights?"

Instances of clients raising highly prejudicial issues are rare. Perhaps people who hold these views are not drawn to engage in the self-reflection required in counseling, or they find therapists who share their views, but it will occasionally happen. You will find many conversations difficult to tolerate as a therapist: hearing unkindness, aggression, witnessing the effects of abuse, and sitting with the pain and grief of your clients. At the top of this list for many clinicians is the effort it takes to listen to and work with prejudice.

All answers need a context, but there are general ideas to consider when you formulate your response. Perhaps this client is testing you, wanting to know if you share his beliefs. It may be an expression of the same hope that you hear in other situations, that you will understand or validate a belief. But what if you can't validate this prejudice? You have to choose whether to be silent, to file the material away in your mind for another time, to interpret, to challenge the sentiment, to observe, or to educate. Silence lets the client think whatever he wants, but is it cowardly? You can file the homophobia away for another time when the client is ready to examine his prejudice. You can interpret the comment if you have other information, for example, "I remember you saying that you were bullied in school, kids called you a *fag*. Could some of your reactions to gays have grown from that?" or "Previously, you have described your experience with gay men as very frightening. Could your worries about equal rights stem from past interactions?" A challenge would be, "Do you believe that only certain people are protected by the Constitution of the United States?" or "Do you believe that we ought to start restricting rights because we don't like someone's sexuality? What would you restrict next?" Your anger comes through in that last answer, so you might shut down any conversation.

When you find yourself having a strong reaction like anger, remember to bring it up in supervision or with a knowledgeable colleague. If you want to observe the question, bringing it to greater awareness, say, "Wow, you have an intense reaction to gays having equal rights. Maybe that is worth looking at." Finally, an answer that hopes to educate sounds something like, "The research shows that gay people don't differ from straight folks except about having same-sex partners. What worries you?" All of these responses are possible, and your choice will depend on you, the relationship with your client, and the treatment.

"Our Company Changed the Work Titles for Most of the Women We Employ, So We Are Able to Pay Them Less and Save Money. Pretty Smart Management, Don't You Think?"

It's easy to imagine the *wink, wink, nod, nod* that follows remarks like this one. On the surface, this comment seems to be prejudicial against women, but we think that is less about bias and more about the client's own craftiness. In this instance, unlike the choices of silence, interpretation, challenge, observation, or education that we suggested to the previous question, we would first consider your client's personality and values. Think about all the information you have: whether the client has a personality disorder; whether the client tends to show off; do familial or historical factors explain this management technique; and are you hearing expressions of low self-esteem and self-protection rather than prejudice. Our initial response would tend toward elucidating personality and values, for example, "Hmmm, that seems deceptive; is it ethical?" or "What if you were one of those women? How would you deal with this management technique?"

How people select and process information will influence their impressions of others. Many of us listen only to the opinions that confirm our existing views. We may watch the news shows that support our existing beliefs and read the position papers that confirm our existing positions. We hope that, because an individual has come into treatment, that he is open to change, but that isn't always the case. Many people exclusively want confirmation of existing beliefs, and we are left with some decisions to make.

"That Guy Wouldn't Have Been Promoted if He Wasn't Black. You've Seen People Get Ahead Just Because They Represent a Minority Group, Haven't You?"

People are rarely honest enough to say, "I hate or fear Blacks, Jews, women, Asians, Muslims, or homosexuals, don't you?" It is usually couched in specific stereotypic gripes, such as, "Blacks get ahead because they have affirmative action; Jews run the banks; women sleep their way to promotions; Asians are good in science; or homosexual couples ruin the institution of marriage." It's tempting to say, "The world is an unfair place in a thousand ways, but I'm not sure what you are really talking about," but that response is low on sympathy. You might do better asking, "Have you been treated unfairly? Are people passing you up at work?" In this way, you address the hurt and will learn more about the source of the complaint.

"We Could Spend Our Money on Schools if We Didn't Have to Worry About Those Militant Muslims Blowing Up Buildings. What Psychological Term Would You Use to Explain Their Terrorist Ways?"

Is it the job of therapy to change people's views or to expose them to the knowledge that there are other reasonable ways of looking at things? Certainly when it is about abuse, violence, and dangerous behaviors, education is required. Other situations leave the choice to you. For this question, we would probably take a middle-of-the-road approach: "Muslims are generally getting up for work, feeding their kids, and arguing with the in-laws just like everyone else. I agree that there is a lunatic fringe in every group. Are you worried about the increased terrorism in the world?" More than anything, we would be wondering why this client is using valuable therapy time to ask about terrorism and try to figure out where the fear originates.

You are in a field where people have problems, so you can't be terribly surprised when you are exposed to the dark side of people's minds. You aren't going to be equally tolerant of all problems. Some will elicit compassion, whereas others will generate pity, fury, hatred, or sadness. In the responses given here, we have advocated a certain range of responses to expressions of prejudice. Other writers strongly disagree with us.

They believe that failing to combat racism is racism. This discrepancy raises important considerations about how you define your job, what is most helpful to your clients, where you make your moral stands, and what you comment on, challenge, or educate in order to raise awareness.

"Will You Think I'm Terrible if I Tell You About My Prejudice?"

Most of us are pleased when a client confesses to a bias; it shows self-awareness and trust in the relationship. The problem can occur after your client makes this disclosure. Therapists often err by responding, "Well, it's normal to have some biases" and leave it at that. That type of response is a well-intentioned effort to normalize a client's reaction, prejudice, or shame. It may be comforting to respond, "That's okay, everyone's prejudiced about something," but this may be too quick of a response that reduces examination. What is the client actually saying? It is probably normal, but even so, the client deserves the right to struggle openly with her thoughts and emotions. When you move quickly to normalize a client's comment, it may stem from your own anxiety about the topic or from a lack of understanding that this particular prejudice is causing extreme discomfort to the individual, even when it seems minor to you. If you are not comfortable with your own prejudices, you will avoid these discussions. So, sit tight, stay with the narrow focus that the client brought in, and say, "That has to be uncomfortable; let's talk about it."

FURTHER THOUGHTS

> "Prejudices are rarely overcome by argument; not being founded in reason they cannot be destroyed by logic."
> —Tryon Edwards

Everyone has prejudices, and the layers can be endless and oblique. As therapists, we are not exempt from this reality, but we are committed to trying to remain aware of our own inevitable distortions. Prejudice may be unavoidable, but that doesn't make it acceptable; it can cause real damage. The results are seen in emotional wounds, financial hardships, and lost opportunities for growth.

You are human and you will have strong, sometimes highly personal reactions to your clients. When you feel hot emotions arising from listening to clients' rants or when your own biases creep into your consciousness, call your supervisor, consultant, or a trusted colleague. The ensuing discussions will be terrifically helpful to you and will improve your work.

SUGGESTED READINGS

Bartoli, E., & Pyati, A. (2009). Addressing clients' racism and racial prejudice in individual psychotherapy: Therapeutic considerations. *Psychotherapy Theory, Research, Practice, Training, 46*, 145–157.

Bieschke, K., Perez, R., & DeBord, K. (2006). Introduction: The challenge of providing affirmative psychotherapy while honoring diverse contexts. In K. Bieschke, R. Perez, & K. DeBord (Eds.), *Handbook of counseling and psychotherapy with lesbian, gay, bisexual, and transgender clients* (2nd ed., pp. 3–11). Washington, DC: American Psychological Association.

Constanine, M. G. (2007). Racial microaggressions against African American clients in cross-racial counseling relationships. *Journal of Counseling Psychology, 54*, 1–16.

Constantine, M. G., & Sue, D. W. (2006). *Facilitating cultural competence in mental health and educational settings.* Hoboken, NJ: Wiley.

Guerin, B. (2003). Combating prejudice and racism: New interventions from a functional analysis of racist language. *Journal of Applied Social Psychology, 13*, 29–45.

Hamer, F. M. (2006). Racism as a transference state: Episodes of racial hostility in the psychoanalytic context. *Psychoanalytic Quarterly, 75*, 197–214.

Heriek, G. M., & Garnets, L. D. (2007). Sexual orientation and mental health. *Annual Review of Clinical Psychology, 3*, 353–375.

Laszloffy, T. A., & Hardy, K. V. (2000). Uncommon strategies for a common problem: Addressing racism in family therapy. *Family Process, 39*, 35–50.

Ponterro, J. G., Utsey, S. O., & Pederson, P. B. (2007). *Preventing prejudice: A guide for counselors, educators, and parents* (2nd ed.). Newbury Park, CA: Sage.

Stone, D., Patton, B., & Heen, S. (1999). *Difficult conversations: How to discuss what matters most.* New York, NY: Penguin Group.

Sue, D. W., Capodilupo, C. M., Torino, G. C., Bucceri, J. M., Holder, A. M. B., Nadal, K. L., & Esquilin, M. (2007). Racial microaggressions in everyday life: Implications for clinical practice. *American Psychologist, 62*, 271–286.

CHAPTER

14

Stigma

Stigma is a type of prejudice, but in these questions and answers, the client is on the receiving end of bias. People are stigmatized because they differ in physical appearance, a deviation from the "norm" that you can see; or because they belong to a racial, ethnic, or other minority; or because they have something in their personal life that others find unacceptable, such as divorce, a criminal past, addictions, or mental illness. You will meet all of these people. Some clients worry about being stigmatized for entering therapy, and that is the primary stigma we address in this chapter.

Linda

Clients keep therapy (or the reasons for treatment) a secret for many reasons. One college freshman told her parents that she wanted to begin therapy because she was having trouble sleeping. True, but she was unable to sleep because she had been raped

(continued)

during the first week of school. A 33-year-old man never told his family about his sessions because his parent's hostile-dependent relationship with each other, and its effect on him, their son, was the impetus for him to get help. A 48-year-old woman kept therapy a secret from her family who were war refugees and would have been appalled at her apparent weakness.

The negative stereotypes of people in treatment are, at one extreme, the weak, indulged, neurotic individuals who have no backbone and refuse to do the independent hard work to fix their lives. At the other extreme, they are not to be trusted, crazy, people who are unlike the rest of us. In the middle, we find the cultural expectations about help-seeking and the preference to rely on family instead of professionals.

Stigma is real, and many people will not seek help because of fear of being discredited, fear of social isolation, and fear of job discrimination. Therefore, individuals and their families go without the services they need.

QUESTIONS

The following questions are answered in the Responses section:

> "My family says that the way to solve problems is to work harder. Why can't I do this by myself?"
>
> "What's the matter with me that I need counseling?"
>
> "Why am I so weak? Lazy? Dependent?"
>
> "My dad laughs at the indulgence of getting treatment. His culture/race/ethnicity doesn't believe in therapy. What do I say to him?"
>
> "What am I supposed to tell people who wonder why I am getting counseling?"
>
> "Do you think that reporting our psychotherapy to my insurance company will somehow come back to haunt me if someone gets hold of this information?"
>
> "Am I going to become a whack job like my Aunt Sue?"

"Should I tell my boyfriend that I'm taking antidepressants?"

"Should I get tested for HIV/ STDs?"

"Do you think I'm crazy?"

And our special favorite, which we answer first:

"Aren't all you therapists a little nuts?"

Linda

I was stopped in the hallway by a teaching colleague who asked, "Linda, did you tell all the grad students in your class that they were crazy?" I said, "Maybe, I don't remember. What did they say?" She answered, "That you announced that anyone who goes into this field is a little crazy." I nodded, "I'm glad they were listening; that's pretty accurate." People who have everything figured out don't need to spend their lives doing therapy. We enter the profession because we are seeking to answer questions, solve problems, fix our lives or our families or even repair the lives of people who have been dead for decades. I laugh when clients ask, "Aren't you all nuts?" because, on some level, I'm in agreement.

RESPONSES

"My Family Says That the Way to Solve Problems Is to Work Harder. Why Can't I Do This by Myself?"

This question is very common. It occurs when a client's family pressures him to end treatment. Never get into a tug of war with your client's family. They have their beliefs and fears. Instead, normalize the comment by saying, "Your family isn't alone in their old-fashioned beliefs. Many people have odd notions about therapy." Then, you can encourage,

"Therapy is one way to work harder and more effectively." You can also ask, "Is your family opposed to all kinds of help—doctors, plumbers, car mechanics?" if you want to get a sense of the general values and attitudes. As always, the main focus remains on your client. "What about you? I don't understand your thinking—why is it better to solve these problems by yourself?" And "How are you feeling about our work? Is it helping you to think about new ideas and solutions?" You can't sell therapy. Your client has to arrive at his own conclusion that counseling has worth.

"What's the Matter With Me That I Need Counseling?"

This could be the beginning of a way to work through unresolved issues about discomfort with one's self, self-hatred, perceived weakness, and/ or cultural stereotypes. "Tell me what worries you." or "You have some problems and decided that two heads are better than one; why are you so down on yourself for that?" or "It seems smart to bring in an expert when you need one," gives you a way to begin to examine your client's concerns.

"Why Am I So Weak? Lazy? Dependent?"

You probably want to get to the root of these assumptions, but it is also reassuring to say, "Therapy is very hard work. It is not for people who are weak or lazy." or "Lazy people don't come into therapy." Then, you may want to examine your client's self-image and negative judgments from others.

"My Dad Laughs at the Indulgence of Getting Treatment. His Culture/Race/Ethnicity Doesn't Believe in Therapy. What Do I Say to Him?"

This question again raises the dilemma of responding to a client whose family, parents, or partner are unsupportive of her receiving therapy. Stigma is quite strong in America, although awareness is slowly increasing, but it's even worse in some other cultures. You can help your client think this through. "I think that you have grown up and know how to find resources that you need to make your life better." or "It certainly is uncomfortable to be unsupported by your family in this." or "Do you need your family's support/approval to move forward comfortably?"

Alternatives might be, "Tell me what you would like to say to your father and we can work on it in here." or "Yes, when it comes to therapy, you can see a clash of cultures."

"What Am I Supposed to Tell People Who Wonder Why I Am Getting Counseling?"

"You don't have to say anything at all, but if you do, you can let them know that you are getting the help you need in order to work through problems and issues that are common to many people." Also, "many people are curious more than critical, so don't assume that everyone who asks is ready to disapprove." There are many successful variations to these responses that you can make in order to empower people to overcome their perceptions of potential stigma.

"Do You Think That Reporting Our Psychotherapy to My Insurance Company Will Somehow Come Back to Haunt Me if Someone Gets Hold of This Information?"

There are laws that govern disclosure of information, but people don't always read all the forms that they sign. You have to admit, "I don't know if it will haunt you, but you are right, information can be released, and we also don't know what the reaction will be." Some clients pay out of pocket because they want therapy to be completely private, but that is expensive. Depending on your client's diagnosis, you can explain that information and explain the mildness or severity of his disorder.

"Am I Going to Become a Whack Job Like My Aunt Sue?"

When a client has a mentally ill parent or relative, he may fear developing the same illness. Talk about the fear. "Tell me more about Aunt Sue. What were her symptoms?" Later you can ask, "Do you see similarities between yourself and your aunt?" Some disorders do appear in families, but the odds are always on your client's side, and he is not doomed.

"Should I Tell My Boyfriend That I'm Taking Antidepressants?"

"It's difficult to always know what is private and what needs to be shared. What is your relationship like?" Each person has to decide what secrets to share and what to keep private. Your job is to help them think it through, weigh the pros and cons, and reflect on their beliefs about relationships and sharing. Ultimately, it is a good exercise for your client to decide where her personal boundaries lie.

Linda

A client came in recently and she was furious. Several years ago, she had dated a guy and, in the beginning of the relationship, she told him, "We have to get tested for STDs." He agreed. She got tested. Unknown to her, he never did. Fast-forward to the end of the relationship: they remained friends, both went on to date others, and then, three years later, he tells her that he has genital warts and had them when they were dating, although he didn't know at that time. She might be infected. She was angry because he had never gone for the testing that would have revealed the problem. She would have been able to make a considered decision about what to do sexually. The lack of knowledge robbed her of the ability to make an informed choice.

"Should I Get Tested for HIV/STDs?"

Here is one question that has little to do directly with therapy but is an excellent example of stigma and allows us to raise issues of ethics and advocacy. Some clinicians learn about advocacy in school, but many others come to it because of their commitment to their work.

It is impossible to be in this field without the desire to help others. That help is usually in the form of counseling and psychotherapy, but many professional organizations contend that advocacy is an aspect of our professional responsibility. Advocacy means active sponsorship and could be accomplished by working against the stigma of mental illness, in favor of broad policies and social justice, or you might advocate to combat poverty, homelessness, illiteracy, civil rights, or even more specific problems such as bullying, date rape, or grandparents' rights.

Advocacy requires a more active stand than some clinicians are accustomed to taking. In the question, "Should I get tested for HIV/ STDs?", whether your client is male or female, gay or straight, your answer encourages the dialogue to proceed in a specific direction. At one end, you might simply reflect, "You seem concerned about having been exposed to an STD." A more active response is, "If you are having sex, testing is a safe and reasonable precaution." Education in the area of ethics would include stating, "If you are having sex, you deserve to know about any risks that you might be exposed to—and so does your partner, hard as that conversation might be." Strong advocacy could include a statement like, "You have made choices about your sexual behaviors. It seems to me that you have certain responsibilities to yourself and others."

You become a different type of change agent when you take an active role in alleviating broader conditions that ultimately affect your clients' mental health and quality of life. This is not a role that all clinicians will adopt, but it does fit into expanded ideas about the role of clinician.

"Do You Think I'm Crazy?"

People stigmatize themselves. Be honest with them: "No, you are not crazy, but you do have problems to work through." This question can open a useful discussion about self-stigmatizing. Your continued conversation allows discussion of the feelings of shame and humiliation that underlie these questions.

FURTHER THOUGHTS

> "Mental illness is nothing to be ashamed of, but stigma and bias shame us all."
>
> —Bill Clinton

Even when people do come in for needed services, the labels put on them by others can be easily internalized and cause them to feel needy, defective, and inferior. Some of your work includes helping them overcome these false beliefs.

Even without stigma, most clients treat the therapy hour as a private conversation. They do not readily share their therapy stories with others.

If you are a client in addition to being a clinician, you are probably the exception. Clinician/clients spend considerable amounts of time dissecting their own therapists and their treatment. In the process, you learn a great deal about yourself and the experience of being a client, sitting in the other chair. Remember, other people don't share therapy accounts quite as easily as we do. Clinicians appreciate treatment because we understand its value, but many people still find it strange and unacceptable. Clients get odd looks and awkward questions when they reveal their treatment. If you learn that therapy is being disparaged, you can reassure your client that this stigma seems to be changing slowly in our culture.

SUGGESTED READINGS

Corrigan, P. W. (2004). How stigma interferes with mental health care. *American Psychologist, 59*, 614–625.

Corrigan, P. W. (2007). How clinical diagnosis might exacerbate the stigma of mental illness. *Social Work, 52*, 31–39.

Corrigan, P. W., & Shapiro, J. R. (2010). Measuring the impact of programs that challenge the public stigma of mental illness. *Clinical Psychology Review, 30*, 907–922.

Levant, R. F. (2006). Making psychology a household word. *American Psychologist, 61*, 383–395.

Stewart, T. A., Semivan, S. G., & Schwartz, R. C. (2009). The art of advocacy: Strategies for psychotherapists. *Annals of the American Psychotherapy Association, 12*, 54–59.

Vogel, D. L., Wade, N. G., & Hackler, A. H. (2007). Perceived public stigma and the willingness to seek counseling: The mediating roles of self-stigma and attitudes toward counseling. *Journal of Counseling Psychology, 54*, 40–50.

CHAPTER

15

Physical
Appearance

Although therapy is primarily about the internal world, your clients react to external appearances, just like you do. Certain appearances have more impact in the early stages of therapy because you and your client are strangers to each other and outward impressions happen first, but many forms of appearance are present throughout treatment. Try not to worry about it, and don't attempt to hide behind your clothes or office; they are not intended to provide a disguise for you. Instead, think about physical looks and office presentation as tools to make yourself and your clients comfortable so you can get to work.

Linda

At the very beginning of January, I had my hair cut from long to very short. All of my clients commented, and several asked, "Oh, a new year, a new haircut?" I agreed. A couple of people asked, "What made you cut your hair?" Because of who those particular

(continued)

clients are, I answered, "I sit here and encourage people to change, and I haven't changed my hairstyle very much since I was in my twenties." This is true, but I was also intentionally sharing that bit of information with clients who are risk adverse. Questions may carry messages, but so do answers. Answers, even simple, true answers, can be therapeutic.

Just when everyone, including me, had gotten used to my hair, one 22-year-old client returned after weeks away from the university. She made appropriate noises about my hair and then said, "My mom has long hair now, but every once in awhile she cuts it short." Pause. "She cuts it short when bad things are happening, when my dad got depressed, and when she had cervical cancer." "Were you worried about me when you saw my hair?" I asked. Pause. "Yeah, I thought maybe something bad happened." I reassured her that I was fine, and that led to a good discussion about the ups and downs of her Christmas visit with her family. It wasn't much of a guess to ask if she was worried. I could have responded with an open-ended question, "What did you imagine?" but her fears were pretty clear, very much in keeping with her personality and history, and the ensuing discussion was what mattered.

This observation turned out to be useful, and haircuts are easy to deal with. Other questions and comments about physical appearance are far more difficult and can be extremely disconcerting. Complete neutrality is a myth. While you strive to be professional and welcoming, it is impossible, even harmful, to disguise every part of yourself. Occasionally in graduate school, students are cautioned so heavily about neutral clothing and appearance that they begin to believe that their individuality is at stake and that they are doomed to varieties of beige in clothing and personality. This is a strange goal when we consider ourselves to be the primary tool in the therapeutic process. A more useful rule of thumb is to keep your physical appearance comfortable, respectful, and not provocative.

There are several matters to think about when you are confronted with questions about physical appearance, and they will be illustrated in the responses that follow. Some questions about personal appearance may indicate that your client hopes to connect in friendly, nontherapy ways. Clients want to know you. Other questions may hint at a client's concern that you cannot understand her life because you have not experienced similar problems or, conversely, if you are similar, that you will be locked into stale ways of thinking. Finally, a few questions about appearance may be less amiable and have aggressive intentions. We cover the range of queries about appearance, dress, office décor, and nonverbal body language, all of which communicate information to your clients.

QUESTIONS ABOUT THE THERAPIST

The following questions are answered in the Responses section:

"Where did you buy that shirt?" "I love your shoes." "Who cuts your hair?" "Where did you get that watch?"

"Do you dye your hair?" "What have you done to your hair?" "Are you going bald?"

"What race are you?"

"Is something wrong/what happened?" (therapists are in wheelchairs, use canes, have scars, etc.)

"Why did they assign me to a woman counselor instead of a man?"

"You look awfully young to be a therapist. How old are you?" "Jeez, you're older than my mother/father. How can you understand me?"

"I have trouble losing weight. You probably know what I mean. Have you always been a little overweight, too?"

"What a crappy office. It isn't yours, is it?"

"I love your toenail polish. What color is it?"

"You are looking very attractive today. Is that a new outfit?"

"You always sit with your arms crossed. Did you know that means you are hiding something?"

"You are giving me that look again—the one that says you are disappointed, right?"

"You yawned. Are you bored?"

Each client is inherently different, as is your relationship with him. In considering the questions and proposed answers, please keep in mind that the answer always differs depending on the client, the meaning of the question to that client, at the time, and at that stage of treatment.

RESPONSES

"Where Did You Buy That Shirt?" "I Love Your Shoes." "Who Cuts Your Hair?" "Where Did You Get That Watch?"

Clothing is obvious and can suggest power, wealth, taste, religion, or values. You are constantly providing evidence about yourself to your clients, so there is no reason to be surprised when they observe you and your office. We suggest that you consider these mild questions as attempts to get to know you better and make a connection that is based on a relationship more equal than that of therapist and client. Answer warmly and neutrally, "Thanks," and provide basic information: "I bought it at Macy's." or "It's new, glad you like it." or "The watch was a gift; I'm enjoying it." If questions about your clothes become a regular feature of therapy, you may need to inquire further, "You often comment on my clothes. What's that about?"

Like clothing, jewelry can be a status symbol, a religious symbol, or a statement about personality. It may have personal meaning to you and perhaps to your client. Therapists who wear religious jewelry such as crosses or Stars of David, head coverings, national dress, or other signs of religion, culture, and beliefs may be asked about it. Many therapists do not wear religious jewelry or outstanding clothing in order to avoid these discussions, but if you do, listen for derivative material, which will give you a sense of your client's reaction. The question is likely to be in the room.

Initial appearances also mark the beginning of transference and countertransference reactions, although they are rarely discussed at that time. In a first session, an adolescent client noticed Elizabeth's shoes and said, "Those are the same as a girl at my high school. She is awful." Although Elizabeth helped her examine the mean girls, the rejection, and the high school judgments, the client did not return. Her mother called to say that she wasn't comfortable. Maybe the shoes set off negative reactions that couldn't be easily erased.

When children ask questions about appearances, most therapists will answer differently, disclosing more freely, providing more information, and answering questions without asking about the origins of the questions. You want to promote your young clients' curiosity. Their questions also provide information about them and can be mentally filed away. The process is not radically different when you work with adults; you also want to promote their curiosity. The difference is that with adults you want to more quickly tap into their ability to be self-reflective, a capacity that is more readily available to them than to children.

"Do You Dye Your Hair?" "What Have You Done to Your Hair?" "Are You Going Bald?"

These questions are getting more personal; they are about the person you are outside the office and are worth thinking about as such. You can inquire, "Are you thinking a lot about hair these days?" Coming from some clients, these questions border on aggressive—use your judgment. If the queries feel like they are pushing at your boundaries, you have the right to draw a line, "That's getting to be too much about me when our work is talking about you." But keep the context in mind, and remember that these questions have a different meaning if they come from a 15-year-old, someone your own age, or someone much older or younger. Gender, culture, and upbringing all influence whether asking questions about personal appearance is acceptable. Appearance questions from the client who holds you in high regard may be merely inquisitive, whereas angry and competitive clients may be speaking aggressively. Label the question accurately, and you will have your direction. "What is your curiosity about my hair?" opens one discussion, while "Ouch, that seems like a real zinger" might open another.

Physical appearance is obvious, available for visual inspection, and therefore more exposing in a certain way. You can adjust some elements of your appearance, such as make up, hairstyle, and wearing professional-looking clothes. Tattoos and piercings are more recent aspects of physical appearance, and you need to decide on the appropriateness of displaying or concealing them, depending on you and the clients you treat. Depending on where you work, you may change other elements of your appearance by removing fancy jewelry so that you are respectful of your clients' economic levels. You have limited control over other aspects of your physical appearance, and you cannot hide your age by too many years, camouflage a pregnancy, or conceal your weight, height, race, or illness. These pieces of your life have stimulus value, and being open to explore them with your client is part of the territory in which you work.

Charlie

I reviewed a videotape of a graduate student's therapy session with a client. As therapist, the student was wearing jeans. I was struck by this and commented that only once in my quarter century of practice have I worn blue jeans to a client session—and that was on an emergency weekend session. I often wear jeans to my university job and teach most of the time in blue jeans, and though I have seen at least one clinician in my office wear jeans (or shorts) to see clients, I couldn't do it; it just isn't me. Although it might not interfere with my professional presentation to a client, it would distract me from my job. I wondered aloud what it might mean to the student, and he said he hadn't thought about it, but he did after that.

"What Race Are You?" "Is Something Wrong/What Happened? (Therapists Who Are in Wheelchairs, Use Canes, Have Scars, Etc.) "Why Did They Assign Me to a Woman Counselor Instead of a Man?"

These questions call for different answers, but the three queries have two things in common: they are visually obvious, and clients are usually reluctant to ask about them. What you can do is answer the question, have a discussion, and get used to being asked about it.

"What Race Are You?"

"I'm Chinese and Irish. I guess you have been wondering about it." or "I'm glad to answer and I am also curious about the question." or "I'm Middle Eastern. Is that new to you?" or "I'm white/black/brown— what were you imagining?" Race is a delicate topic and may be questioned in the most circumspect ways.

Elizabeth Marklein, a Northwestern graduate student

At my placement this year, Thomas, a 20-year-old African American client described how white people in his past have hurt, ignored, and harassed him in various ways. His white fraternity brothers called him gay and spread rumors that he had AIDS. As he expressed the hurt he felt, I felt a need to address my white skin color. I asked, "What does it feel like to be talking to a white therapist?" because I felt our racial difference would likely influence his ability to trust me. Thomas replied "Fine," and continued to tell his story.

Even though he avoided the invitation to discuss it further, Elizabeth learned more about Thomas that may be helpful to him later. Perhaps he has trouble with directness or confrontation. Whatever directions they go in the future, Elizabeth's comment was good modeling. He referenced race obliquely, and she put it on the table. Now, either of them can go back to it.

"Is Something Wrong/What Happened?"

Similarly, this question calls for an open response. With reference to physical infirmities, note it directly, "Does the wheelchair surprise you?" Scars and markings will be commented on sideways, such as, "My best friend has a nasty scar on her chin and she . . .," which provides an opportunity to say, "I assume that you noticed my scar. Did you wonder about it?" More often than not, clients may wonder, but they remain silent so you don't have many opportunities to get comfortable with the topic of differences. Your ability to discuss your client's observations neutrally may mark the first time in his life that such a discussion was possible.

"Why Did They Assign Me to a Woman Counselor Instead of a Man?"

Gender is the most obvious of all physical differences, with race and age close behind, and it certainly will be subject to expectations, even stereotyping. Clients often have preferences for working with a man or woman therapist, but as therapy progresses, those differences are minimized as the alliance grows. Start with a simple observation, "I guess you would have preferred a man. Why?" Other comments that imply, "How can you understand menstruation, erections, or other gender-specific activities; you're a woman/man," can be answered, "That's certainly true. You are going to have to help me understand. As you do, we will both know more."

Children begin to notice racial difference around age 4, so they may become curious and will ask about your skin, hair, or race more freely than adults do. With adults, you cannot know in advance which clients will have strong reactions to you if you are noticeably different from their expectations. When you inquire about differences, you are not looking for expressions of prejudice; you are just checking to see if there is a discomfort, confusion, or other reactions that might be helpful to discuss. You also want to take advantage of any opportunity for your client to learn more about herself. You want to set the tone of open conversation. Finally, we don't encourage you to provide long stories if you respond to your clients' observations. Clients don't especially want to hear how you got into a wheelchair or why you wear a headcovering, or how many African-American therapists are in the United States, but it is the elephant in the room until you give clients permission to voice their thoughts about these areas.

Charlie

I didn't have my schedule book out at the end of a third session with my client Mike, so I reached under my desk and pulled out my briefcase to get it. Mike noticed the Barack Obama sticker I had pasted on the side, and he commented dryly, "I guess we know where you stand on things." He cancelled our next appointment, and then he called and left a message that he was very busy and would call when his schedule freed up. He never did. Although he had always been a reluctant client, I wonder how much his observation of my politics sent him over the edge. I wish we could have talked about it.

"You Look Awfully Young to Be a Therapist. How Old Are You?" "Jeez, You're Older Than My Mother/Father, How Can You Understand Me?"

These two questions are more often posed as comments, such as, "You remind me of my daughter/my mother's best friend/my professor." The questions are asking whether you can understand your client's life because you are so different and have not experienced (or experienced the problems so long ago that you are out of touch) similar problems of being young, old, fat, attractive, healthy, tall, or all the other ways in which we are physically different from each other. Just ask, "Do I seem too young/too old to be helpful?" You aren't going to get older, younger, or taller anytime soon; you acknowledge physical appearances because your openness defuses your client's discomfort and broadens the topics you can safely talk about.

Mary Miller Lewis, Ph.D., a specialist in geropsychology

I tell students that a 60-year-old man may feel embarrassed, or protective, or neutral, or excited, or ashamed to come into the office to talk to a 25-year-old woman. Try to notice these reactions and offer to examine them. Openness helps alleviate clients' anxieties and encourages them to recognize that, even though you are not alike, you can understand their worlds and be helpful.

"I Have Trouble Losing Weight. You Probably Know What I Mean. Have You Always Been Overweight, Too?" "What a Crappy Office. It Isn't Yours, Is It?"

The aggression in these types of questions is less interesting than the fact that your weight or your office is seen as an important reflection of you as a person or professional. What does this mean to your client? Do you lack willpower, good taste, or money? Are you less of a therapist? Listen to the words and decide if they are aggressive or ill-considered. If aggressive, note, "Wow, that's pretty hostile. What are you upset about?" or "It seems to bother you that I'm not slim or that I have a simple office." If it doesn't feel hostile, you can observe, "Are you worried that my weight/office means that I will be less able to help you?" or turning the discussion to a deeper unvoiced concern, "Does it scare you if I am not perfect?"

Clients will wonder what your clothes, weight, or office says about you, often because they wonder what these kinds of things say about themselves. However, these aspects are usually quite peripheral to your ability to be a good therapist. By considering them in this latter way, exploring clients' thoughts about you can become grist for the therapeutic mill rather than an affront to the core of your professional self.

"I Love Your Toenail Polish. What Color Is It?" "You Are Looking Very Attractive Today. Is That a New Outfit?"

These two questions provide good illustrations of uncomfortable personal inquiries if you are picking up a sexual undertone. Pushing it even further are questions like, "Will you teach my girlfriend how to dress?" and "Will you wear this sexy shirt again next week?" You know what to respond if a guy says these things in a bar, but not in your office. These questions add sexual tension, flirting, coaxing, or intimidation to the session. It feels like your client is willing to change the relationship from a professional one to dating or lovers. Responses that can pull the conversation back on track could include "Thanks. Are you having relationship problems?" or "I think we have more important topics to talk about." or "Let's get back to talking about (your problem)." or "This is therapy, not the local bar; let's talk about your problem." If and when your efforts to redirect the focus don't work, you need to think about the questions more seriously and manage the situation differently. Chapter 11, Sexuality, is devoted entirely to the topic of sexual questions.

If the comments escalate, you want to try to answer in ways that get you back to work but don't humiliate your clients. "This is a professional relationship; it doesn't include sex." or "Therapy works because we don't complicate it with all the outside stuff, like sex." or "You are commenting on my sexuality. Let's figure out what you are looking for, and maybe we can figure out a way for you to have it in a more appropriate part of your life." or "Sexual comments don't work well with therapy relationships." or "You seem to want to change this relationship into something else; I will not let that happen." Sometimes the flirting or sex talk comes from a desire to get closer. After all, your client may be feeling understood for the first time, and that is a powerful experience. At other times, pointed, uncomfortable inquiries are intended to diminish the power of the therapy relationship. If you say nothing and the comments are repeated, you will find yourself dreading certain clients or entire days of work. Don't let it get to that point; you and your client have work to do. If, "Let's get back to . . ." doesn't work and you see the inappropriateness of your client's questions as part of the overall therapy issue that he needs to address, you can comment directly on the material: "That question is an example of what we have been talking about regarding your awkward conversations/inappropriate statements/sexualizing of relationships" (or whatever you understand the problem to be).

"You Always Sit With Your Arms Crossed. Did You Know That Means You Are Hiding Something?"

Body language analysis is very popular on television and is beloved by the tabloids. Reading body language is not particularly reliable and can be manipulated easily. Of course, if a teenage client sits on the floor with her back to you, she is sending a message, but if either of you are simply sitting with your arms or legs crossed, don't make too much out of it.

Don't get into pop psychology. Answer, "Yes, I often sit with my arms crossed. It feels comfortable, but I never thought of it as hiding anything. What are your ideas about that?"

"You Are Giving Me That Look Again—the One That Says You Are Disappointed, Right?"

Clients and therapists watch each other for interest and approval. Clients notice when you lean forward or move to the edge of your chair. They believe, rightly or wrongly, that they are talking about the right things. Conversely, when your eyes glaze over, they may wonder if you are bored with them.

"I can't see my face. What does the look say to you?" Of course it matters what you were thinking or feeling at the moment, but initially, the client's perception is more important. When your client's reaction is understood, give it a moment while also considering what you were thinking. It could be helpful to disclose your thoughts, for example,

"You're observant. I was still thinking about your comment about your mother." or "I don't know exactly what face I made, but I was thinking that I don't yet understand your reaction to your boss."

"You Yawned. Are You Bored?"

If you are groggy when you are with this client, examine your reaction carefully; it may be diagnostic of the client or the relationship. Observe yourself, "I'm sorry. I'm not feeling well." or "I'm not bored, just a bit tired, but I am also interested in you." Alternatively, if your client is correct, you can admit, "I'm sorry, I feel lost in this conversation and my mind was wandering." or "I'm not bored, but I feel excluded from this conversation, and I'm afraid my mind went elsewhere." or "No, I'm not bored. I'm following your train of thought about your boyfriend." If extreme reactions show on your face too often, this is a good thing to examine with a supervisor or colleague.

QUESTIONS ABOUT THE THERAPEUTIC ENVIRONMENT

Linda

My therapist's office was in the sunroom of his home, so there were more personal photos scattered around than you would ordinarily see in a clinician's office. In my comings and goings, I noticed one picture of the man's three sons in a group photo. Many, many months later, I realized that there were also two daughters in that picture. I was embarrassed. Being a special, only daughter myself, I guess that I was just not ready to see that he had daughters of his own. The photo hadn't changed; I had.

Certainly, most forms of therapy depend on talking. Both parties acquire a great deal of information through their ears, but the other senses, especially our eyes, also collect information during sessions, either accurate or distorted. Linda's example makes us want to change the phrase, "Beauty is in the eye of the beholder" into the psychological version, "Reality is in the eye of the beholder," meaning that the client sees what the client sees, otherwise known as transference. If your first client of the day has an overeating problem, you may look thin. Two hours later, another client can walk in suffering from bulimia, and you might be seen as fat. You might be seen as young and out of touch, or young and state of the art. The physical, visual world is not seen as consistent as we would imagine; it is subject to interpretation. Beauty, your appearance, the magazines in your waiting room, your desk, your artwork, and your shoes come alive in the eyes of the beholder.

The following questions are answered in the Responses section:

> **"Why do you have so many pictures of your sons in your office?"**
> **"Why don't you have more personal pictures here?" "Why are all your pictures in this clinic so PC?"**
> **"Did you see Lindsay Lohan on the cover of your People magazine?"**
> **"Why is your office so messy? I can't stand it."**

We don't want to scare you into a self-conscious frenzy of hypervigilance. We don't want you to police the visual world you present so that you avoid stimulating clients' imaginations. On the contrary, we want you to appreciate and feel comfortable working with the opportunities presented by visual perception.

We want to highlight three interesting issues by discussing questions about visual perceptions: (1) you can choose whether to focus on reality or on perception; (2) it may not be the right time for you to respond to perceptual distortions; and (3) transference is an issue throughout the process of therapy, and sometimes you address it directly and sometimes you leave it alone.

RESPONSES

"Why Do You Have So Many Pictures of Your Sons in Your Office?"

You may not have sons; it might be a nephew or another clinician's photo. It doesn't really matter, especially not in the early months of therapy. Follow what people see—you will learn about the world through their eyes. You will see their environment. It is not about reality; it's not about being correct, but it is about knowing your client better. Just ask, "What is it about these pictures that grabbed your attention/disturbed you?"

"Why Don't You Have More Personal Pictures Here?" "Why Are All Your Pictures in This Clinic so PC?"

First, you want to explore your client's world; then you may choose to educate him. "This is a clinic in which we share offices, so the rooms tend to be pretty impersonal. Sounds like you are wondering why I don't get more personal here." If you want to respond to the political correct-ness comment, you might say, "We want to put up pictures that reflect all types of people and families. Sounds like these pictures got something going inside of you."

"Did You See Lindsay Lohan on the Cover of Your *People* Magazine?"

It might not be your office or your magazine, and you might not care about Lindsay, but is this the right time to explain any of that? Timing is always important. Lindsay is one way into the client's world. "What is Lindsay up to now?" In this way, you get to hear from the client what is important about Lindsay, JLo, Nicole, Paris, or Brad and Angelina—and how it pertains, in some way, to her life: that is what you are interested in discussing, whether it is infidelity, eating disorders, addictions, or sim-ple envy. Another way of asking is, "I don't follow Lindsay. What did you see?" When you have gone as far as the real topic takes the two of you, it is not hard to shift back into work by saying, "Who cares about them? What does this say about you?"

"Why Is Your Office So Messy? I Can't Stand It."

This is a serious question, and perhaps this client feels that you are not a safe person to work with. Any repeated distress about your environment—difficult parking, inoperable elevators, inaccessible entrances—is important and worth pursuing. Sometimes these questions reflect reality, but some-times they are saying more. Acknowledge the reality, and ask clients about what more they might be saying. "My mess disturbs you. Have you any idea why that is so?" or "Does my office seem especially messy/disordered today?"

or "Yes, the parking often is a real nightmare, and today it seems to have angered you." It gives clients the opportunity to say more. There is a good chance that your client remembers someone messy and that person had poor boundaries or they are feeling out of control and need some organization. Don't apologize, set them straight, or make excuses; you want to help your client figure out why the mess is distressing while also reassuring them that the work can be done reliably with you.

Certain clients will evoke reactions in you about your appearance. You can see it when you find yourself dressing carefully, worrying about your hair, nails, or straightening your office excessively. Perhaps the client is brittle and needs a perfect world. You may find yourself not wanting to unsettle clients with personal carelessness. Perhaps your client is narcissistic and has ridiculed your clothing. Perhaps your client has made you feel young, like a sexual object, inexperienced or unworthy. Perhaps you feel that you need a perfect setting for you to do the work. When you have strong reactions, in all cases, ask yourself, "What does my client evoke in me?" You will learn a lot about your client and even more about yourself.

Linda

In the final session, saying goodbye at the door, a client looked puzzled and said, "I always thought you were taller." In her eyes, I probably had been taller and more imposing in the beginning of treatment. I was very moved by seeing the effect that her internal growth had on her external perceptions. Height, just like beauty or ugliness, is often in the eyes of the beholder.

FURTHER THOUGHTS

"Why not be oneself? That is the whole secret of a successful appearance. If one is a greyhound, why try to look like a Pekingese?"

—Dame Edith Sitwell

Learning to become a clinician is internally transformative, so it is easy to minimize the external world. However, it is wise to think about how you want to appear to both of the important people in your session, you and your client. You send messages, so send them with awareness and intention. Some clients are very sensitive to the total presentation. Linda is no longer surprised when clients comment on her office, especially about its calmness and protectedness. Of course, she has spent years making sure of those features, a very different scenario from training, when she occasionally had sessions in converted storage rooms or shifted from office to office, carrying a box of tissues and a clock in her bag.

Appearances matter because you are trying to create a safe, professional, confidential environment. Clients sit across from you for the better part of an hour, not having much else to look at, so they notice your expressions, your clothing, and your office furniture, even if you have no control over this. Even your voice on your message machine matters, because that may be the first contact that a potential client has with you. Caring about appearance is not superficial; don't confuse attention to these details as insignificant or shallow. Clients are trying to get a sense of you, just as you are of them, in order to determine how safe it is to expose and explore their lives.

SUGGESTED READINGS

Barocas, R., & Vance, F. L. (1974). Physical appearance and personal adjustment counseling. *Journal of Counseling Psychology, 21*, 96–100.

Lazarus, J. A. (2005). *Entering private practice: A handbook for psychiatrists.* Arlington, VA: American Psychiatric Publishing.

Levitt, H., Butler, M., & Hill, T. (2006). What clients find helpful in psychotherapy: Developing principles for facilitating moment-to-moment change. *Journal of Counseling Psychology, 53*, 314–324.

Nihalani, N. D., Kunwar, A., Staller, J., & Lamberti, J. S. (2006). How should psychiatrists dress? A survey. *Community Mental Health Journal, 42*, 291–302.

Wiger, D.E. (2007). *The well-managed mental health practice: Your guide to building and managing a successful practice, group, or clinic.* Hoboken, NJ: Wiley.

CHAPTER

16

Dreams

Dreams, more than many other elements of therapy, have captured people's imaginations. Not surprisingly, clients often assume that you will use dreams in treatment and, for the most part, they are drawn to the idea of dream interpretation. They hope that their unconscious processes will be revealed in treatment and deciphered by the two of you. You don't need oracle training to work with a client who brings in a dream—you are interviewing the dreamer with your existing skills.

Linda

In the final meeting with a group of students who were completing their externships, one soon-to-be social worker told us her dream. Jane said, "I dreamed that I was in a cabin in the woods. I wanted to get out and walk around but had a hard time in the forest. I got all scratched up, my feet hurt, and I had to fight my way through the tangle of trees. Finally, exhausted, I returned to the cabin. Then I wanted to go out again and it was easier, but I struggled in the forest

(continued)

before I found my way back to the cabin. I went out a third time and my trip was easy. I even took off my shoes and kind of skipped through the forest before I returned. When I got back, I knew that it was the same cabin, but it looked different." Everybody listening loved the dream. What did the dreamer think? Jane said that it described her year of training: very hard at first, confusing, and she struggled. Over time, doing therapy got easier and she became more confident. I was struck by the idea that, after an important journey, especially one that has transformed us, even home looks different.

Clients have often read novels that vividly describe dreams, seen movies that make use of dreams, and picked up a little Dream Interpretation book at the checkout aisle in the grocery store that explains how to analyze the images or predict the future. So, the chances are good, whether you work with dreams or not, that you will be asked about them, even by clients who shy away from treatment that emphasizes the unconscious. The questions and answers in this chapter are less about underlying issues or dream symbolism and more about having accurate, inviting information for your responses.

QUESTIONS

The following questions are answered in the Responses section:

"What are dreams?"

"So, do you want me to tell you about my dreams?"

"What about those strange dreams that I have when I'm not really asleep?"

"If I have a dream, should I tell you?"

"Are you going to analyze my dreams and tell me what they mean?"

"How do we do this dream analysis thing?"

"Do those little books about the meanings of dreams that you buy in the grocery store checkout line have any value?"

"If I have the same dream over and over, does that mean it is particularly important?"

"My girlfriend cheats on me in my dreams. Does that mean
    that she will cheat in real life?"
"Violence/shooting/killing/raping occurs often in my dreams.
    Am I more likely to act this way in my awake life?"
"Is it weird that I don't have any dreams?"

RESPONSES

"What Are Dreams?"

Clients do not want you to respond with a course on sleep stages and dream analysis. However, they do want to know if you are familiar with dreams and comfortable working with them so you can answer concretely and scientifically, "Dreams are mental images that integrate thoughts and emotions during REM, rapid eye movement sleep." or with some clinical information, "There are many different ideas about the clinical meaning of dreams. They might be wishes, fears, efforts to gain control, compensation for personal shortcomings, statements of repressed emotion, an effort toward organizing thoughts and feelings, unfinished business, or perhaps random neuronal firings." Professionals who have spent years studying dreams can't resolve these many possibilities; dreams are likely these things and more.

Rarely, however, in our experience do clients bring up the issues of dreams in therapy because they see them as random neuronal firings. Clients offer us their dreams in the hope of understanding more about their lives or for resolving their confusion, pain, or fear. For instance, when Linda's client Dita was first dating Greg, she said, "I had a funny dream last night," and with a little encouragement, she continued, "My mother was driving me halfway across the country and then we met Greg. She handed me off to Greg for him to take me the rest of the way. The next day, I told Greg about the dream, it was embarrassing." Later in the session, with no further reference to the dream, she admitted that she was falling in love with Greg. This dream seemed to represent her wish and, less so, her day-to-day experience. We have seen that clients' dreams can be enormously helpful in therapy, so usually we want to answer questions about dreams in ways that invite examination. For instance, "Dreams might give some real insight into our work here. Do you have one in mind?"

At the same time, when a client mentions an important dream or asks questions about dreams with only a few minutes left in a session, you are headed into a brief, regrettable discussion if you pursue the topic, so defer. Dreams need time; if you can't devote the time to a wandering, free-floating conversation, acknowledge this by saying, "It is too interesting, so let's remember it for next week."

Charlie

I became even more convinced of the utility of my dreams after a personal experience years ago. I had a vivid and perplexing dream in which one of the main characters was an undergraduate from a large class I had taught years before. Although I care about my students, why this relatively unremarkable young lady was pulled from the recesses of my brain was beyond my understanding. After several days, it finally dawned on me that the initials of her name were identical to those of an academic administrator with whom I was currently having some very testy moments that evoked some dramatic emotional associations for me. I recognized the pattern in which the characters of my dreams are often indirect images masked by the initials of their names to represent other people with whom I have present interactions. Having let her in on the code that my unconscious uses, my wife Tracy now believes that when I have a dream about Tiger Woods (T. W.), I am really dreaming about her. Although this is often true, I also believe that sometimes I might just be dreaming about the world's most famous athlete.

"So, Do You Want Me to Tell You About My Dreams?"

A surprising 80% of clinicians report using clients' dreams in therapy, at least occasionally. If you have some training or experience working with dreams and enjoy using dreamwork in treatment, you will probably welcome this question with the same openness that you would respond to a client offering to share any intimate material. "Yes, I enjoy working with dreams." or "Yes, I think dreams can facilitate our work here." If it begins to look like dreamwork will be a helpful or welcome addition to therapy, you might encourage clients to use some technique, for example, "You will remember dreams more easily as we continue to talk about them." or "If you want to increase your memory for dreams, consider jotting the dreams down on paper after you wake up so that we can explore them."

Dreamwork has found its way into mainstream therapy, no longer being the sole province of psychoanalytic clinicians who believed Sigmund Freud's statement that dreams are the "royal road to the unconscious" or Gestalt founder Fritz Perls' philosophy that dreams can help people reclaim the lost parts of their personality and become more integrated or whole. Still, dreamwork is not recommended for psychotic clients, because doing so can lead them away from contact with reality. Be aware, too, that for some clients, dreamwork has a way of sneaking around defenses, so if you don't want to go in that direction, consider skipping discussions about dreams.

If you don't want to hear dreams, say so casually. "Generally I don't work with dreams. We can learn about you in other ways." or "Although dreams do have their place in people's lives, our time here might best be spent addressing the more immediate concerns of . . ." Remember, your client is offering to bring in very personal, often confusing or frightening, material and inspect it with you. So, if you turn it down, do so gently. You are turning down a gift.

"What About Those Strange Dreams That I Have When I'm Not Really Asleep?"

Don't assume that when clients ask questions about dreams that they are talking about dreams that happen only while they are asleep. Clients may use this language to introduce a hope, fantasy, goal, or more disturbingly, a delusion or hallucination. So inquire, "Can you describe what these strange awake dreams are like?" or "When do you have these strange awake dreams?" or "Tell me about one of them." Keep an open mind about what might come next, and don't convey the idea that your client has said something wrong.

"If I Have a Dream, Should I Tell You?"

Certainly you have the right, and responsibility, to say "No" to questions about using dreams in therapy if you are not in a position to use them constructively and competently to inform good treatment. If this is the case, you need to be honest about it. If you don't have the interest, knowledge, and facility in the area, simply say so, while not rejecting your client. "Certainly we can talk about anything in here, but dreamwork is not an approach that I have found useful for clients."

"Are You Going to Analyze My Dreams and Tell Me What They Mean?"

"Only you can analyze your dreams. I can guide you and ask some questions, and together we can work to explore their meaning for you. Ultimately, your associations to the dream images will lead us in useful directions." Your attitude toward your client's dream matters enormously. Clients need to know that you are not going to impose yourself on them.

Linda

Goldie, age 14, loved her dreams and ended a previous therapy after an unpleasant encounter about one. She told me that she had a dream with all kinds of images. "I was at an amusement park and I was eating tater tots (those frozen, oddly shaped potatoes). I asked my therapist, 'What do you think the tater tots mean?' He said, 'I think that they represent the anger that you feel toward your parents.' 'But I like tater tots,' I told him, 'and I know that I can get pretty angry with my parents, but I don't see the tater tots that way.' He went on to say, 'Well, I'm the therapist here, so I know better what it represents.'"

Goldie was mortified by his arrogance, and she was even more scared at having her voice so blatantly stripped away from her. Although she stayed to the end of that session, she did not return for another.

"How Do We Do This Dream Analysis Thing?"

Clients have the right to ask about the type of work the two of you will be doing. Naïve clients may be requesting straightforward information, and educating them is appropriate. Even informed clients might wonder if therapy with you will include dreamwork. This is a place for simple, clear information: "I can be your dream interviewer, but I am not the dream expert. Only you can be the expert on your dreams." You may want to explain how the two of you will go about your work with dreams by saying, "First, I want you to tell your dream with as much detail as you remember. Then I'll ask more specific questions and we'll talk." At the conclusion of the dream retelling, you can continue with prompts like, "What images stand out for you?" Then, "Try not to censor yourself. Let your mind roam from that image, and tell me what comes to you."

You can also note certain images and ask about them, "What are your associations to the deck of a ship that appeared in your dream?" You can reference an activity in the dream and ask, "What are your associations to being pulled from your bed?" As the descriptions unfold, you can ask, "Has anything happened in your waking life that might have set off the vivid image of a fight between two women?" At different points, you will want to inquire about images or people who struck you as salient, "What emotions are connected to Nellie from middle school?" These explorations can lead to broad insights and deep emotions. There also comes a time when you can ask your client, "Do you want to do anything about this understanding?"

Usually questions about dreams show the client's genuine interest in this area of exploration. Rarely, but it happens, the questions are neither simple nor straightforward. They can be asked with a sarcastic, challenging tone and indicate contempt for you and for the therapy process. If the question is aggressive, it is intended to mock psychotherapy as venturing into the worlds of crystals, psychics, and UFOs. This statement also provides information. It speaks to your client's aversion to, or fear of, revealing herself in this way. A gentle confrontation may be in order. "From the tone of your voice, I wonder if you are mocking the use of dreams?" or "You sound sarcastic. Is that your intention? Should I assume that you are not interested in looking at your dreams?"

Another way in which questions about dreams can be complicated is when they are used by a client to resist some aspect of therapy. At times when clients feel threatened or ill-at-ease about the current conversation, they might divert the discussion by offering a dream as a juicy and tantalizing psychological item. If you think that the allusion to a possible dream might be resistance, you can state, "Let's file that away because I am not sure how that might be useful for our current discussion," and keep the conversation on track. Or, you can put a mental bookmark in the current discussion, knowing that you can always return to it, and you can examine the dream. Wherever you begin, and however meandering, the issues that are pressing on your client will reoccur. Listen carefully.

"Do Those Little Books About the Meanings of Dreams That You Buy in the Grocery Store Checkout Line Have Any Value?"

"The books are fun to look through. They can't get into your head—only you can do that—but the books may have some good ideas about certain dream symbols and their meanings." This helps remind your client that she is in charge of her understanding, not the little book and not you.

You can reassure your client that the meaning of her dream is unraveled by her with your assistance. There is no absolute truth to be revealed or to be found. "This is your dream saying something about your life. Our goal is to find the meaning that it has for you by drawing connections between your dream and other aspects of your life."

If pressed on the idea of there being some ultimate truth to be revealed, you might say, "Certainly there are some aspects of a dream that might have universal meaning. For example, a trip may reflect a personal journey, a death may suggest that the dreamer is dealing with loss in some way, winning the lottery probably is a positive event, but does a tree always represent your father and a house always represent your mother—I can't go that far."

Linda

A client of mine, Kayla, had a classic dream. She said, "I had a rough couple of days at work and felt horrible. By the time I went to bed, I was convinced that I had not succeeded in any area of my life. I dreamed that I had been kidnapped and held for two days while the kidnappers tried to reach my father and negotiate my ransom. They finally got him on the phone. I heard them talking to my father and then, in the dream, they handed me the telephone.

I saw my father's expression as he told me in his usual disgusted voice, 'Try to get the kidnappers to call me at a reasonable hour. This is too early for me.' I hung up on him."

This dream captured Kayla's father's dislike of being inconvenienced, or as she has come to understand, "It's always about him." The connection that she made to her life, and the discussion for the rest of the session, was how much she would have loved to be able to rely on her father when days were rough.

"If I Have a Dream Over and Over Again, Does That Mean It Is Particularly Important?"

Clients may be more disturbed by repetitive dreams because the dreams begin to feel persecutory. In this question, it sounds like this client is giving the repetition some importance, and most clinicians who work with dreams are interested in those that recur. "Actually, the majority of people report having recurrent dreams. Do you think there is some issue on your mind that you continue to visit regularly?" or "Maybe there is some feeling or idea that you are trying to work out over and over. Let's see if we can figure some of it out."

"My Girlfriend Cheats on Me in My Dreams. Does That Mean That She Will Cheat in Real Life?"

This question suggests that your client gives a lot of power to dreams rather than to himself. Your client wonders whether the dream is sending him a message; is he smarter when he is asleep than awake, or is he fooled when awake but astute when asleep. Let's bring this back to where it belongs—with the awake, thinking, feeling client. "People believe all kinds of things about dreams, including your fear—that you are sending yourself a message when you are asleep that you do not want to receive when you are awake. There is no real evidence to support this idea. It does make me wonder if you worry about her likelihood to cheat." Or, if it seems more appropriate, you may remind your client, "In your dream you may be processing outside information. Your dream could reflect information that you gather when you are awake and process when you are asleep. Do you suspect that your girlfriend will cheat on you?" or "This is your dream, it is not her dream, so all aspects of the dream come from your mind. In this way let's see what the dream says about you, not her."

Some dreams come directly from the day's concerns and are magnified by dramatic images. In class, after reading Judith Herman's brilliant and disturbing book, *Trauma and Recovery*, one student said, "I put the book down and went to sleep, but I had a dream that I was attacked by a man. Afterward I stood up and thought that no matter what, my life will never be the same. I woke up terrified and shaking, and almost wept with relief that it was just a dream." She really understood Herman's book.

"Violence/Shooting/Killing/Raping Occurs Often in My Dreams. Am I More Likely to Act This Way in My Awake Life?"

This is a common question that follows particularly violent, sexual, or aggressive dreams. The dreamer wonders, is this who I really am? It is a fear-based question. For many people, dreams are frightening because when they sleep, they relinquish conscious control. Clients may be uncomfortable when they confront their unconscious, and they may have a sincere struggle sorting out reality from fantasy, especially if fantasy is vivid. You can answer in a way that reassures your client and explores the dream, for example, "Let's remember that dreams come from an irrational part of your mind, and the emotions that are expressed can be very strong. This does not mean that you will act on these impulses. We will know more about your feelings as we explore further."

Linda

Years ago I worked with a woman who spontaneously reported a violent dream in our third session. She had no previous therapy, and in the few times we met, she was pleasant but guarded. The dream was filled with bloody images and penetrating objects. Had the dream been less disturbing, she probably would have brushed it aside. Although the dream sickened me because I guessed where we were headed, I approached the material as I normally do and invited her to examine the images and associate to them. Sadly, but not surprisingly, it led to the disclosure that she had been raped 8 years earlier and had kept the incident entirely secret. Without the dream, that discussion would have occurred, but it would have happened much, much later. Dreams open new conversations because the conscious protections may be lowered.

"Is It Weird That I Don't Have Any Dreams?"

Dreams are not likely to be essential for your work with clients, so having a client who can't remember his dreams doesn't pose a problem. However, this client seems to be asking whether he is weird. Normalizing the experience, while also leaving the door open for future thoughts on the matter, you might say, "Actually, everyone does have brain activity associated with dreams during certain stages of their sleep cycle. Some people, however, simply don't have any memory of them once they wake up."

FURTHER THOUGHTS

"Dreams are often most profound when they seem the most crazy."

—Sigmund Freud

Expect to get questions about dreams. Sometimes clients feel silly bringing up dreams; other times they are frightened by them, confused by them, or excited by them. Clients are telling you that they trust you when they bring in a dream, because they have no idea where the discussion will go. When you value your client's dreams, you communicate that you value your client.

Much has been learned about dreams since Freud. Look for underlying physiology, medications, the day's activities, hormones, and pain levels in addition to enjoying dreams as exploring a new realm of your client's world. When you work with dreams, remind your client that there is no absolute truth contained in dreams; instead there is the potential for great subjective meaning and personal learning. Talk and think in metaphors for dreams. Even without specific courses in dreamwork, you already practice many of the skills involved in working with dreams. For example, you are an active listener, you make connections to your client's ongoing concerns, and you know how to place new material into context.

Dreams can be alluring because of their mystery, yet much of dreamwork is pragmatic. Therapists are particularly helpful when they encourage clients to associate to the dream images, help clients reach their own interpretations of the dreams, interpret dreams as related to current waking-life problems, and work with clients to develop ways of changing their behaviors based on their new learning. If working with dreams interests you, get further training so that you can work with them effectively.

SUGGESTED READINGS

Baumann, E., & Hill, C. E. (2008). The attainment of insight in the insight stage of the Hill dream model: The influence of client reactance and therapist interventions. *Dreaming, 18,* 127–137.

Crook-Lyon, R. E., & Hill, C. E. (2004). Client reactions to working with dreams in psychotherapy. *Dreaming, 14,* 207–219.

Crook-Lyon, R. E., & Wimmer, C. L. (2005). Spirituality and dream work in counseling: Clients' experiences. *Pastoral Psychology, 54,* 35–45.

Eudell-Simmons, E. M., & Hilsenroth, M. J. (2005). A review of empirical research supporting four conceptual uses of dreams in psychotherapy. *Clinical Psychology and Psychotherapy, 12,* 255–269.

Eudell-Simmons, E. M., & Hilsenroth, M. J. (2007). The use of dreams in psychotherapy: An integrative model. *Journal of Psychotherapy Integration, 17,* 330–356.

Hill, C. E. (1996). *Working with dreams in psychotherapy.* New York, NY: Guilford Press.

Hill, C. E., Spangler, P., Sim, W., & Baumann, E. (2007). The interpersonal content of dreams: Relation to pre-session client variables, process, and outcome of sessions using the Hill dream model. *Dreaming, 17,* 1–19.

Knox, S., Hill, C. E., Hess, S. A., & Crook-Lyon, R. E. (2008). Case studies of the attainment of insight in dream sessions: Replication and extension. *Psychotherapy Research, 18,* 200–215.

Pesant, N., & Zadra, A. (2004). Working with dreams in therapy: What do we know and what should we do? *Clinical Psychology Review, 24,* 489–512.

CHAPTER 17

Therapists' Reactions

Your subjective experience during sessions is an indispensable element of therapy. As a clinician, your understanding of and ability to work with your thoughts and emotions provides information about the subtleties going on in your client and in yourself. With this understanding, your reactions—emotional, physical, and intellectual—are transformed from phenomena that you might fear into tools that you can depend on and use productively.

Linda

I remember the day that I actually learned what countertransference meant. I was already at my first job treating Paula, a young woman who was determined to self-destruct. Paula and I agreed that she was kamikaze-like in her behavior, willing to harm herself if her actions also punished her mother for past years of poor parenting. Her mother was now forced to take care of her 28-year-old daughter who could not, or would not, take care of herself.

(continued)

Each week, Paula happily told me a new story of her self-destructive behavior, such as getting fired from work or rejecting friends. As she grew increasingly satisfied, I sank lower and lower into a pool of personal ineffectiveness and intense anger. During one particular morning session, as we sat across from each other, the blaring siren of a fire truck got louder and louder. Paula asked excitedly, "Is it coming here?" and I responded without a moment's reflection, "Are you hoping for mouth-to-mouth resuscitation?"

As soon as I spoke them, I was stunned by the cruelty of my words. The two of us just stared at each other. In my frustration, I had mixed my primitive understanding that she wanted to be saved and to be cared for with my anger at her refusal to take better care of herself. I was furious and helpless that she continued to destroy her life and angrier than I had realized. Fortunately, I was able to figure out what I had done and explained my reaction, saying something like, "I think I'm angry that you don't take better care of yourself." She seemed vaguely interested in her ability to rile me, but unfortunately, our discussion had a bigger impact on my behaviors than on Paula's. I'm afraid that I proved the point about countertransference: As therapists, we often respond first and analyze afterward.

I had heard the stories about countertransference when I was in school; everyone has listened to them. In the beginning of my work, I imagined that countertransference would stomp into the consulting room like a large buffalo and announce its presence with loud, unmistakable noises. Instead, I have learned that countertransference is softer, more like a shadow that drifts through the room, providing a glimpse of something elusive, matters to think about further, but usually not clear.

Countertransference, in the definition we use, encompasses all thoughts and feelings evoked in you with regard to a client, not just the neurotic reactions, unconscious responses, or uncomfortable emotions such as love and hate, but all the rest like irritation, admiration, competitiveness, exhilaration, and despair. It shouldn't come as a surprise that you have some strong reactions. After all, most close relationships stir up strong emotions. More than other clinicians, psychodynamic therapists rely on countertransference, but all theoretical viewpoints acknowledge that therapists have reactions, although they may use them differently. Therefore, we encourage you to develop ruthless personal honesty in order to understand and use the reactions of which you are already aware and those evoked by questions.

QUESTIONS

The following questions are answered in the Responses section. These questions could be examined with regard to other issues, but they provide excellent material for examining your reactions to clients:

> "Why are you angry with me today? I've missed other appointments/not done other homework assignments."
>
> "Are you falling asleep? You look distracted. Are you?"
>
> "I was surprised that it took you so long to call me back to reschedule our appointment. Is everything all right?"
>
> "Why did you call me by someone else's name?"
>
> "I was here for my appointment and you never showed up. How could you do this to me?"
>
> "How can you continue to see the bright side of things when my life is a mess?"
>
> "How can you forget my boyfriend/story/mother's name/trauma/upcoming graduation?"
>
> "Why aren't you behaving like my former therapist?"
>
> "Why do you always need to be right? What about what I say?"
>
> "Why are you being mean to me?"

RESPONSES

"Why Are You Angry Today? I've Missed Other Appointments/Not Done Other Homework Assignments."

There are many variations of this question, but the point is that you finally commented to a client about her missed appointment or other repetitive behavior. You previously held back, and now your feelings finally show. People who become therapists want to be helpful and to be liked, so it is disconcerting to find yourself angry, irritated, or unengaged. Of course, this is perfectly normal in doing therapy, but it doesn't feel good. In fact, it feels awful to dislike a client, get angry, or dread an upcoming session. This is countertransference, defined as all your reactions evoked by your clients and the relationship that you create together.

Similarly to Linda's example about countertransference, the previously withheld anger implied in this question also says something about the therapist. Another clinician might have commented on the first or second missed appointment or an incompleted homework assignment. We imagine that this therapist wanted to be agreeable and pushed aside the continued missed appointments. However, being an effective clinician includes mild confrontations early in order to avoid the buildup of frustration and anger that surprises clients (and you) later on.

You mislead clients when you appear to be endlessly accommodating and pleasant. Then, when they have gone too far, you startle both of you with your anger. For this response and similar ones, you don't need to explain in detail, but acknowledgment of your client's accurate perception is helpful, such as, "You are right. I ought to have said something earlier about your missed appointment/lateness/cancellations . . . It is not a good trait—don't imitate me." Then return the focus to the client and get back on track, "Now let's talk about the missed appointments."

The general guideline is to be honest about what you think and feel at the moment; next, reflect on the circumstances that evoked your reaction; then decide whether to share, how much to share, and how to phrase your comment. This is not a timed quiz. If something important is happening and you don't realize it until you are trying to fall asleep that night or in consultation with another therapist, you can come back to the matter in another session.

"Are You Falling Asleep? You Look Distracted. Are You?"

It happens; that awful, sleepy, nodding-off feeling. Sometimes you are tired, but our experience is that certain clients elicit a sleepy reaction in you when you feel invisible or unnecessary in the room. When you are an engaged partner in the session, you feel energized, not drained. A different cause of sleepiness, distraction, or wandering thoughts can be anger, or the desire to distance yourself from the client or from the difficult material being discussed. Your reactions are good diagnostic tools, but it is still a mistake to fall asleep. It's essential to your work as a therapist to be honest with yourself and try to figure out what causes your reaction. In the moment, you can admit, "Yes, I'm having a strange reaction to our session." If you know why, say so. "When you talk about your wife in that manner, I have a hard time staying with it." or "It does seem like we have been over this material before. Do you know why we have returned to it?" or if you don't yet understand your reaction, admit, "I have to think about it." If you were distracted and missed words, consider disclosing that fact, "I did feel a little distracted while you were talking. I'd like to return to your last comments to make sure I understand them because the details of your story are important to me."

If your sleepy reaction happens with a specific client more than once, it is time to have a long discussion with a consultant about your client's personality, defenses, presentation, and the work you are doing together. Also, talk to your own therapist about the etiology of your emotional responses.

Intense engagement at one extreme or distracted thoughts at the other are common countertransference reactions and are worth examining. Did something about the client or conversation capture your attention or bore you? What does it say about you, about your client at this time, and about the relationship? The answers to these questions (and only you have the answers) will provide excellent information and lead you in the direction of deepening the therapy.

"I Was Surprised That It Took You So Long to Call Me Back to Reschedule Our Appointment. Is Everything All Right?"

Some therapists admit that the least favorite part of their job is returning client phone calls. Generally, there is something uncomfortable about not being able to see your client. Also, phone calls need to be kept brief and focused, a departure from your usual stance of exploring and expanding the dialogue. Sometimes, there are specific reasons for the differences in how you respond to calls. If you immediately reply to one client but delay replying to another, you can learn a lot from reflecting on the internal processes that influence your decision. Although your insight regarding your reactions—an eagerness to respond or a dread of having to make the call—will not be included in your response, it may be informative of your overall relationship. So, to this client you might say, "To tell you the truth, returning phone calls is the least favorite part of my job, but nothing is wrong. Thanks for asking. Did it worry you?" or "Sorry I worried you. I waited until I had more time to devote to the call." or "Sorry, I have been delayed."

"Why Did You Call Me by Someone Else's Name?"

This question refers to another ordinary reaction in which your associations lead your thoughts elsewhere, so you substitute a name, event, or experience that does not belong to your client. You can't very well say to Susan, "Well, Emily also has an abusive boyfriend, and I was recalling my work with her." You can, however, think about the associations that led to your remark and use that information in the client's interest, for example, "Sorry, I think that our discussion about abusive boyfriends got me confused for a moment." There will be many times during treatment sessions that you will associate to other clients and to people from your own world, past and present. Those associations can be very important in getting to the heart of the discussion occurring in the present. Use the information to understand your client's problem but disclose very cautiously, for example, "The behavior you described sent my mind along an interesting path that might be useful to our discussion." Then return to your client with, "I have this idea I want to share with you . . ."

"I Was Here for My Appointment and You Never Showed Up. How Could You Do This to Me?"

Hopefully, this is a rare event. This scenario calls up the same issues as previous questions but adds a significant dimension, the interplay of reactions. Your countertransference, not showing up, may be a reaction to your client, and now there are further consequences because your client is hurt by your behavior. Your client will have certain feelings about your behavior and interpret it in light of his previous experience, in this instance, probably as rejection. These errors are not the way that we advise clinicians to bring emotions into the session, but when they surface, you work with them.

Mistakes about time, double-booking, or unreturned calls may be simple accidents of forgetfulness, but there is often more going on when you look beneath the surface. It is your error, so check your life first. Are you overwhelmed, tired, burned out, or distracted by personal matters? Even when you can trace the mistake to your own busy life, take additional time to also understand these kinds of slips as a possible interplay between you and your client or as relevant to other aspects of your client's life, past and present. You will treat many people who have suffered neglect, rejection, and abuse, so your innocent, or not-so-innocent, behaviors can replicate your client's past experiences.

For example, Linda forgot to write down a changed appointment time with AmiNoel and didn't go to the office early enough. On the surface, it seems innocent, but AmiNoel had a mother who was schizophrenic and often disappeared without warning. That fact, coupled with Linda's usual excessive punctuality, makes it possible that she was acting out the unreliable mother role. She apologized, owned the transgression, and then tried to remain aware of the emergence of issues of neglect or unreliability. Frightening to most clinicians is the realization that we too act out before we process our countertransference.

Linda

I received a phone call from a clinician who wanted to schedule a consultation as soon as possible. Rich was rattled when he came in, and after hesitation and great embarrassment, he told me, "I've been treating Lisa for months, and it has gone well. She is beginning to trust me. Then, all of a sudden, I have this crazy sexual attraction to her. I feel horrible, but I'd like to jump her." These intense feelings had never happened before with a client, and Rich was confused. He was miserably uncomfortable. We talked at length about the client, her past, and their work together.

Finally I asked him, "Was she ever sexually abused?" He didn't know; she had never mentioned it. I explained that the quick way his reaction developed made me wonder if his client had

(continued)

a history of sexual abuse. It seemed that without realizing it, Lisa was presenting herself to him in the only way she knew, sexually, and he was reacting to her. This hypothesis turned out to be true. Rich's reaction, although it made him miserable, was filled with important information that would ultimately help his client. It is to his credit that he took great care to understand it rather than act on it.

"How Can You Continue to See the Bright Side of Things When My Life Is a Mess?"

Previous questions have looked at the seemingly negative reactions on the part of the therapist. Here is the other side to the countertransference coin. There will be many times when you go out of your way for a particular client, when you admire or appreciate a client, when you reassure a client, and when you are charmed by a client. None of these reactions are wrong or abnormal, but they may be signs of countertransference in another direction.

This question seems to represent a mild empathic breach where the therapist lost track of her client's emotions and, instead, she responded to something else in the room. Perhaps the therapist wanted life to be better for her client and therefore reassured her client without sufficiently dealing with the feelings expressed. Perhaps the therapist admired her client's strengths without appreciating the insistence on negativity or victimization. Perhaps the therapist offered encouragement prematurely, when examination was needed. Only the therapist (working with her client in that session) can have the answer. You can tell whether you were on the mark by your client's reaction to your comment. Whatever "bright side of things" comment the therapist had made, the client felt unheard. In this instance, we think that it is logical to return to the client's actual emotional state and recognize, "Yes, I seem to be more optimistic than you are. Let's go back to the mess." Or you can own your experience and say, "Yes, I do want things to be brighter for you, but that wasn't the point you were making."

Linda

My class laughed when I admitted that I get defensive in personal or social situations, but when I am doing therapy, I hold myself to a higher standard. I'm sure that I am not alone in that behavior. Most clinicians that I know try very hard during each clinical hour to be present and honest. That said, we all still make mistakes, and some of them come directly from our personalities.

"How Can You Forget My Boyfriend/Story/Mother'sName/ Trauma/Upcoming Graduation?" "Why Aren't You Behaving Like My Former Therapist?" "Why Do You Always Need to Be Right? What About What I Say?" "Why Are You Being Mean to Me?"

We use these remaining questions and their answers to attend more specifically to understanding therapists' vulnerabilities. Everyone has their own vulnerabilities, so forget about trying to obliterate or hide them. Instead, make friends with your weaknesses. There is a Native American saying, "If you are going to walk out on the thin ice, you may as well dance." Therapy sessions often have the feeling of walking on thin ice. In your own dealings with colleagues and with supervisors, pay attention to your vulnerabilities, and your work will be easier. The responses try to give you an idea of how common vulnerabilities have an impact on treatment, just like they do in all close relationships. These sensitive traps will be sprung during treatment, and you will find that escape is difficult.

"How Can You Forget My Boyfriend/Story/ Mother's Name/Trauma/Upcoming Graduation?"

This type of question brings up different possibilities for vulnerability. You have offended your client, and you may be very tempted to defend yourself and cover your lapse. Try not to be; instead say, "I'm sorry I didn't remember all the details about your boyfriend/story/trauma. However, I do remember you talking about it and know how important it is to you

Charlie

I am not particularly good with remembering names. If I see a client on the street years after I have treated him, I can remember his personality pattern, presenting concerns, and strengths and weaknesses as a client, but not his name. I do remember clients' names when they are in session with me, but my shortcoming can be awkward when I want to say "And Lisa says . . ." and instead I have to say, "And your wife says . . ." Sometimes I try to preempt the awkwardness by saying "I'm sorry, I am not very good with names," when there is a natural place in a conversation to use someone's name and I haven't used one. On the other hand, there is a certain paradox that, once I have announced my memory difficulties with names, my forgetfulness is usually less pronounced with those clients.

for me to understand your relationship with boyfriend/story/trauma better. I'd like to go back to the relationship/story/trauma now if you are ready."

It is important to not let your own defensiveness get in the way when you respond. It is not uncommon to sometimes miss the details of your clients' stories. Accept responsibility, say you are sorry, and move on to understand what you missed or forgot. If, in your judgment, more needs to be explored, ask, "Did I hurt your feelings with my forgetfulness?" or "My forgetfulness has brought up strong feelings in you."

"Why Aren't You Behaving Like My Former Therapist?"

Questions that compare you to former therapists act as a magnet for insecurities like competitiveness, possessiveness, and defensiveness. Start with, "Are there some ways that your former therapist behaved that were particularly helpful to you?" Then, instead of just reacting to your competitive fantasy about the former therapist, ask about the treatment. You can always learn a lot from clients' previous experiences. "What was your past experience with therapy like?" or "What did you find useful about your previous therapist? What didn't you like?" or "Tell me about that treatment." or "I want to understand your previous therapy and the relationship you had with your therapist. It's important for us." If it seems appropriate, you might add, "Therapy is like all relationships—no two are alike. I am optimistic that we can work together in ways that are similar and different from your former therapist."

You will be tempted to reassure clients. Of course, you want to be regarded highly as a therapist; this is your life's work, but your job is to understand and examine emotions and events first. If reassurance is necessary, that comes later. You will be regarded highly by your clients because you do your work, not because you tell them what they want to hear.

"Why Do You Always Need to Be Right? What About What I Say?"

We have included this and the following question "Why are you being mean to me?" in our list of questions in order to examine some personality characteristics of the therapist. In the first example, we have the therapist as expert. Perhaps this therapist has narcissistic tendencies and a desire to be correct, expert, authoritative, skilled, knowledgeable, and all those other adjectives that were helpful in school performance but will drive you to make this mistake. You train and read and study and train some more and have a great deal of information swirling around in your head. You want to use it, to offer it to clients, and you want them to admire, respect, and listen to you. Well, that doesn't always happen. Even with all your help, clients stumble around and find their own ways of doing things. Try, "What did I say that made your words invisible?" or "Please go ahead and correct my ideas. Tell me where I went off track." Clinicians are thoughtful people. Therefore, you are probably aware of places where your vulnerabilities have already shown up in your life outside the office. You have to expect that they will creep into your work as well. The commitment to becoming a therapist is an agreement for a lifetime of introspection. We need to cultivate the same curiosity for ourselves as we have developed with and for our clients.

"Why Are You Being Mean to Me?"

We strongly doubt that the overwhelming majority of clinicians are mean to their clients, but in this final question, we again want to highlight how personality characteristics can lead you in negative directions. We do know that therapists can be punishing under certain circumstances; that therapists can respond aggressively, especially when under threat; that therapists can tease or belittle clients, often without awareness of the results; that therapists can be glib; that therapists who are generally the most empathic of creatures also get critical, unsupportive, and insensitive when they are provoked. Try this as a response, "That couldn't have been easy to say. Can you help me see how I may have been mean?" or "I didn't realize that I was mean—what did I say?" or "Maybe I am being rough. I'm frustrated at our (problem)," but it doesn't stop there. Explore your client's experience of the interchange with her.

FURTHER THOUGHTS

> "Most of your reactions are echoes from the past. You do not really live in the present."
>
> —Gaelic proverb

The responses here do not finish this piece of work. The real activity of questions regarding your reaction to clients comes from more than some good examples of responses and applies to all countertransference experiences. It is important to understand your reaction to these questions. It is wise to examine the exchange that evoked the emotion to which your client is referring with her question. Stay in touch with your emotions. Be honest about what you feel. Attempt to figure out what your reaction says about you, your client, and the interaction, or in some instances collision, between the two of you. Supervision and your own therapy are excellent places to learn more about your reactions, where they come from, and what they mean. We are more aware of our reactions when they are negative or disturbing, but most reactions are positive.

Bridget (pseudonym), a first-year Master's student

Josh is an attractive man in his mid-twenties who puzzles and fascinates me. He came into therapy to discuss a depression that has resulted from a recent breakup with a longtime girlfriend. During our third session, Josh disclosed that he had sex with a man for the first time, and then he quickly assured me, "I'm positive that I'm not homosexual, but I am happy that I tried sex with a man." I was completely caught off guard, and I hoped my face didn't reflect my confusion, because I knew Josh was feeling vulnerable and exposed. "Okay," I said, thinking that I needed to be calm and act normal. I had no idea what to say, so I just sat there silently, listening and nodding.

Shortly Josh continued, "So, my friend told me that shrinks try to change people's personalities. Are you going to do that to me?" I responded, "Hmm, that's an interesting thought. What do you think about that?" "I dunno, I guess I'm just a little scared. I mean, I don't want you to." I agreed. "Yeah, having someone change your personality sounds scary to me!" We both laughed and I continued, "To be honest, I don't want to change your personality, and even if I wanted to, I couldn't." Josh seemed pleased. "Oh, really? Okay, good, I was a little nervous." "I can imagine. What right or abilities do I have to change your personality? You're here because you want to work on and figure out some things about yourself. Those are the things we can work together on. So, it's more of a collaborative process." Josh answered, "Yeah, okay, good. I feel a little relieved."

We have been working together for about three months now, and he has not brought up either his sexual encounter or fears about me changing his personality since our third session. I have a theory about why Josh asked about personality change after disclosing his secret. I think that he was wondering if he was gay and was perhaps hoping that I would tell him that I was capable of changing his personality and, thus, his sexual orientation. As I rethink the third session and his question, I realize that there is probably much more that both of us want to know about Josh, and I'm intrigued. He is a fascinating client.

We all have personalities and we all have reactions. Who you are will dictate what you do. This is what writers mean when they talk about using yourself as "a clinical instrument." We all have the responsibility to learn to play our instruments well. Being a good therapist doesn't mean that you never have a countertransference reaction; it means that you are committed to use your reactions as data. These are also the sort of encounters to discuss with your own therapist. In this way, you will learn more about yourself and your client, allowing the work to become even more meaningful.

SUGGESTED READINGS

Gelso, C. J., & Hayes, J. A. (2002). Countertransference management. In J. C. Norcross (Ed.), *Psychotherapy relationships that work: Therapist contributions and responsiveness to patients*. New York, NY: Oxford University Press.

Gelso, C. J., & Hayes, J. A. (2007). *Countertransference and the therapist's inner experience: Perils and possibilities*. Mahwah, NJ: Erlbaum.

Gelso, C. J., Latts, M. G., Gomez, M. J., & Fassinger, R. E. (2002). Countertransference management and therapy outcome: An initial evaluation. *Journal of Clinical Psychology, 58*, 861–867.

Lewis, J. I. (2009). The crossroads of countertransference and attributional theory: Reinventing clinical training within an evidence-based treatment world. *The American Journal of Psychoanalysis, 69*, 106–120.

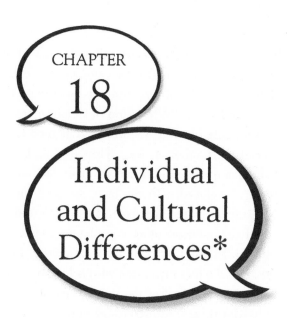

CHAPTER

18

Individual
and Cultural
Differences*

There will be days when you think about clients and wonder, "What do I do with our differences?" You can validate the differences, but don't get distracted by them. People are typically more alike than different if they can stay related in the moment long enough to recognize

Lianna, a 28-year-old student intern

She went into the clinic waiting room to greet her 68-year-old client Tony for the first time. Before this meeting, they had a brief, friendly phone conversation while setting the appointment, and Lianna knew that her client was a veteran who had been referred

(continued)

---

* This chapter was written primarily by Carol Kerr, Ph.D., Chief Psychologist, Graduate Clinical Training Program, Marin County Health and Human Services, Division of Community Mental Health. For 25 years, Carol has practiced, taught, and supervised in public mental health clinics "where a diverse group of students serve a diverse group of clients, and we all learn all the time about the power and richness of individual and cultural diversity and its role in clinical work."

to therapy for grief because his wife died in an auto accident. He stood up, smiling, when she came up to greet him. As they walked down the hall and entered the treatment room, Tony asked in a cheerful voice, "What kind of Oriental are you?" Many thoughts and feelings arose in Lianna in that moment, but she recognized that the key question was, "How do I reply while I am also establishing a therapeutic alliance?" Her answer was to respond, not react; she stayed with the facts, because she knew that she could investigate the feelings, both the client's and hers, once she understood the question more completely. Lianna said, "I was born in Hawaii. My mother's parents immigrated there from Japan in the 30s, and she met my father, who is Dutch-American, in Honolulu." "I was in Hawaii after the war," Tony responded as he took a seat. "I liked it there. I wanted to take my wife there."

that fact. Your effective therapeutic alliance is built on the relationship in the present, and that includes both similarities and differences. The quality of your attention in the moment and your attunement to the client's experience in the present is far more important than any real or imagined differences.

In this instance, the frank observation of differences by the client and an open, honest response from Lianna got the therapy started in a surprisingly quick and direct way. It would have gone very differently if Lianna had avoided or redirected the question with the traditional answer, "I wonder why you are interested in that?" By deflecting a direct inquiry about differences, she would have suggested that Tony should not be curious, not observe differences, or not expect any personal disclosure from Lianna, who will be asking Tony many personal questions.

Your ability to create connection while you recognize, respect, and understand differences is essential to the practice of psychotherapy. Good academic programs in counseling, psychology, and social work always provide coursework in *multicultural competence*, a descriptor for a set of skills that in combination allow you to effectively recognize differences while you establish points of connection and common purpose. But even outstanding lectures, readings, and a range of personal cross-cultural experiences do not result in clinicians feeling well-prepared for the types of direct questions that can arise out of the perceived or imagined differences present in the consulting room—or even in the waiting room before the first session.

The kinds of questions and answers explored in this chapter arise in response to variables of age, gender, race, ethnicity, language, religion, size/weight, physical disability/ability, sexual orientation, legal status/arrest history, immigration history, family composition, social class, and economic status. These are just some of the differences among and between people that can give rise to questions, voiced or unvoiced. We have compiled a selection of questions and responses with the goal of examining specific underlying concerns of establishing a common sense of safety, inviting interest in the obvious but unspoken doubts or fears, and contending with prejudice.

QUESTIONS

These questions were all asked by clients who strongly identified with the issue at hand. They are answered in the Responses section.

"How can a man understand what it is like to be raped?"

"How can you possibly relate to my fibromyalgia?"

"Have you ever been poor?"

"Do you have any idea what it is like to be Black and live in this city?"

"Were you born in this country?"

"How do you feel about gay sex?"

"Are you a Christian?"

"Have you been through withdrawal?" "Do you have a drug of choice?"

"Going on vacation at Christmas again?"

"Are you old enough to help me at all?"

"Don't you think most Southerners are racist?"

"Does your husband criticize you for being fat?"

"Do you believe in angels?"

Some of these questions have also appeared in other chapters. We offered possible answers then, but we reintroduce them here in order to discuss responses that specifically attend to the reality of individual and cultural themes. We originally thought that we would be able to embed diversity questions and answers throughout the book, but we have since been convinced that sprinkling these questions is too much like serving bagels at brunch and imagining that anti-Semitism is resolved, or legislating Dr. Martin Luther King, Jr. Day as a national holiday and believing that we have overcome racism. The major reason to give individual and cultural diversity a chapter of its own is to emphasize the importance of directly addressing the topic, at least in your own awareness, in the same way you address questions about your experience or confidentiality.

RESPONSES

We live in a culture that attempts to obscure differences and perpetuate the myth that everyone has the same opportunities and experiences. Therefore, questions like the ones raised in this chapter confront you more directly than usual. Brave clinical work involves addressing issues of cultural and individual differences that are spoken and approaching those that remain unspoken. It will be productive. At the outset, you may want to begin by receiving the question well. "I am glad you brought this up." or "That's an important question." or "Your question can really help our work." or "Your question speaks to your attention to these concerns." In this way, you validate the risk that your client has taken, and you also get some time to formulate your response.

"How Can a Man Understand What It Is Like to Be Raped?"

"Yes, I am a man, so I can really see why you would worry that I can't understand your experience as a woman. We will both have to pay close attention to when that might be in our way." If you sense reluctance, consider reassuring your client with, "If we can't work within that difference, I'll work with you to find a female therapist, but I think I have skills that could help you, and I'm hoping I can be useful and helpful, even if I'm male." or "I've definitely felt helpless, but I haven't been assaulted in the way you were. I'd like us to work together to find a safe way to help with how the assault affects your life."

Clients need to feel safe. We all navigate in a psychosocial environment by noticing and evaluating, often at an automatic or unconscious level, whether we are like and unlike someone else. Trust develops from a sense of common and mutual regard. For purposes of psychotherapy, one fundamental question that clients have is, "Are you enough like me that I can be safe?" Each individual's history and present circumstances determine whether and which differences are threatening—or intriguing. So from the beginning of treatment, the therapy team, you and your client, will negotiate how your alikeness and difference figure in how you can work together.

Questions based on factual, expected, or imagined differences are a source of particular anxiety, because they cross over into the complex and fluid domain of social judgments and attitudes about gender, race, ethnicity, and other important identifiers that inform each person's sense of self. These moments of inquiry are rich with potential for you to feel that you are being either agent or object of stigma, prejudice, discrimination, and rejection. We try to use these moments to create connections that promote the therapeutic alliance in the face of the inevitable differences.

"How Can You Possibly Relate to My Fibromyalgia?"

Some of what therapy can do is remove artificiality and get down to the bedrock upon which firm and reliable systems can be based. Acknowledge the reality of your differences in health, and then find a way to use it constructively. This maintains your alliance with your client and probably will increase his confidence in you. "I have not had the experience of fibromyalgia myself, so I will really need to connect to your experience, as well as do some reading on my own, so that I can relate to the kind of pain and havoc that this disease is causing you."

"Have You Ever Been Poor?"

If you haven't been poor, this question can be responded to with, "I have been pretty lucky and had enough of the basic things for most of my life. I've had to go without things I wanted, but I haven't had to raise kids without enough food for them." You could also add a more general acknowledgment that, "Nothing is fair about how poverty burdens people's lives, and I think therapy could help if you're willing to work with me." If a client experiences you as genuinely intent on understanding his experience in the present and in being helpful, despite the obstacles that differences can impose, you are positioned to move forward in the therapy. In both responses, the therapist validates the difference and its effects *and* asserts that therapy offers an opportunity to collaborate despite the existing difference. The answers all have two components: (1) you directly acknowledge the reality of the difference, and (2) you affirm your conviction that it is possible to find a common ground while also respecting the differences between you.

If you have been poor, or lived with any of the other experiences that we use in the questions, you may have a starting point but still have to acknowledge, "Yes, but that alone doesn't make me able to understand the uniqueness of your life." or another response that notes commonality while still appreciating difference and the continued need for working together.

"Do You Have Any Idea What It Is Like to Be Black and Live in This City?"

This is related to the previous question and calls for you to be obvious and direct, "Well, I'm not Black and shouldn't be guessing at what that is like. I've lived in this area long enough to know you probably experience all kinds of both direct and indirect discrimination. I'm interested in how you see its effects for you—and how I can learn to understand your experience." After exploring what those effects are, reinforce your intention not to have parallel painful experiences in the therapy relationship with, "And we need to watch together for anything I do or say that could feel like I am repeating those bad experiences. We can't make the differences between us disappear, but we can work to keep them from getting in our way."

And, if you are Black, but don't live locally, it can be important to observe that you want to understand the specifics of the local community, and even your own experience with racism shouldn't be understood to mean you will automatically understand your client's.

"Were You Born in This Country?"

Any answer to this question and the ones that follow need to be straight-forward and at the same time invite some explorations of the implications of your answer. Be candid and invite exploration: "I was (or wasn't) born here." Say where you were born in either case, followed by "I'm interested in how that might matter to you," and be open to different responses from your client as well, ranging from "Are you legal?" to "My brother-in-law comes from (the country you just mentioned); he's a good guy."

"How Do You Feel About Gay Sex?"

This question can be answered, "Sex questions always need some context—so I will ask you a couple of questions in return. I really want to understand your question, but basically I think what is most important about sex is that it is healthy. I mean, it is a normal part of being human to be sexual. And people can be normally heterosexual, homosexual, or bisexual. But like any other activity, sex can also be hazardous if it's not practiced safely." Then, go back to the questions you warned them about. "What are your thoughts about gay sex? And in what ways does it matter to our working together?"

Although they are very different queries, "Were you born in this country?" and "How do you feel about gay sex?" are both "locator" questions. Clients will try to locate or position you in a context that relates to their own values, experience, or identity. Not knowing can be a barrier for some clients. Once the two of you have crossed the obstruction that was caused by not knowing, you can explore what the topic means for the therapeutic alliance, for example, "Do you find it easier when you talk to people who were born inside or outside the U.S.?" or "If I had answered differently, would that have gotten in the way of (or helped) us working together?" You can go further and inquire about the projections, such as "Were you concerned that I would be prejudiced about your birthplace/sexual behaviors?" or "Do you run into opinions about your birthplace/sexual practices?"

Some clients need to ask these kinds of questions even when you have some obvious common denominators. When Dora had her first opportunity to provide services in her native Lao to clients who did not speak English, she expected an automatic bond to be created by the common language. She was surprised at how many challenging questions she immediately received about class, education, and exactly where she was born. Even though the common language and country of origin provided an initial connection, their experiences differed. Clients felt increasingly safe as they were able to discuss their personal immigration experiences, education, and certain traditional practices.

"Are You a Christian?"

When clients ask you this question, you often don't know what answer they are hoping for as they locate you in relation to themselves. They may—or may not—want you to be Christian. Giving a simple descriptive response and then exploring what the answer means in the therapy context usually works. "I was raised in the Christian Methodist tradition, but I began questioning some things about it when I was in college and haven't really gotten back to membership in any specific church. Tell me how my believing in Christ, or not, could be important in our work?" or "I do believe in Christ, the same as I believe in other important religious figures, but I am very interested in knowing how we will include your religious beliefs in our work." Sometimes, the answer is more clear-cut: "No, I am not a Christian." or "Yes, I consider myself a Christian," with either response being followed by, "Can you tell me how this comes into our work together?"

A similar "tell me how" inquiry can also be used when a question challenges your position on politics, values, or personal issues and it is not yet clear what values the client holds in relation to the question. It can be tempting to dismiss or minimize differences, because we worry that we will not be able to build or sustain a strong alliance and be helpful. You don't have to be identical, but you do need to convey openness, attention, and respect.

Clinicians often wonder, "Should I pretend to understand or pretend to be someone I'm not?" No, pretending doesn't work. You can acknowledge that you don't understand fully and demonstrate that you remain interested. This usually furthers the therapeutic connection. On the other hand, clinicians have a real concern of, "How much can I ask before I sound stupid?" The real issue is not to ask questions stupidly. There is an art to asking questions without asking too many of them. Questions that facilitate conversation are those that build on comments already spoken or naturally bridge to related material. It is also important not to expect the client to be your only source of learning about important individual or cultural differences that are relevant and unfamiliar to you. You have a professional responsibility to do your own research and advance your knowledge outside of the therapy hour about social and historical realities that have shaped your client's environment.

"Have You Been Through Withdrawal?" "Do You Have a Drug of Choice?"

These questions present a different challenge. In previous questions, we suggested some level of disclosure, depending on the question, and presented several reasons why revealing yourself can benefit the progress of therapy. Here, we have the opportunity to look at alliance building when you do not choose to answer. You do not have to answer every question a client asks, but you do need to respond to the question in some way that sustains their desire to talk to you and answer your questions. Clients and therapists have different jobs in the process, so if you feel the question crosses a personal boundary you want to observe, say that. For example, "I know I've been asking you (or will be asking you) questions about drug use, but I need to wait until we are further along in therapy and know each other better before I talk about details of my own experience with substances. I want to postpone your question for now. But we'll remember it, and if we need to get back to it, we will." Other arguments for nondisclosure to this and similar questions are made in Chapter 10, Personal Questions.

When you set a boundary and you assert your right to choose the time of any disclosure, you model the right to establish boundaries, a skill that many clients lack and learn during the course of treatment. You are also educating your client as to how the therapy conversation will evolve. The art is in setting limits while still acknowledging your client's question and appreciating how he is using it to establish a connection. If you choose not to disclose at all to the drug question, remain inviting, "It's fine to be curious, but I just can't answer all of your questions. And I actually know a lot about withdrawal, even if I'm not ready to disclose more personal details right now."

If you have no knowledge of drugs and withdrawal, or any of the other differences that arise, it may be difficult, or impossible, to understand your client's experience. If it doesn't happen with drugs, it will happen with something else. "Will I understand?" is an existential question that is always in the therapeutic process. You will understand more about the differences if you can get a dialog started. You will never understand them entirely, but you can still do effective psychotherapy.

"Going on Vacation at Christmas Again?"

This is a good example of a category of question that is usually not asked directly but is implied. Perhaps your client needs information about individual, cultural, or socioeconomic differences that may be barriers, but he is afraid to ask. So, if it isn't asked directly, it is your job to turn the statement into a question. For example, "Going on vacation at Christmas again?" or others like "I love your car." or "I bet you don't live around here." identify ways that the two of you differ with regard to economic status or privilege. The comment, "You probably get along great with your kids" is inquiring about both parenthood and experiences of frustration or failure. When you give attention to these comments, you invite a common interest in what is real (or imagined) and what is often not said. "Hmm, I do (go on vacations/have a new car I like/get along with my kids, or not). I'm interested that you've noticed that and wonder what brings it up. Maybe there's something important for us to talk more about?"

Questions about obvious or possible differences—which are always present—are often avoided or postponed in ways that limit or disrupt formation of a treatment alliance and relationship. Although the questions that are asked can seem awkward, the ones that are present but unasked can definitely limit the potential therapeutic relationship. So in addition to answering questions, you need to learn how to raise potentially unasked questions that are not always easy for either of you to explore. There is no better way than forward.

Ida was completing an internship in a setting where almost all clients were younger, white males. She asked all her clients at some time in the first session, "How do you feel about doing therapy with a middle-aged Latina woman?" While it sometimes evoked an initial negative judgment or expressions of doubt, every client engaged and stayed in treatment through the year. Her validation of their possible discomfort with differences and willingness to explore the effects right from the beginning was an effective engagement tool. These moments of direct encounter allow the therapist to model the exploration of what is thought and felt and how it can be safely talked about in therapy and beyond.

"Are You Old Enough To Help Me At All?" "Don't You Think Most Southerners Are Racist?" "Does Your Husband Criticize You For Being Fat?"

This set of questions provides common examples of queries that are intentionally or inadvertently insulting to you or others. You are challenged to address the element of genuine inquiry without being snared by the "ism" (as in ageism, sexism, racism, or sizism). At the same time, it can be important not to ignore the explicit or implied values difference when it will affect the therapy. Usually questions like these have a lot going on. They can feel like tests, so you choose one issue and respond to that. The following answers demonstrate different responses.

"Are You Old Enough to Help Me at All?"

A challenging question like this one about age can certainly be experienced, and even be meant, as devaluing of the therapist's experience and equating age by itself with skill and experience. It also conveys the client's fear that he is beyond help or being discriminated against because he has been assigned a young or young-looking therapist, so you need to start there. "I am younger than you, and I can see you would worry that I don't have the experience to deal with problems as difficult as the ones you're facing. Are you willing to be surprised?" or "And because I am still being supervised, I actually have a whole team who can

Tammi Vacha-Haase, Ph.D., Colorado State University, specialist on aging

I usually tell students that the most honest and direct response is to agree with the client: Yes, there is an age difference. However, therapy is a collaborative effort, with what the client knows about being a 50/70/80-year-old Latina/African-American/Korean/Southern man or woman and what the therapist understands given his or her training. The client and the therapist work together, pooling their individual resources, to improve the older client's quality of life.

I also remind students that their client will react to their presentation. So, if as therapists they act professional, competent, authentic, and comfortable, that sets the tone for the session and influences how the older client responds. If in the therapist role they appear unsure,

(continued)

uneasy, and worry the client will see them as being young, then they may actually set into motion a self-fulfilling prophecy.

Bottom line, younger therapists rarely are asked this question by their older clients, those over 65, or even into their eighties and nineties. I believe the therapist's approach matters, but I also think older clients tend to be grateful for those who are truly interested in helping them, and thus, may not care about the age difference, or out of appreciation and respect do not comment directly about the therapist's age. I would say that the majority of older clients feel very positively toward younger therapists who are genuinely invested in their well-being, and overall, the therapist's age is of little importance.

help us work on your goals. If you won't give up on me before we start, I won't give up on you."

"Don't You Think Most Southerners Are Racist?"

This is a joining question that is loaded in several ways, including the unpleasant fact that it invites you into regionalism, if not racism. And depending on the client's allegiances, it is not clear what answer she desires. Sometimes it is wisest to step back and invite more exploration. "Well, that is a lot of generalizing that I'm not so comfortable with myself. I definitely think racism exists and is a problem in many different ways. What's your specific experience with racism been like?" or "That is a very broad statement. What are you really trying to say?"

"Does Your Husband Criticize You for Being Fat?"

This question could be hard to hear with calm objectivity but is certainly rich with information. It also has the potential to develop a connection with your client and model how to state limits or values and explore a difficult question in the context of therapy. Depending on your own comfort level, any of these responses could work: "Ouch. Yes, he does." or "If he did, I'd probably say to him, 'Back off, you short person.' I think each person's size is what it is. But health does matter. How do you handle personal criticism?" or "Hmm, I wonder what brought that up now. There seems to be something about my size that disturbs you."

Sometimes the therapist may need to raise a point during the therapy, particularly when a client's -isms affect treatment. For example, in this chapter's opening anecdote, Lianna's client referred to her as an Oriental, a term she associates with negative, inaccurate, racist labeling. When her client used the term again later in therapy, after they had a good alliance, asking if she liked Oriental food, she said, "You know, Oriental is a really broad category and lumps everything together. I feel about that phrase a little like I think you would about the term Dago— it's not always used kindly or accurately. I do like lots of native Hawaiian dishes, and Vietnamese and Japanese food. Thai food is a little hot for me." This response mixes authentic disclosure with psycho-education and an added perspective the client might be able to connect to—and then also answers the essential question.

"Do You Believe in Angels?"

This question was asked by an 8-year-old girl. We often forget that a wide gap exists between adults and children, so this question reminds all of us that individual differences extend to our young clients, too. You could reply, "I don't know if I do. I am interested in the experiences people have that make angels real for them. Can you tell me why you are interested in angels?" or simply, "I want to know more about them. Tell me what you know. I think people around the world, for a long time, have been interested in angels." Your own experiences in life will be very different from your clients' experiences no matter how similar or different they might seem at the beginning. Don't deny the differences and don't overfocus on them. You are both in the same room in the present and have some shared reason for being there.

FURTHER THOUGHTS

"Every person is like all other persons, like some other persons, and like no other persons."
—Clyde Kluckhohn and Henry Murray

"Will clients distrust me because I'm different?" Clients will trust you once they see your genuine interest and find something you do have in common, like surviving the first psychotherapy hour, loving the Cubs,

272   CLIENT QUESTIONS AND RESPONSES BY TOPIC

having a dog, or being on the same side in their struggles. Perhaps what you have in common is that you both wonder what you have in common. Connections are found in unlikely places but are always available; perhaps the strongest connection is your common desire for your client's increased health. One of the most fundamental competencies in the helping professions is skill in responding to individual and cultural diversity.

What about you? Are you prejudiced or overly value laden in relation to certain differences or categories of identity? Everyone has "blind spots and dumb spots." No one is immune. One critical task is to always be open to discovering these and learning from oversights or mistakes. Sometimes you need to lead with disclosure, including how different from the client you feel, as well as how similar you might be. The other critical task is to master ways to bring differences into the room and talk about them with respectful curiosity about how they can inform your work together. Multicultural competence is always a work in progress, because cultures are living, evolving traditions. The path to competence involves mindful practice and continuous curiosity and consultation.

SUGGESTED READINGS

Caremil, E. V., & Battle, C. L. (2003). Guess who's coming to therapy? Getting comfortable with conversations about race and ethnicity in psychotherapy. *Professional Psychology: Research and Practice, 34*, 278–286.

Constantine, M., & Sue, D. W. (Eds.). (2005). *Strategies for building multicultural competence in mental health and educational settings*. Hoboken, NJ: Wiley.

Hereck, G. M., & Garnets, L. D. (2007). Sexual orientation and mental health. *Annual Review of Clinical Psychology, 3*, 353–375.

Kluckhohn, C., & Murray, H. A. (1953). Personality formation: The determinants. In C. Kluckhohn, H. A. Murray, & D. M. Schneider (Eds.), *Personality in nature, society and culture* (pp. 53–67). New York, NY: Knopf.

La Roche, M. J., & Maxie, A. (2003). Ten considerations in addressing cultural differences in psychotherapy. *Professional Psychology: Research and Practice, 34*, 180–186.

McIntosh, P. (2000). White privilege and male privilege. In T. E. Ore (Ed.), *The social construction of difference and inequality* (pp. 475–485). Mountain View, CA: Mayfield.

Tatum, B. (2002). *Why are all the black kids sitting together in the cafeteria?* New York, NY: Basic Books.

CHAPTER

19

Involving
Others

When you and your client appear to be sitting privately in your consulting room, don't be deceived. You have both brought crowds along with you. The people, the relationships, and the experiences that have shaped the two of you all have something to say. Although this chapter primarily deals with real people, appreciate the power of past and present influences on you and on your client.

Linda

I have one client who sits and talks to her purse during sessions. She also talks to me, but several times during each session when we are in the middle of a discussion, she leans over, nods vigorously, and scolds her purse. In her purse is her telephone, and in her telephone is her boyfriend. Her boyfriend has hijacked therapy. Talking to her purse is indicative of some of her problems; she has given up her life in favor of organizing herself around her unreliable,

(continued)

dramatic boyfriend, and it is easier to talk about others instead of talking about herself. Other people have taken over this funny, bright, creative woman's life. Our work is bringing the treatment back to her, but it is slow.

You can see how ubiquitous others are in treatment, whether they are internalized voices, sounds from the other end of a cell phone, or, as in this chapter, people who are actually brought in or invite themselves into the individual therapy relationship. Mechanical interference happens with increasing frequency because people seem to believe that they must be reachable all the time, so Blackberrys, phone tones, and dings from text messages are regular intrusions. Human and animal guests also make appearances. We have conducted therapy sessions in which clients have invited a twin, a partner, a dog, a baby, a secret lover, a spouse, a roommate, a best friend, a business partner, a teenage son or daughter, and assorted family members.

We have also fielded calls from other therapists, lawyers, parents, spurned lovers, concerned friends, doctors, retaliatory spouses, insurance agents, and complainers from collection agencies. All of these people have a place in treatment, even when the modality is primarily individual therapy. It is always strange when a client shows up unexpectedly with a best friend in tow, a large dog, a crawling child who eats from the less-than-clean carpet, or is carrying scribbled notes that contain instructions from other players in their lives. Some of these surprises feel intrusive, but at other times we want to invite people to be part of the process.

Always, in answering questions that involve others, you are called on to think about boundaries. When you involve other people, anyone may disclose information that had not previously been revealed. Also, clients fear that information will be leaked, and therefore they may conceal their thoughts or behaviors. On the plus side, you have potential benefits from another person's perspective. Always, you must deal with your own reactions to the introduction of others into treatment. In this chapter, we talk about the variety of people, external not internal, who may become involved during treatment, questions that arise because of these interactions, and different possibilities for responses.

QUESTIONS

The following questions are answered in the Responses section:

> "Do you want to see photos?"
> "Can I bring my fiance with me to a session?"
> "Can I bring in my friend? She's in the waiting room."
> "I had to bring my dog. Can he stay?"
> "Will you call so-and-so while I'm here?"
> "Do you mind if I take this call?"
> "My friend says blah blah. What do you think?"
> "My phone psychic had some great advice. Do you agree?"
> "Will you tell my teacher/partner/parole officer that I have a real excuse for not doing something?"
> "Will you please talk to my husband's/mother's/marriage therapist? I think it would help me. She said that she would be happy to talk to you."
> "When I go off to college I want to get into therapy at the counseling center. Can my therapist there contact you?"
> "Would I benefit from medication? Should I see a psychiatrist?"

RESPONSES

"Do You Want to See Photos?"

"Sure." When clients share their pictures, you have an opportunity to see and learn more about the people and events in their worlds. After you look at the photos, you can ask, "Was there something specific that you wanted me to see?" Sometimes clients just want to introduce significant people to you because, "I talk about him so much, I thought you ought to see him." Often, they want to bring in photos or letters in order to have actual physical data to support their ideas or to do a reality check with you, wondering, "Am I right about this?"

"Can I Bring My Fiancé With Me to a Session?"

Until you know your client's motives and plans, this is a tricky question, so you have to ask, "What do you have in mind?" Your response will be very different if your client responds, "I want you to tell her to get off my case about something" versus "We are stuck and can't figure out my role with his kids from the first wife. I would like to have him here to get some ideas about what to do." With the former request, we would probably focus on how this client could talk with his fiancé himself, even if it meant a little coaching. The latter request is far more appropriate, and we would probably say, "That could be useful, let's talk about it. I need to know what you have in mind, and to consider what goal we would focus on in one or two meetings." Later, it is easy to clarify that, "One of my concerns about having him come in is being clear about what you want kept private about our work here and what you want to share with him."

If the client is able to articulate these parameters, we would probably look forward to the meeting. There is a lot to be gained from such collateral contact. If her fiancé does come in, we see our role as clarifying the purpose of the meeting, acknowledging the time-limited nature of this contact, staying clearly with the problem, and suggesting future ideas for them, whether that means another visit, reading material, couples therapy with someone else, or focused conversations between the two of them that build on our session.

"Can I Bring in My Friend? She's in the Waiting Room."

When your client has asked about a friend or family member in advance, it is easy to prepare a focus and purpose of the visit and structure the session appropriately. However, when the visit is unexpected, it may be best to meet the friend, say hello, and then say to your client, "This is a surprise. Why don't you come in and we will take a few minutes to talk about it." You will be able to make a more informed decision after the two of you discuss it. "Why is your friend here? What is the goal?"

As a rule, don't allow anyone to pressure you into an impulsive decision about who enters the consulting room. When you say "yes" to be agreeable or because you don't think it is a big deal, you give the wrong message about boundaries and the privacy of the work you do. Safe, thoughtful boundaries permit answers of both "yes" or "no." Particularly if your client has had problems maintaining safe boundaries, or if he or she has been the victim of other people trampling those boundaries, either emotionally or physically, you want to keep in mind that when you allow or invite others into a session, it may not be a light visit but rather a reenactment of something you do not want to replicate.

To retain your focus when there are others in the room, don't forget which person is your client.

Linda

Nicole, age 50, came into treatment after a tragic family boating accident. I had been seeing her for about six weeks when she said, "The question that people ask me most often now is, 'How is therapy going?' I tell them that I like you a lot, and even though I've been in therapy before, this time is different. But it makes me wonder, how can I assess how therapy is going?" The fact that Nicole asked this question while I was writing this book probably made me more enthusiastic than usual. I did validate and rephrase her question, prepared to have an actual discussion of assessment and goals, but she veered off in an entirely different, novel direction.

She said, "My cousin asks all the time because she feels guilty (about the accident), my friend is curious about therapy, my mother wants to know what I talk about, and my sister asks because she thinks that therapy is a waste of time and money." I had not given much thought to outsiders' motivations when they ask about treatment, but clients are affected by questions that can be motivated by sincere concern, curiosity, guilt, or criticism—all from people outside the room with their own agendas.

"I Had to Bring My Dog. Can He Stay?"

This is similar to the friend question, except you can't leave the pooch sitting in your waiting room reading magazines. You still have choices. You have the right to say "no" and end the session, but you could also give it a try. It is worth knowing why your client brought the dog. It will certainly have meaning if you turn the dog away. We have both had clients bring in dogs, both puppies and grown, refrigerator-sized dogs.

It always dilutes the session's focus, but the dilemma becomes whether a compromised session is better than no session. Unless you are allergic, maybe it is best to try to have a session and then say, "Fido is great, but he did distract us." If you have been excessively accommodating with this client already, and this is yet another example, you may choose to postpone the session and discuss boundaries at your next meeting.

"Will You Call So-and-So While I'm Here?"

This question arises in the context of a conversation in which you are already engaged, so your answer depends on the purpose of the call to so-and-so. What is the aim? Certainly your client is asking for your help, but about what? Is he asking you to call his tax attorney? You have to consider whether it is your job to make the call or if that action will usurp your client's autonomy. If it is appropriate to call, decide whether you want to do it during the session or wait until later. Colleagues tell us that they have phoned parents, psychiatrists, parole officers, or another treatment facility while the client is in the room so the problems get straightened out immediately. "Let's take care of this now because we can all participate." This request happens less often with high-functioning clients than with severely impaired people or with children. If it can wait, then it makes less sense to disrupt the session. Tell your client, "I'll be sure to call your couple's therapist this week, and we can talk about it next time." or "I'll call your teacher/psychiatrist/father, and if the information is important, I'll get back to you right away. Otherwise, we can go over it next time." If, in your opinion, it is the safest way to get something done, you may opt for an immediate call.

"Do You Mind if I Take This Call?"

Most of the time, your office feels like an intensely private space for both you and your client. You work hard to create a safe place where no one enters unexpectedly, where you have protected time to spend on a problem, where you pay undivided attention to your client's world—and then, from the depths of the client's pocket or backpack, a phone jolts you with the music from *Thriller*. The world is back, forcing itself into your room.

This is the client's time to use as she wants, so we usually let the client decide whether to take a call. If she wants to use our limited therapy minutes on the phone, it is her decision. If it happens more than once, and it is not a child at home, the school, or some emergency, we would notice out loud, "You have been taking calls during our sessions. It is your time, but is this really the way you want to use it?" In this way, you make an observation, and the client will think about it. If it continues, and you develop some understanding of the intrusion, you can offer your reaction to, or interpretation of, the phone calls. It may lead to a productive discussion in the direction of boundaries, the client's tolerance for intrusions, problems with anxiety, a need to feel important, a willingness to let others trample on their time, or any of the other possibilities that come to mind when people allow phone calls to take precedence over their immediate situation.

"My Friend Says Blah Blah. What Do You Think?"

Listen to the friend's advice, comment, observation, or suggestion, and you can decide whether you want to say, "You are lucky to have good friends." or "Your friend is very observant." or "You need to explain the context for that remark. I don't understand it." or "I have a different perspective." or "What was your reaction?" If it is someone who has been regularly introduced into the sessions, such as a family member or significant other, you have a sense of this person and have a history of information to recall and rely on about whether they are dependable observers. It is important that clients have friends and develop good support systems, so we don't want to undermine advice from others. We don't want to be the only source of insightful discussions and shared emotions. If we do our jobs well, we are working toward unemployment. It is also fascinating to see how observant some friends can be. There is a lot to learn from the other people who frequently interact with your client.

Charlie

Sharon was a client who had a tendency to talk about the advice (directives?) she was getting from two of her friends. She "brought
(continued)

them in" so often that I could predict their comments before Sharon revealed them: Kelly was her friend who would be bossy and tell her how to handle situations with aggressive posturing; Jan was more yielding and made suggestions along the lines of "you get more bees with honey than vinegar," or by being sneaky about her undertakings. Both of these positions became active voices in our sessions, because they each had merit and were each alive in my client.

Where complications came in was when my client did not want to disappoint either of these friends by following the advice of the other. Sharon's feeling of being torn occupied a great deal of our work. Jan and Kelly became the instruments with which we could identify Sharon's dilemma about whether to be aggressive or passive. Eventually we were able to examine the conflict as being inside, not outside, and that allowed Sharon to make clearer decisions.

"My Phone Psychic Had Some Great Advice. Do You Agree?"

A very bright but judgment-impaired client came in and announced to Linda that her phone psychic said that she was "too giving, too understanding, and treated other people far better than they treated her." The client adored this fortune cookie pronouncement, and Linda wanted to scream at the way her client gobbled up the platitudes, but instead asked, "Can you give me some examples of how these qualities play out in your relationships?" and led the discussion toward, "Do you have any ideas about what you are specifically looking for from other people?" understanding that the client needed more advice or consolation than she was getting. Usually horoscopes, phone psychics, tarot cards, or the I Ching are harmless and help you to further understand what your client is working on, so ask about it, "I'd like to hear what Omar, the phone psychic, had to say about your future," and listen carefully to the selections that your client remembers and repeats, because those are the ideas that made an impact.

Will You Tell My Teacher/Partner/Parole Officer That I Had a Good Reason for Missing Something?"

Being complicit in any lie is always a bad idea. Clients cannot trust us if we are willing to lie to others. If we lie *for* them, we are also capable of lying *to* them. "Will you . . .?" also comes up about insurance, such as, "Will you say that we had extra sessions so they will pay more and cover my co-pay?" "Will you change the date?" "Will you say that my wife came in, not me?" "Will you snitch if I tell the bookkeeper at your agency that I make less money so I can get the sliding-scale price?" The answer always has to be, "I can't lie. Certainly it is unlawful and unethical, but for us, it is also about mental health, our relationship, and our essential need for honesty."

"Will You Please Talk to My Husband's/Mother's/Marriage Therapist? I Think It Would Help Me. She Said That She Would Be Happy to Talk to You."

There are many times when coordinating treatment with other therapists is advisable, but it can also lead to competition and chaos. Think it through carefully before you agree to be drawn into anyone else's therapy. You can discuss all of your client's concerns before you commit to any conversations with another clinician. Clarify your role and that of the other therapist. Be clear about your goals. And always get signed releases—even when you don't think you need one, get one—this helps impress on your client the seriousness with which you consider his request.

The conditions under which it might be a good idea to coordinate with another therapist are when family therapy or couples therapy is going on simultaneously to individual treatment. Also, when you are treating children, you may get involved in extended treatment conversations, but it still gets complicated. Agreeing to talk to others often raises the question of what to say and what to omit. Clients have the right to worry about personal information getting loose. "Let's talk about it in here first. I want us to think about our goals in talking to this other therapist. Also, I need to know what you want me to keep private or want to share."

"When I Go Off to College I Want to Get Into Therapy at the Counseling Center. Can My Therapist There Contact You?"

This seems like a legitimate request in order to coordinate treatment and help your client adjust to a new situation. Such a contact could help build on the work that this client has been doing with you. At a minimum, it makes your client feel secure. Still, we would also wonder why she feels unable to explain her therapy without assistance. It is probably most helpful to encourage your client, "I believe that you could describe our work better than I could. Before you leave town, we will go over the different problems that we have talked about. Let's discuss what you have learned here and what you want to accomplish at college. Then if you want your college counselor to contact me, sure, I'm open to it." This discussion could also foster a greater understanding about what she needs from a new therapist.

"Would I Benefit From Medication? Should I See a Psychiatrist?"

The decision about whether medication is indicated for a particular client is deeply important and highly idiosyncratic. Many people attach a stigma to receiving chemical assistance for their mental health. Others are looking for relief from any bottle. Clients sometimes have unrealistic expectations about the magic results that psychotropic medications hold, and they minimize the potential negative side effects. For other clients, the opposite is true—they disparage the potential benefit from drugs because they fear negative physical reactions. People benefit from the right prescription and proper use of medication when they need biological intervention.

You are not an expert in this area, but it is your responsibility to examine your client's symptoms, beliefs, and desires about medication before you answer. "Those are serious and important questions. I need to understand your thinking. What symptoms do you have that medication might help?" Then you are in a better position to suggest, "I can give you the names of some psychiatrists. You can get a medical consult, and then we will have more information." Encourage your clients to get their medications from psychiatrists rather than from family practitioners. Keeping up with research and understanding medication uses and interactions is what psychiatrists are trained to do.

Your treatment of clients who are lower functioning, either physically or psychologically, and who need a coordinated support network will necessarily involve more outside people. This could be day treatment or hospital personnel, family members, nutritionists, guardians, caregivers, or attorneys. Clients involved in the court system or drug abuse programs will have other people involved. Working with children always involves parents and often school personnel. Psychiatric medications mean that other practitioners have a hand in treatment. Coordinating physical care with psychological care can be cumbersome and involve multiple people and slow-moving institutions. It can also be a good way to enhance both professional endeavors. Although often indicated for complete care, consultations can change the nature of the privacy between you and your client.

FURTHER THOUGHTS

"He who controls others may be powerful, but he who has mastered himself is mightier still."

—Lao Tzu

We have spent this chapter proposing responses to client's questions about involving others in treatment. For a moment, let's turn to you and think about the crowd you carry into the treatment room. You will be forever surprised by how much your own upbringing and your family, as well as former supervisors, teachers, and therapists, show up in your office. Sometimes a therapy interaction sparks a memory of a much-beloved elementary school teacher, other times it may be a feared, racist neighbor. Often we are not aware of the original source of a belief we bring with us.

Be open to the reality that you will deal with actual, imagined, past, present, invited, and uninvited people from your client's world and that you will learn from all of these voices, welcome and otherwise. Because so many other people are indirectly involved in all of our identities, it makes sense that our clients would sometimes want to involve significant others directly in their therapy as well. Certainly, therapists can be effective and mediate a discussion or keep it focused so that there is a chance of resolving a problem, and in those instances, therapy is enhanced by the involvement of others.

When clients ask to bring in another person as a visitor, the main concern is whether it facilitates the client's therapy. If it helps your client to talk to his mother or partner with you present, it may be a good idea. One task for you is to gather information about the goals and anticipate as much as you can to make it a good exchange. When clients bring significant others with them into therapy, you may come to better appreciate the job your elementary school teacher did when she had playground duty and had to coax unruly children into playing nicely.

SUGGESTED READINGS

Bea, S., & Tesar, G. (2002). A primer for referring patients for psychotherapy. *Cleveland Clinic Journal of Medicine, 69*, 113–127.

Burns, W. J., & Hatziyannakis, C. V. (1998). Knowing when to refer. In M. Herson & V. B. Van Hesselt (Eds.), *Basic interviewing: Practical guide for counselors and clinicians* (pp. 197–216). Mahwah, NJ: Erlbaum.

Leigh, A. (1994). *Referral and termination issues for counselors.* London, England: Sage.

Lloyd, G. (2003). Why refer to a psychiatrist? *Clinical Medicine, 3*, 99–101.

Martire, L. M., & Schulz, R. (2007). Involving family in psychosocial interventions for chronic illness. *Current Directions in Psychology Science, 16*, 90–94.

Norcross, J. C. (2006). Integrating self-help into psychotherapy: 16 practical suggestions. *Professional Psychology: Research and Practice, 37*, 683–693.

Sherman, R., Shumsky, A., & Rountree, Y. B. (1994). *Enlarging the therapeutic circle: The therapists' guide to collaborative therapy with families and schools.* New York, NY: Brunner/Mazel.

Yalom, I. (2002). *Gift of therapy: An open letter to a new generation of therapists and their patients.* New York, NY: Harper.

Zambonie, B. D. (2006). Therapeutic considerations in working with the family, friends, and partners of transgendered tndividuals. *The Family Journal: Counseling and Therapy for Couples and Families, 14*, 174–179.

CHAPTER

20

Out of
the Office

It's a strange experience, after working in a soundproofed room with promises of confidentiality and clear attention to boundaries and privacy, to sit down in a coffee shop or movie theater, to enter the grocery store or dressing room, or to pull off your sweaty clothes in the gym locker room and see a client. Of course clients exist during the in-between hours, and so do we.

Linda

After working hard in therapy for months and changing some pretty bad marital behavior, Marjorie suggested, "I would like you to meet my kids and see how great they are. Why don't you come over for dinner?" Declining politely was the easy part. "I can't do that. As much as I would enjoy meeting your kids, it would be uncomfortable." The harder part was deciding whether to address the meaning behind the invitation, which was Marjorie's wish to

(continued)

let me know, "See, despite the other areas of life that I've messed up, I am a good mother." My decision was to remain aware of her need to feel competent, save that discussion for another time, and, in the moment, to acknowledge her genuine talent for being a good mom.

Extending the relationship outside of the office is generally frowned upon, although most of the therapists we know have gone to a client's wedding, graduation, baseball game, or visited someone in the hospital. Clinicians who treat children sometimes visit their homes or schools, and those who work with severely mentally ill clients or individuals plagued by phobias will also do some of their work outside of the office. Practitioners in nontraditional settings are often working in places other than the conventional office. And, for all the people who work outside of offices, there are still boundaries and clinicians still attend to them.

But most of us stay in the office most of the time, and the walls of the consulting room remain the accepted physical boundary for sessions. Creating a safe alliance is an essential element in treatment, and your office becomes the private, predictable place where that can occur. Keeping the treatment bound by time and place allows you and your clients to do your work. So, when you consider leaving that space and engaging clients elsewhere, you have to think hard about it.

Clients' questions about meeting outside of the office and invitations to get together can be motivated by different wishes. Usually, they indicate the desire to be connected, to level an unequal relationship, or to have you share in an event. Less frequently, the questions reflect a fear that clients will unexpectedly encounter you in some awkward situation. Occasionally, invitations to meet outside of the office may signal the initial step toward beginning an inappropriate dual relationship. In the questions and answers that follow, we address a variety of questions, different motivations, accidental meetings, and cyberspace connections.

QUESTIONS

The following questions are answered in the Responses section:

"Can we meet for coffee?"

"Do you want to attend a lecture/book discussion/ballgame?"

"Do you belong to the Y? Do you mind if I join?" " Do you want to work out together at the gym?"

"Can I go to the same 12-step group as you?"

"Will you come and see me while I am in the hospital for surgery/having a baby?"

"Will you attend my graduation/wedding/musical performance/ speech/business grand opening?"

"What do I say if I run into you on the street or at the movies?"

"Why did you ignore me in the supermarket/party/art fair/ church?" "Why did you talk to me in the supermarket? No one knows that I see you."

"Can we have our session someplace else?"

"I have a great business idea, and we work so well as a team. Why don't we go into it together?"

A more modern consideration that we examine in this chapter is that outside of the office can now mean Facebook, MySpace, web pages, blogs, YouTube, Twitter posts, and other cyberspace locations that make therapists more and more visible to their clients.

The following questions about electronic contact are also addressed:

"I read your website. I didn't know that you are married/do hypnosis/have children/write books/raise Collies/moved from California/play drums. Is it true?"

"I saw your blog/posts on Facebook." "I stumbled on your YouTube video where you were singing karaoke and seemed pretty wasted. Do you always party like that?"

"Can I show you these pictures on my phone or the computer that I have with me? "Can we log on to your computer and look at my stuff?"

RESPONSES

"Can We Meet for Coffee?"

You need to understand the intent behind this question, so ask, "What are you thinking?" Meetings outside of the office, even innocent engagements for coffee, have the potential to erode the nature of the therapeutic relationship. Outside get-togethers increase the possibility that your judgment will become clouded, your client will develop expectations that cannot be met, you will alter the essential nature of treatment, or the two of you will change the therapy into something else. Many of these sorts of questions are innocent, based on cultural differences or in a naive understanding of what is expected. Clients feel close to you, and additional contact, like having coffee, seems like a good way to spend time together. Once you have a better understanding of your client's wishes, you can say, "As enjoyable as that would be, meeting outside would change our relationship, and I wouldn't want to take the chance on compromising our work together." If, in your opinion, your client wants and needs more time, think about increasing the frequency of sessions.

If your client needs a further explanation of why you keep the relationship confined to the office, you can briefly mention your reasoning about strong boundaries. "There are real reasons why I can't have an outside relationship with you. Therapy works because it is private, confidential, and confined to this time and place. You can trust it and know that my goal is figuring out what is in your best interest. Once those boundaries are loosened or gone, it isn't a unique place any longer."

Occasionally, you will meet a client who wants to change the therapeutic relationship into some other affiliation. Your client may feel under-the-microscope, uncomfortable, exposed in some other way, or excessively ill at ease and attempt to undermine the authority and place of therapy by taking it outside of the office. These rare clients need to hear a firm "No" regarding meeting for coffee and the reason why. "I am aware that you have some discomfort about being here, but this is the safest place to talk about your problems, and that is what we are here to do. I know therapy isn't easy, but you are doing well and will get more comfortable."

"Do You Want to Attend a Lecture/Book Discussion/ Ballgame?"

Most invitations are attempts to be friendly, to get to know you better, to pursue a shared interest, or to equalize the relationship. The wish to make the relationship balanced or normal is understandable because the necessary disclosures in therapy expose the client and put power into the therapist's hands. Clients share some profoundly personal aspects of their lives with us; we do not share our lives with them. We put our hearts and minds into the session, but the revelations are predominantly one-sided, making clients vulnerable. Sharing regular activities can be an attempt to redress the one-sidedness of the relationship. We are fond of many clients, and if we had met them under other circumstances, we might have become good friends, but it didn't happen that way. Multiple roles compromise our work. The goal of treatment is to make one person—the client—healthier, not to make friends or to expose the therapist to new events. You can say, "Thanks for thinking about me. I don't usually see clients outside of the office, but I'll be interested in hearing about it." or "It's nice of you to include me, but I have a policy of avoiding any dual relationships. It could hurt therapy."

"Do You Belong to the Y? Do You Mind if I Join?" "Do You Want to Work Out Together at the Gym?"

Most clients do not want to be next to you on the treadmill at the gym or in yoga classes, in swimming pools, or in sports leagues. As one client told Linda, "I know that we belong to the same gym, and I worry that I'll run into you in the locker room and one of us will be naked." "Which one of us?" Linda asked. "Well, you've already seen me emotionally naked, so that might be manageable, but I don't think that I could deal with you naked." It's hard to disagree with that observation, and her clarity is admirable.

Seventy-five years ago, the Freudians would have had a field day with that interchange, but practically speaking, without espousing one theory or another, therapists and clients do better when they don't have to deal with the complexities of public outside engagements, whether it is a church or a gym. "Do you mind if I join?" is best answered, "It's a fine gym/church, and I go there to get some exercise/spiritual renewal. I don't want to offend you by not being terribly social if we run into each other while I'm there."

At the same time, there are situations where overlapping relation-ships are inevitable, but they can be limited. "Do you want to work out together at the gym?" might best be answered, "As much as it might make the time pass quickly, I have to decline." You are not rejecting your client; you are simply acknowledging that you have the right to some free time at the gym.

"Can I Go to the Same 12-Step Group as You?"

Melissa Perrin, Psy.D., addictions expert

Your client's need is to get better faster by following you into your sphere of perceived mental health. In this joint endeavor, your cli-ent's wish is to also become healthy. A secondary hope the client may have is to have more opportunities to connect with you, get to know you, and occasionally, to receive more treatment without going into the office or paying for it. It is crucial to maintain sepa-rate boundaries between your office and the 12-step meetings. For your continued health and recovery, clients and meetings should not go together. You need the safety and space of your consistent meetings, where you are able to express yourself honestly and work through rough patches without having to worry about professional appearances.

Twelve-step groups have also anticipated this issue, and in Tradition 8 of the 12 Traditions (the suggested guidelines of behavior within the 12-step groups) it states that "when recovering individuals are not able to work through issues on their own, they must seek out paid professionals." The interpretation of this tradition includes the expectation that clients and therapists have relationships that are professional, thereby eliminating attendance at the same meetings on a regular basis, except in small communities where 12-step meetings are limited in number.

Most clinicians who work a healthy recovery program that adheres to the 12-step programs will talk openly with a client about the boundaries of personal recovery work as it relates to the 12 Tradition guidelines, and the health and well-being of both individuals. This usually leads the session into productive discussions of balance, moderation, delayed gratification, and boundaries. I suggest a direct answer to "Do you mind if I go to that meeting also?" of "I cannot tell you whether you can attend that meeting or not. Tradition 8 states that we cannot have a professional relationship while attending the same meetings. Therefore, if you decide to go to that meeting regularly, I can refer you to another clinician so that you can continue to receive therapy. This professional relationship will need to end. Let's talk about what will serve you best."

"Will You Come and See Me While I Am in the Hospital for Surgery/Having a Baby?"

Think about whether you want to do this, and only go if you want to. If not, say, "I'm not able to visit, but I would like to give you a call." If you believe that a visit is a good idea and you want to do it, say, "Yes, I would like to, but let's wait and see how you feel about a visit from me after surgery/giving birth. You call me if it still feels right, and I'll come over if I can." These events are rare and don't set any strange patterns or evoke other expectations, but they can be awkward.

There may be other times when you go to the client. Linda treated a woman who was terminally ill, and when she could no longer get to the office, Linda went to her home as long as her client wanted the visits. That was a choice made with the best interest of the client in mind; there are no hard-and-fast rules about visiting very ill clients.

It is trickier when you work in nontraditional settings where you might meet out of the office frequently. Hinda Pozner is a social worker in Maine who worked with autistic children in their homes.

Hinda Pozner

I traveled many miles each day, going from suburban areas to farms to backwoods homes, never knowing if a goose would try to bite at my heels or a poodle would be coming home from the groomer. Adults and siblings asked me many questions that sometimes, unfortunately, had no immediate answers. But, I always tried to respond in ways that were specific to that child, that situation, that home, and that diagnosis. Because of the complexity of the diagnosis of autism, and the uniqueness of each child, sometimes there were no answers. I could provide therapeutic tools, encouragement, and truths. This type of intervention left a few moms and dads questioning my effectiveness and my motives. Others wondered if their child would be removed from their home if I said so, and some wanted desperately to know if their child could ever be typical.

Another common dilemma in small towns is that families share information at church and at the mom-and-pop stores, and they compare notes. Then, they would ask me, "Why is my neighbor's child doing this or that and my child isn't?" or "Why do you go to her house more often than my house?" or "Why are you helping that child at school?" I could not answer questions about other children. At times it felt like I needed a neighborhood release because of confidentiality. So, when I had to say, "I can't discuss this with you," I was taking a chance that barriers to an honest and effective therapeutic relationship might develop.

Working in people's homes has the tendency to blur boundaries, and you will have to respond to questions that aren't usually relevant in an office. You will be confronted with neighbors who want to stay during treatment, questions from family members that cause you to doubt the family's literacy or whether the parents can understand the information you provide and follow guidelines, and always, you have to respond in ways that ensure that the environment remains safe for *you*.

"Will You Attend My Graduation/Wedding/Speech/ Business Grand Opening?"

Celebrations are wonderful times, and clients often attribute at least some of their successes in school, business, or relationships to their growth in therapy and understandably want you to share in the festivities. Appreciate the invitation by saying, "That is a wonderful invitation. I need you to think some more about whether you would really be comfortable with me in attendance, and I need to think about whether it interferes with our work here." Then ask yourself, do you want to attend? If you don't for any reason, decline warmly. If you would like to go, ask yourself, "Why?" Consider discussing your interest with your supervisor or another therapist. It is an honor to be invited, but will your presence make you or the graduate/bridal couple uncomfortable?

One compromise that many therapists make is to attend a wedding or graduation ceremony and skip the family festivities that often follow. You can always decline and say, "Even if I'm not there, I'll be thinking about you." Linda went to a wedding and for the first and only time accepted an invitation to attend the reception because she was very fond of the bride/client. The strange stares from the family were manageable, but midway through the beautiful reception, Linda was called by a bridesmaid because someone thought the bride was having an anxiety attack in the women's bathroom and needed her therapist, not her mom. It was awkward for Linda and the bride. In situations like weddings or graduations, you can prepare ahead of time and discuss the particulars with your client, but surprises do occur.

Charlie

I am more likely to attend a significant event when invited by an adolescent client rather than an adult, because it seems to be more important for the therapeutic alliance. Rich was a high school junior I was seeing in therapy. Although he was a thoroughly likable young man, he was pretty unsuccessful in most of his endeavors because he didn't put a lot of thought into his undertakings. During one session, Rich asked me if I would attend one of his football games. He was proud of the fact that, although he was not a big kid, he was a starting player on his team. I really didn't want to spend a Friday night at one of his games, so, as I thanked him for his invitation, and pointed out the pride he felt in this accomplishment, I also stated, "You know sometimes these situations can be awkward, for instance, what would you say to one of your family or friends if they saw me there?" Rich replied, "Well, I expect that you would sit with my family. They all know you, and if a friend asked about you I would just say that you were one of my dad's friends." Clearly he had put much thought into this invitation, and I saw how important it was for him. I attended his game and took several pictures of him playing so that we could share the event together in his next session.

With adolescents and children, if you accept an invitation to attend a graduation, you may need to explain more. "I'm thrilled for you and will be at the ceremony, but I won't attend the party. That's for your family. We will celebrate in here when you have your next session."

With regard to events that are more available to the general public, like a speech or a business opening, your anonymity will be more possible, so your attendance would be less conspicuous. If you work with more severely disturbed clients, you may have additional out-of-the-office contact that is an acknowledged aspect of your work together. Even then, you may be blindsided by invitations.

Lee Rodin, L.C.S.W.

Years ago, I worked with Jim, a slow-moving, depressed man of 42. Jim had been in treatment with me for seven years when he asked, "Will you come to my house to see my model train set?" I had never gone to a client's house and said, "Let me think about it." I talked it over with my consultant, who said she wasn't sure; it could be okay or it might be strange. She asked how I felt about it, and I said I wasn't comfortable going.

At the next session, I told Jim, "I discussed going over to your house with my consultant, and she thought it would be better not to, because it would be a breach of boundaries." Jim didn't react much at the time, but the following week, he sat down and said, "This is my last session; I won't be coming to therapy anymore." I was stunned. "Why?" I asked. "I was really shocked last week when you said you'd talked about me with someone else. I didn't even know you had a consultant and wouldn't have told you certain things if I thought you would tell anyone." I said, "Everybody has a supervisor or consultant. It's the way we check ourselves to make sure we're doing a good job and not missing anything," I continued, "I wanted to do the best job I could for you. It's the same person who was my supervisor at the agency, and you knew about her." Jim replied, "I thought you stopped talking to her after you left the agency. The two of you have been talking about me, laughing together about me." I was unable to convince him that we weren't laughing at him and that there was nothing malicious in the conversations, and he quit.

(continued)

I have thought about this over the years. I regret that I put the responsibility on my consultant. I could have said, "I feel uncomfortable about going to your house because it would be relating in a different way. I'm not sure it would be the best thing for the therapy." Also, now I would directly handle his accusation that we were laughing at him by stating, "After working together for seven years, and seeing my commitment to you and our work together, do you really think I would laugh at you? Do you think your perceptions and experience could be so off that you could work closely with someone for so long who would laugh at you?" At the time, these questions felt too personal, that I would be coming forward as an individual, stepping out of the professional persona. Now I realize it was the one most important point to address. Maybe Jim would still have left treatment, but I would have known I was authentic and had tried everything.

"What Do I Say if I Run Into You on the Street or at the Movies?"

In smaller towns, or if you work near home, you run into clients more often than you do in big cities. This may be pleasant or unpleasant for either of you. Therapists like their privacy and want to be able to scold their children, kiss their partner, buy cookies, and wear sloppy clothes without being scrutinized for a later discussion, but it is part of the job to deal with it, if it comes up. Many clients keep therapy a secret and like to protect the relationship, so they are uncomfortable running into you outside of the office and may ignore you, which is their right. You can ask, "What feels comfortable to you? You can ignore me or say hello. It's your call." If a client tells you that she will just pass by, inquire, "That's fine, but I'm curious, what are you worried about?" This always leads to an interesting discussion about therapy, privacy, secrets, or stigma.

Linda

I was in the lobby of the local movie theater and a couple walked by. They had been in marital therapy with me for most of the year, ending recently. The wife waved and called out a greeting. I waved back and heard the husband lean over and ask her, "Who was that?" Although you may be concerned about being seen, it also happens that clients often pass you by and don't recognize you when you are in a different context.

It doesn't take long for your friends and family to realize that, when you bump into a person on the street and don't make an introduction, it may be a client. If asked later, you can say to friends or family, "It's someone I know from work." Or, if you stop to say hello you can tell your companions, "Go on ahead, I'll catch up."

"Why Did You Ignore Me in the Supermarket/Party/ Art Fair/Church?" "Why Did You Talk to Me in the Supermarket? No One Knows That I See You."

Both varieties of this question come up quite often. Clients are very different about whether they want to know you on the street or in places outside of the office. Even if they want to say hello, it can be disconcerting to some. It is perfectly appropriate to mention your policy, for example, "I make a practice of not saying hello unless you want me to, or if you say hello first." Or, you don't have to say anything beforehand and can discuss your policy after an incidental encounter. Saying a casual hello on the street is not nearly as awkward as winding up at the same wedding or sitting in the next booth at a restaurant (one client noticed Linda and asked to have her table changed) when the encounter is extended.

Linda

In my old office building, the suites circled a center stairway. After a client left to go home, I walked out to go to the bathroom. I went in one direction while she went in the other, but we met at the landing in front of the staircase. She was startled and sputtered, "But, you're out of your office. You aren't supposed to be out of your office!" Knowing that she had a good sense of humor, I responded, "It's okay, I leave the office, but I never leave the building." We did have a follow-up discussion about how strange it was to meet me out of the usual context.

"Can We Have Our Session Someplace Else?"

Simply put, "No." Once, when the elevator broke without warning, one therapist met a client who had a heart condition in the back booth of a nearby coffee shop. It was far from ideal because she relentlessly scanned the room, worrying about interfering noises or intruding people. Another time, when there was smoke in the building and everyone was evacuated, another clinician, always determined to keep therapy going, tried to move the session to her car, but that particular technique was not repeated. Sessions in places other than the office need to be reserved for client emergencies. Generally, it is far better to reschedule the session.

Charlie

Fifty-nine-year-old Ben presented himself interpersonally as bumbling through life. He had first come to me six years earlier when his wife of 30 years was diagnosed with cancer. He was stunned and did not know how to react. I saw him twice a month for about a year, and he left feeling better. Now, I was seeing him mourn her death 15 months before. With no children and no relatives in this area, as well as having only intermittent, part-time work, he was feeling very lost and alone. We had arranged a session to fit his schedule, and as luck would have it, there were no rooms available in the house where I practice. All seven treatment rooms were in use during the hour that we had scheduled.

I called Ben about 20 minutes before our session and told him the situation. He chimed in, "Well, I am already on my way, so why don't we just meet at the coffee shop on the corner and have our appointment there." I had considered this possibility, and I know that some other therapists in my practice have done this before, although I shy away from it. In this situation, I was grateful that he made the suggestion rather than me. I also appreciated his use of the term "appointment," which implied that he was open to changing location, not the nature of the meeting. Had he said "Let's meet for coffee," I might have reacted differently.

Instead, I said, "Well, that is an option, maybe a better one than rescheduling. My biggest concern is one of confidentiality." He replied: "I am a little worried about that too, but if we can't find a private space, we can reschedule at that point." It was clear to me that he was eager to get together and that he was going to be a partner in weighing the benefits and risks of this unusual situation. We met at the coffee shop, scouted out a private booth, and had a very productive session together. I duly noted the exceptional nature surrounding this interaction in my notes. At the next session, I checked it out with him. I wondered whether he continued to feel that our meeting at the coffee shop was okay. He gave me a smirk and said, "Yeah, of course it was fine—better than not meeting." I agreed with him. This session stretched the boundaries, but it didn't violate them.

"I Have a Great Business Idea, and We Work So Well as a Team. Why Don't We Go Into It Together?"

This question raises the dilemma of a business dual relationship. Dual relationships are addressed in all of the ethics books because they can lead to therapy being compromised, often seriously. At the most basic level, a dual relationship adds another dimension to treatment; you are no longer exclusively the mental health practitioner who is concerned only with your client's best interests. You now have an interest of your own that could conflict with your client's interests. Dual relationships are trouble that you can generally avoid. Acknowledge your client's compliment by saying, "We certainly are a good team in here, but I could never ethically have a business relationship with you, because that could have a bad impact on our work."

"I Read Your Website. I Didn't Know That You Are Married/Do Hypnosis/Have Children/Raise Collies/Moved From California/Play Drums. Is It True?"

As noted earlier, cyberspace has created a new set of out-of-the-office questions. Cyberspace allows for a different means of out-of-office contact, but the reasons or motivations for questions are not new. What is new and feels different is the amount of knowledge that can be learned about you if you appear on the Web. So, it is useful to think ahead and be prepared to deal with questions involving information that you may not have known was available.

Answers to website questions are pretty standard: Either it is you or it isn't. "Yes, what was your reaction to reading my website?" More importantly, what did this new information mean to your client? Did it raise reactions that ought to be examined? Ask: "Did it surprise you to read about me?" You are being seen by clients and future clients, so be cautious about the material you include.

Websites will become increasingly common. If you want one, think about it carefully before you create it, and research other websites to see what type of content fits your work. You can use web pages effectively to market your practice, post professional biographical information, and list practice information and policies.

Websites are more static than blogs and therefore easier to create once and leave unchanged. Blogs have the potential to create a dialogue and present timely information. Linda recently created a psychology blog, so she had to carefully think about what type of material she would post. The question she asks herself in order to determine what is in and what is out is, "Will I be okay with some imaginary, very sensitive client reading this particular post?" Linda's posts are about psychological ideas but not about therapy. This area is still very new for clinicians. The guidelines and ethics for blogging will continue to be developed. For now, read your words as if you are a stranger; it will help you to decide what to put into cyberspace and what to keep in your personal journal.

"I Saw Your Blog/Posts on Facebook." "I Stumbled on Your YouTube Video Where You Were Singing Karaoke and Seemed Pretty Wasted. Do You Always Party Like That?"

You are entitled to a personal life, but if you put material into cyberspace, clients may find it. Photos pasted into your album are kept on a shelf in your home; photos posted to your blog, Flickr, MySpace, or Facebook and others are far more available to the scrutiny of clients. This sort of question will become increasingly common and gives all of us a lot to think about. You give up control of your information when it is on the Web, so think about it ahead of time. Clients will be curious. The present level of contact is only an introduction to whatever the next generation of cyber-communication is going to be.

When getting questions like these, take a moment to shift from feeling violated to a more therapeutic frame of mind. Your brain may scream, "How did you simply stumble upon a video of what I do in my private life?" but remember that you can be a figure of major intrigue to your client, and some clients are very curious. Even when clients search out information, they can have strong reactions to seeing you out of context. An appropriate response could be, "How did you react to seeing me in a different context?" or "You know that I have a life outside of this office as well. What was it like to see a snapshot of that life?"

"Can I Show You These Emails/Pictures on My Phone/ Computer?" "Can We Log on to Your Computer?"

"Sure." Clients used to bring in notes, journals, photo albums, or letters. Now they bring in laptops; it is still bringing in their world to share, just in a new form. When the question shifts to, "Can we log on to your computer and look at my stuff?" or "I brought my flash drive. Can we use your computer to look at some material?" it changes into a more personal request. For us, personal computers are not to be opened up to every client. It might be different at an agency where a computer terminal is shared by all of the staff members, but it feels similar to inviting a client into the kitchen area or staff room—just a little too intimate, so we would decline.

FURTHER THOUGHTS

> "You often meet your fate on the road you take to avoid it."
> —French proverb

Our work has exposed us to many strange experiences and questions about extra-office encounters. In this chapter, we stayed with reasonable questions and away from those that describe unethical behavior. Regarding questions that pull for unethical behavior, a clear "no, that is unethical," or "that would constitute insurance fraud," or "that is unethical and a bad idea for other reasons as well," doesn't take too much thought. Sometimes, however, you need to explain further—not shame—because your client is genuinely confused. Always wonder how each question fits into your client's psychology or into the therapy relationship.

Generally, meeting outside of the office compromises much of what is empowering about the therapy relationship. Therapy is a unique relationship because its goals are furthering the best interests of the client and focusing exclusively on the attainment of client mental health. But it is also a real relationship that works best when it is contained, uncontaminated and protected from the complexities of other types of relationships in which people engage. We are saying, "think about your outside-the-office activities," we are not saying, "give up your life." Because you provide a very personal service, your outside behaviors matter, and clients hope that your in-the-office persona and the one outside are consistent.

Many clinicians have nontraditional work settings and spend time with clients out of the office, although most training concentrates on one-on-one, in-the-office psychotherapy. This singular focus does not make use of other settings, potential roles, and techniques that will be responsive to clients with specialized needs or those who could benefit from other strategies.

Atkinson et al. (1993) considered different roles that counselors may assume depending on various client needs and work roles, which they listed as Adviser, Advocate, Facilitator of Indigenous Support Systems, Facilitator of Indigenous Healing Systems, Consultant, Change Agent, Counselor, and Psychotherapist. As you can easily imagine, there would be times when these roles draw the therapist out of the office, so thinking about them and their place in your work can be instructive.

SUGGESTED READINGS

Atkinson, D., Thompson, C., & Grant, S. (1993). A three-dimensional model for counseling racial/ethnic minorities. *The Counseling Psychologist, 21,* 257–277.

Clinton, B. K., Silverman, B. C., &. Brendel, D. H., (2010). Patient-targeted googling: The ethics of searching online for patient information. *Harvard Review of Psychiatry, 18,* 103–112.

Hunt, C., Shochet, I., & King, R. (2005). The use of e-mail in the therapy process. *Australia and New Zealand Journal of Family Therapy, 26*(1), 10–20.

Kessler, L. E., & Waehler, C. A. (2005). Addressing multiple relationships between clients and therapists in the lesbian, gay, bisexual, and transgender community. *Professional Psychology: Research and Practice, 36,* 66–72.

Pope, K. S., & Keith-Spiegel, P. (2008). A practical approach to boundaries in psychotherapy: Making decisions, bypassing blunders, and mending fences. *Journal of Clinical Psychology: In Session, 64,* 638–652.

Reed, G. M., McLaughlin, C. J., & Milholland, K. (2000). Ten interdisciplinary principles for professional practice in telehealth: Implications for psychology. *Professional Psychology; Research and Practice, 31,* 170–178.

CHAPTER

21

Keeping in Touch

Do you remember the final day of camp when you were a kid, or the night of high school graduation, or packing up after your freshman year at college? You probably swore to keep in touch with the people who had been so meaningful to you during those intense days. You meant it. Maybe you kept in touch, maybe not, but you understand the normal desire to maintain a connection with people who make a difference in your life.

Linda

Heather came into treatment because she had a miserable breakup and was despairing of ever finding a good guy. We talked about many aspects of her life, past and present, including her intermittent eating disorder and body image issues. Therapy helped, and when she left, she was dating a nice man, had improved the relationships with her parents, and was working at a new job. I did not hear from her again until two years later, when she returned married and pregnant. The pregnancy reawakened her body image and eating disorder issues. She was terrified. She equated pregnancy with obesity, and her anxiety skyrocketed. Again, she worked hard in treatment and left. After that, every year for about 10 years, I received a Christmas card, first with one child posed against the fireplace, then two children, and eventually three children. She kept in touch with me, and I understood the beautiful children to mean that she was able to tolerate additional pregnancies, so her body image problems must have remained manageable.

Keeping in touch has always been a fact of life during therapy and after treatment ends. Now, keeping in touch can also include the world of cyberspace—same issues, new packaging. This chapter examines questions that arise during and after therapy about being in contact. Also, we attend to some of the underlying concerns, such as whether you will be around if your client needs you, and especially after therapy ends, clients wonder where you are and if you are okay.

QUESTIONS

The following questions are answered in the Responses section:

> "What can I do about this problem between sessions?"
> "Can we keep in touch between sessions?"
> "Can I e-mail you?" "Can I check in online?" "Can I text you?"
> "Will you be my Friend on Facebook/MySpace?"
> "Can we have sessions online?"
> "Can we stay in contact?" "Can I stop by and maybe we could get coffee?

RESPONSES

"What Can I Do About This Problem Between Sessions?"

If it is unwise or impracticable to have additional sessions, most therapists are comfortable providing ideas for clients to use between sessions, or they refer clients to outside resources for help to extend the work being done. Consider offering reading materials, behavioral ideas, or thoughts to hold onto when clients are on their own. Linda sometimes jots down a thought on a sticky note and hands it across to a client to affix to a computer screen or in a notebook.

There are also many groups, books, classes, and websites that can be good adjuncts to therapy. Information about physical health, mental health, online support groups, or relaxation downloads can all be useful. Be careful, though, not to recommend any site that you have not checked out yourself. And, don't throw everything at your clients. That would be about your anxiety, not theirs. You might overwhelm them with information and unwittingly suggest that you are not confident in the therapy process. Say, "Let's figure out what makes sense for you," and then you can tailor your ideas to the problem at hand.

When you work with children, depending on their ages, you probably want to consult with and inform parents when you give their children additional places to get information, like the library or Internet.

You will respond differently to each client based on your client's personality and presenting problem. A client who is obsessed with working on a solution to his problem is the one you might tell to lighten up. On the other hand, your client who has trouble maintaining her focus could use some skills to practice between sessions. For clients with interpersonal concerns, their homework might include practicing social relations, and depressed clients might commit to a couple of healthy activities. The point here is to work with each client to identify ways that she can continue her gains.

Our friend and colleague, Chicago psychologist Margit Kir-Stimon, Ph.D., has developed a couple of excellent ways to stay in touch during and between sessions.

Margit Kir-Stimon, Ph.D.

At times I've had clients who, because of learning disabilities or other neurological issues, have a difficult time keeping our conversations in their working memories. I find this to be typical of adult ADD clients. One client, when he became excited by our subject matter, asked me to e-mail the ideas to him. Otherwise, he knew that the discussion wouldn't stick. I did, and this evolved into a different way to work together. After our sessions, I e-mailed the gist of the conversation to him. This technique was effective as a cognitive prompt. It became useful for maintaining an emotional connection, and the client had a concrete document to read and remind him about the content of our work. In many ways it was helpful to me as well. I got the chance to digest our sessions, think about content, and improve my specific recall of material. While it is not feasible to offer this technique to all clients, I do suggest it to people who have difficulty retaining the substance of sessions.

When you decide to keep in touch by phone or Internet, be sure that the means of communication is secure and confidential.

"Can We Keep in Touch Between Sessions?"

When a client successfully runs the marathon, it is fun to get an e-mail immediately. If it is a sad situation, like a bereavement, we would also want to be informed, although it seems like a phone call is a better alternative, and we would return the communication by phone, or at least with an offer to phone. Another example is when a despondent client cannot come in every day during her crisis and does not require hospitalization, but you deem it necessary to stay in contact between meetings. We might say, "Let's plan a nightly five-minute check-in." Staying in touch or checking in regularly between sessions needs a good reason and requires a lot of work, so clinicians tend to offer it sparingly. Before agreeing to keep in contact on a regular basis, think hard about the implications for managing boundaries and for the message it sends to the client about his or her ability to manage independently. Finally, excessive keeping in touch will breed resentment in you—quicker than you think.

If you have provided your e-mail address and a client oversteps boundaries (e.g., forwarding every e-mail he receives from his ex-wife), it is important to address this and reset boundaries as you would in any other boundary-crossing situation. Just because you have made yourself available online does not mean that overcommunicating is okay.

Linda

I have one client whose depression made it difficult to stay focused and accomplish normal tasks. When she asked about ways to change this pattern, we came up with the idea that she would create a reasonable, daily, written schedule. She was very willing to try. The old behaviors made her feel terrible about herself. Not ready to go it alone, we agreed that she would e-mail me her schedule every day, and I would read it but no response was required. My reading it made her feel more accountable and less alone in the endeavor. It isn't a big deal to me to take a moment to read it each day, and the exercise has been useful to her in keeping a focus and prioritizing activities.

"Can I E-mail You?" "Can I Check in Online?" "Can I Text You?"

These questions come up all the time. "Feel free to e-mail me between sessions if it is important, but I don't e-mail back extensively. I'll let you know that I received your e-mail, and we can discuss your thoughts at our next session." or "I prefer to communicate in person. If you want to jot down your thoughts and bring them in to our next session, I think it would benefit us to talk about them then." or "I rarely check e-mail and would not want you to get the wrong idea if you don't hear from me in a reasonable time frame." If a client is having a particularly difficult week, you might offer, "If you'd like to check in on e-mail or leave me a voice mail to let me know how everything went, I'd be glad to hear from you." In an emergency, you might insist on it.

All of these methods are best used for quick confirmations, not for serious conversation. Tone is often absent when e-mails are sent, and misinterpretation occurs frequently. In addition, your writing persona may be different from your in-person persona. Nonetheless, different therapists have to decide how available they would like to be to clients via e-mail. Be clear, because boundaries can get blurry depending on how much or what type of communication via e-mail is acceptable to you. Keep these ideas, and the particular client, in mind when you decide what to answer.

In our experience, most clients are very considerate and send us e-mails the way that people have previously phoned—sparingly and with good reason.

"Will You Be My Friend on Facebook/MySpace?"

These questions usually come via e-mail, and it may not be brought up by your client during a session. If you simply ignore the request, you may appear to be rejecting. Unfortunately, the amount of information that is placed on the sites is probably inappropriate to be shared with clients or for you to receive as therapist. It may be best to do nothing until a session and then say, "I see you found me on Facebook/MySpace. I wanted to talk about why I feel uncomfortable accepting your friend request. To me, this feels too revealing of a large quantity of information. You may feel capable of handling that type of contact and the information you read, but it puts me in a tough position."

Other social networking sites are just for professional purposes, like LinkedIn, and they do not necessarily include much personal information. In a situation where a client reaches out through one of those sites, it may feel okay to accept the connection request and perhaps casually mention it in session or not at all. Sometimes a professional connection on a social networking site is just a professional connection.

When a client says that she saw your post about anxiety on Cannotstopsharing.org, don't be surprised. When you are in cyberspace, many people, clients included, will find you. Some information is more easily obtainable, and your client may choose to bring up certain facts and not others. We suggest that you inquire, "What were you interested in?" Often clients want to know who you are, not just your credentials, in deciding to trust you.

Charlie

I have a client who suffers from depression who forwards e-mails to a broadcast listserve he has identified as "May Be Worth Reading." He asked if I wanted to get his missives, and I said, "Sure, though I may not read them all." Some of his postings are fairly interesting and give us some material to review together. We also talk at times about the fact that he forwards some material at 2 A.M. or 4 A.M., which allows us to talk about these and his other symptoms.

"Can We Have Sessions Online?"

Different states and professional organizations have distinct provisions regarding online sessions. Whether your profession considers online sessions unethical, we are opposed and would tell a client, "Online communication is difficult. Therapy needs thoughtful time and space. In this fast-paced world, it is a very good thing that we take 45 or 50 minutes without technology to have an uninterrupted face-to-face discussion." Anyone who has tried to have conversations can verify that online communication lacks nuance and tone. It is a far cry from old-fashioned, crafted letter writing. Electronic connections can be instantaneous and, too often, impulsive. Keep online communication uncomplicated. It is effective and convenient to use for reminders, to respond to appointment requests, to change meeting times, and for quick follow-ups. If it begins to get lengthy, write, "This is too important for e-mail or texts; let's continue in the office."

There are exceptions that we can imagine, for example, an elderly client in bad weather, but a phone call still makes more sense. The same is true with a disabled client, but again, why wouldn't you talk on the phone and at least have a voice connection. The notion of online therapy waters down the essential nature of the process.

"Can We Stay in Contact?" "Can I Stop by and Maybe We Could Get Coffee?

These questions are occasionally asked as therapy ends, and you will have a different answer than when you are asked during treatment. For example, you could say, "I would love to hear from you and know how you are doing. Here is my work phone number or e-mail." or "When you are back in town, call me and you could stop by the office." Then, if it happens, arrange a time to meet in your office.

There are real losses at the close of treatment, and keeping in touch may have different meanings to different clients. We believe that the uniqueness of the therapy relationship creates a complicated bond, and you remain important in the lives of your former clients.

The majority of clients, maybe as high as two-thirds, contact their former therapists. In a small study that Linda did years ago, "Who am I after therapy ends?" she was able to document the goals of contact and hypothesize who we, as former therapists, become after therapy ends. Most often, when clients contacted their former therapists, they wanted to let the therapist know they were doing well, to report their progress and successes, and generally to provide an update on their lives, a shared wish on the part of many therapists, no doubt. Those who actually made contact also described other reasons, including the desire for mentoring advice, getting help with a problem, or requesting a referral for a friend. The people sampled described their former therapists with words like "caring, warm, kind, and empathic." Even those who said that therapy had mixed results emphasized that their therapist's human caring qualities were significant for them long after therapy had ended, a sentiment substantiated repeatedly in research.

Post-therapy contact raises our interest in the question "Who are we and how do we exist in the minds and hearts of clients after therapy ends?" We believe that we are maintained as people who not only care—most clients have people in their lives who care about them—but as people who know them and understand their internal worlds. Understanding is a more unique relationship than affection. We are people who are helpful when life is not going well. We have shared the disappointment of failures and the pride in hard-won successes. We were there for the growing and have become co-authors of the stories they continue to create. Sometimes, we are contacted when they need to reestablish faith in their abilities, which is similar to, but not identical with, continuing to be a nurturing internal representation. We remain the holders of hope and faith, and we persist as touchstones to mitigate isolation and doubt. Staying in touch after therapy doesn't mean that professional responsibilities cease. The relative balance of focus on the client may alter slightly and the exploration lessens, but our role in our clients' lives has been as their therapist, so remember that you don't want to undo the work that has been so important to them.

FURTHER THOUGHTS

> "I've learned that people will forget what you said; people will forget what you did; but people will never forget how you made them feel."
>
> —Maya Angelou

Linda

Last month I got an excited voice mail. "Hi, this is Jay Wolsky (pseudonym). I was a patient of yours 15 years ago. I came for a dental appointment and saw your name on the building directory. This is great! I'm doing well and I hope you are. I'm a lawyer now—I wonder if that surprises you. I'm married. Here's my number if you get a chance to call me back—I would love to say hello." It was wonderful to hear Jay's voice and contrast it with the days when he was underemployed, very glum, and having serious health problems. He clearly wanted to tell me that he had succeeded. I was delighted that he still felt the enthusiasm to give me a call, and I did call back for a short chat.

Our experience has been that clients are respectful, and although it seems to be a pervasive fear that clients will bombard their therapists with unwelcome communications, we have not found it to be true. Therapy used to be conceptualized as a process that clients complete and then they are launched, never to return. These days, most therapists believe that they are likely to enter and leave clients' lives as different events must be faced or when refreshers and tune-ups are needed.

One of the aspects of this work that we like the least is when clients leave and we do not know what has happened to these people who we cared about and with whom we shared many intimate conversations. Strangely, though, this feels right. We sign up for part of their journey and have to trust them to continue.

SUGGESTED READINGS

Edelstein, L. (1998). Post-termination Relationships: Who Am I After Therapy Ends? Paper presented at the 106th annual convention of the American Psychological Association, San Francisco, California.

Fisher, C. B., & Oransky, M. (2008). Informed consent to psychotherapy: Protecting the dignity and respecting the autonomy of patients. *Journal of Clinical Psychology: In Session, 64,* 576–588.

Koocher, G. P. (2003). Ethical and legal issues in professional practice transitions. *Professional Psychology: Research and Practice, 34,* 383–387.

Younggren, J. N., & Gottlieb, M. C. (2008). Termination and abandonment: History, risk, and risk management. *Professional Psychology: Research and Practice, 39,* 498–504.

CHAPTER

22

Life Events

You expect to go through life events with your clients, but you imagine that their life events, not yours, will be at the forefront of your discussions. It is unnerving when the situation is reversed and you find that they are accompanying you through the changes in your life. You have to be honest when questions are asked, but the degree of disclosure depends on your client and your relationship. The difficulty in answering questions about your life events is finding the way to stay connected when you might require privacy.

Linda

Recently, Dotty, a client whom I have seen for many years, walked in, sat down at the front edge of the couch, and looked earnestly at me. "At my book club," she said, "a friend told us that her therapist has a brain tumor and didn't tell her." Then Dotty asked very seriously, "Would you tell me if you were sick?" I thought hard about what I would really do, and there seemed to be only one answer, whether it suited my private nature or not. "Yes, I would tell you." She relaxed like a balloon losing air.

Dotty was a client of long standing, an adult who battled cancer years earlier, and a woman who would be shattered by dishonesty on my part. Those factors permitted only one action. As much as I would hate to talk about illness with a client, as private as my life feels to me, I believe that I owe that level of revelation to some clients. But, because therapy is a relationship, I wouldn't be the only person dictating the conditions. I treat other clients who would not ask, "Would you tell me if you were sick?" because they would not want "Yes" as the answer. And from me, I can imagine coming up with other varieties of answers for other clients with whom I have different relationships.

QUESTIONS

The following questions are answered in the Responses section:

> "Are you pregnant?"
> "Is that an engagement ring/wedding ring?"
> "Is it true that you are moving/quitting your job/leaving the agency?"
> "I heard that your husband/partner/wife/mother/father died. Is that true?"
> "You haven't been looking well. Are you ill?"
> "I ran into your sister/daughter/son/husband at a party/wedding/bar/game, and we got to talking about you. Is it true that . . .?"

RESPONSES

"Are You Pregnant?"

If you are, it is past the time to have announced it. "Yes, I am. I guess it isn't a secret anymore, so let's talk about it." or you are not and something else is going on, such as sudden weight gain, hostility, or

Linda

One of my favorite stories came from a friend who was asked, "Are you pregnant?" by a young, intuitive client who suffered from a personality disorder. My friend sincerely answered "No," only to learn several days later that she was pregnant, reminding us that we are not the only sensitive people in the room.

pregnancy issues in the client's world. "No, I'm not. Is pregnancy on your mind these days?"

Pregnancy invariably changes the balance of your personal and professional life. Your personal life and the fact that you are a sexual being is right there in the room. This is one life event that women cannot hide. Eventually you must disclose the pregnancy and deal with the emotions and practical matters that follow. Many clients will feel protective; some may feel jealous, and others may feel competitive for your attention; men may have additional erotic fantasies; and many clients will have other types of reactions. While your clients are experiencing all kinds of feelings, so are you. Physically, you are changing and perhaps experiencing morning sickness or fears of a miscarriage. Maybe you feel less engaged with your work. Emotionally, you are vulnerable and want to protect the fetus from clients' fantasies and yourself from the natural curiosity that your clients will have about you and your family. Practically, you need to think about maternity leave.

You may want to avoid much discussion about your pregnancy. However, you do need to acknowledge it and respond with facts about your due date and your plans, if you have them. "I'm figuring out how much time I'll take off. Right now, I feel good and am thinking that I'll work until (name a date). I'll let you know more as I decide."

Sociologists and anthropologists confirm that it is entirely normal for other people, even strangers, to feel more solicitous and act in ways that are more personally disclosing or inquiring when they are in the presence of a pregnant woman, saying, for example, "How are you feeling?" "I wonder if you will get varicose veins like I did?" "Will you have the baby in the hospital?" These kinds of questions are not pathological or deeply transferential, so you will need to sort out a way to respond that simultaneously respects your boundaries and maintains the relationship. When in doubt, do what is normal and respond similarly as you would if someone in the market or the elevator made a well-intended, but intrusive, inquiry.

Clients may worry about losing you and may be confused by the range of their reactions. You are still the therapist, so it falls to you to ask, "What about you? Are you having some reactions to my pregnancy?" Even if your client says "No," monitor changes and ask again at reasonable intervals. Some clients will feel protective of you, reluctant to talk about aggressive emotions, and even suggest, "Cover your stomach. We don't want the baby to hear." It will be tempting to collude with your client's avoidance and keep the pregnancy completely private, but in fact, the role of being a pregnant woman has a very public component, and you collude in denial if you don't accept that fact.

With adoption, you don't have to deal with pregnancy questions, but then you have to explain the presence of your new baby and deal with the same changes that motherhood will bring to your professional life. Similarly, if you are an expectant father whose schedule might require adjustments, you need to bring this important life change into the room in a way that respects your client and your own boundaries.

Either mothers-to-be or fathers-to-be can say, "I have some good news that I want to share with you," and after the congratulations that will follow, address the implications for the continuing therapy: "I plan to take (name an amount of time) off and then come back. We have plenty of time to discuss whether you want to see someone else during our break." Other matters to eventually discuss are about your availability, "I will/will not be available by phone during portions of my leave," and methods of imparting information, "I'll leave a message on my machine after the baby is born so you can call in and know the details right away."

"Is That an Engagement Ring/Wedding Ring?"

For clinicians, an engagement ring question may evoke concerns about modesty, fear of envy, or ambivalence about display. You don't know what it means to the client without getting more additional information. "Yes, I've just gotten engaged," and listen for the material that follows. It helps to think about your responses ahead of time. "Thanks for your good wishes." or "It seems like my ring has brought up some feelings about your own life. Why don't we talk about it?"

The same is true of wedding rings, for men and women. Clients may notice, especially if you have taken time off. Answer simply. You can say, "Yes, I recently got married. I'm happy about it." Clients rarely go past a few additional questions about when and where and your new spouse's name. Unless you have a good reason to avoid the questions, we suggest responding with some facts and then moving back to the client's problems. If other concerns have not been expressed, they will seep out in the derivative material, so listen for the comments that follow your announcement. With a wedding, you may want to tell clients ahead of time that you are taking some time off and will be married. Then, if there is processing to be done, you can begin in advance and avoid some of the surprises.

"Is It True That You Are Moving/Quitting Your Job/ Leaving the Agency?"

This question isn't terribly important unless it is true. If a client has heard from other sources, your disclosure is late. You might need to own up to, "Yes, but I'm not going anywhere until (the date), so we have plenty of time to talk about the implications for our work." Then, ask about reactions.

Students have to deal with leaving placements every year, and it is horrible because you have to say goodbye to everyone within a short period of time. Some clients will have forgotten that you told them about your departure in the early sessions of treatment. Students need to follow the guidelines of the agency and their schools when they announce their departures, and different theoretical approaches advise varying times for advance notice.

If the move was initiated by you and is not a placement that has ended, you can begin the discussion with, "I'm sorry that you heard about it elsewhere. I wanted to be the person to tell you that I am moving/ leaving. I've been thinking about it for a long time and recently made my final decision. I'm here until (the date). We have plenty of time to talk about it and make the right plan for you." You may have to deal with clients' feelings of abandonment or rejection because the move was within your power, so listen for those emotions or descriptions of other events in your clients' lives when important people let them go.

"I Heard That Your Husband/Partner/Wife/ Mother/Father Died. Is That True?"

Of course, it happens. You have a real life with real people who might get hurt or sick or die. Some therapists don't tell their clients about deaths and illnesses in the family. That is an option, but don't be shocked if clients are hurt when they find out. Keeping your bereavement a complete secret robs clients of the chance to behave like autonomous adults and offer sympathy to you. You can say, "Yes, sadly, it is true." You could mention a few details and state whether you will be taking time off. Clients don't want all the particulars, but they do want to express their sadness to you. After all, you have been very present for them.

If you plan to be away for any event other than a vacation, clients are likely to ask, "Why are you taking time off?" You have to provide some answer. Replying with, "a family illness" seems skimpy, even if you are private and don't want to discuss details. We would advise a reasonable amount of disclosure, such as, "I want to take time to be with my mother. She is very ill." or "My sister has to go through some tests, and I want to be there." Aim for respect and honesty but not too much disclosure. Revealing deep sadness in your own life goes against the privacy that most therapists cherish. Also, even minor discussions about your losses have the potential to bring up strong emotions that you certainly prefer to deal with privately.

Nancy Newton, Ph.D., Professor at The Chicago School

Lately I have had to travel out of state to care for my brother. Between trips, I also have had to schedule a battery of health tests for myself. The tests caused considerable anxiety until I received good results. These life events have disrupted the schedule for my

(continued)

clinical work. I told some clients that I needed to travel for a family emergency, but other clients who I see less regularly were not told.

Phoebe came in after having been out of touch for a couple of months with her own family problems. As soon as she sat down, she turned to me seriously and said, "I've been so worried about you. Are you ill? I've been imagining that you have cancer." I immediately responded with an explanation about my brother and my travel. Then I asked her, "What made you think that I had cancer?" flashing back to my series of tests.

"I saw a bottle of pills on your desk." The pills were a collection of vitamins that I carry when I travel, so I explained them. I encouraged her to tell me the other matters that worried her. "My good friend is moving out of the country, and another friend is having a baby so she is unavailable." "Maybe these events caused you some worry about me, too." I gently suggested. The talk moved further along, into her fear of losing me just like she was losing her friends.

I found the entire interchange illuminating. Not only because she included me in her circle of potential losses but also because, although she hadn't known it, her fantasy of my imagined illness was very close to the reality of my month of worrisome tests.

"You Haven't Been Looking Well. Are You Ill?"

Illness brings up fears for you and fears of losing you. Let's look at both extremes of potential answers. You admit honestly to an illness, saying, "Yes. I have a condition/am going through tests/am being treated for something," and your client may be relieved to understand your appearance and honored to be trusted with the information. But your client is now also burdened. Can your client be angry if you miss work? Can your client express disappointment that you are less attentive? Can your client tell you that she is afraid that you will die and leave her? Do you want to hear all of those honest expressions?

If that was Scylla, here is Charybdis: You say nothing, you deny your illness and lie, "I've been fighting a flu." Some clinicians don't mention illnesses because the disclosure and the ensuing discussions are almost as much of a burden as the illness itself. Others don't tell clients because they are in denial or because they are afraid that clients will quit. If you choose that direction, you protect your privacy and can deal with your illness in secret, but you have modeled lying. You have demonstrated secret keeping instead of talking openly, endangering the alliance. Even worse, your client may sense that something is wrong, and your lie tells her that her sense of reality is off, reenacting damaging childhood experiences that taught her not to trust her own perceptions of reality. In this last instance, you have to admit something or you may do harm to your client.

Usually, when therapists conceal illness or bereavement, they are protecting themselves from their own strong feelings and from their clients' reactions, which might be difficult to handle. This is an understandable motivation. Perhaps there is a middle ground, answering clients' questions to a certain extent with, "Yes, I am being treated for an illness. If it becomes serious or I have to miss work, I will explain more, but right now, I need to use my energy to deal with it. Can you handle an arrangement like that?" If you do reveal an illness, you have to think carefully about how much to reveal and what language to use in recounting the problem. It may bring up discussions of your client's losses and other people in their life.

"I Ran Into Your Sister/Daughter/Son/Husband at a Party/ Wedding/Bar/Game and We Got to Talking About You. Is It True That . . .?"

If you live near your work, people will know you and share stories. It is not your neighbor's responsibility to keep your name out of conversations. After several years of treating Barb, Linda found out that Barb's best friend is Linda's accountant. It was luck that everyone in that situation understood boundaries.

More complex is the high school senior who walked into his therapist's office and asked, "What do I do if I'm at a party with your son and I see him doing drugs? Do I tell you? That seems like a crappy thing to do to a classmate, but I don't like lying to you either." This is an extraordinary adolescent, grappling with serious considerations of teenaged ethical conduct. It arose because the client had just realized that he was in some classes with his therapist's son. It hadn't come up sooner because the son had a different last name.

You go about your business just like everyone else, and if clients inadvertently or intentionally gather information about you, you deal with it. First, clarify the situation so that you understand the tangled relationships, and then you might say, "Yes, my son plays in that league. Are you connected to it?" or "My wife does work at that school; she teaches art. Why?" Or, while you are thinking that you might have to murder your sister/child/friend for talking to a client, you compose yourself and clarify, "What exactly did my sister say about my marriage/life/musical ability?" and go from there. You can confirm and move on, or you can defer with, "That will not be useful for us to discuss." It is more likely that your clients will never tell you all the information they have learned about you.

You don't withhold personal information in order to be mysterious; that's for the movies. You stay in the background so that your clients can remain in the foreground. When you inadvertently become the focus, it may feel like an invasion of your privacy because it is a strange turnabout. These questions can all become very useful as you examine your client's reactions to your life events as a first step to understanding what these events mean to them. You don't have to answer in ways that make you uncomfortable, but you do have to remain gracious and deal with questions professionally so that, as your discussion progresses, clients will be learning about themselves.

FURTHER THOUGHTS

"I always avoid prophesying beforehand because it is a much better policy to prophesy after the event has already taken place."
—Winston Churchill

Life happens. You cannot keep your practice entirely pure and free from impinging events. Although you may want to set up therapy as a private sanctuary, it isn't possible and probably not even desirable. Certain happenings, like pregnancy or illness, cannot be concealed. Other events present choices. As you make decisions about the degree to which to include your life events in your work with clients, consider that any event that affects you strongly may seep into therapy. Don't be surprised when clients pick up your affect. When they do, remember that you owe your client honesty and you owe yourself privacy. Unfortunately, sometimes these obligations conflict, and important decisions will need to be made.

SUGGESTED READINGS

Baum, N. (2006). End-of-year treatment termination: Responses of social work student trainees. *British Journal of Social Work, 36*, 639–656.

Field, R. (2007). Breaks and endings in independent practice. In A. Hemmings & R. Field (Eds.), *Counselling and psychotherapy in contemporary private practice* (pp. 158–177). New York, NY: Routledge.

Norton, J., & McGrath, A. (2007). What do we tell your next therapist? A collaborative approach to forced termination of therapy and case handover. *Australian Journal of Counselling Psychology, 8*, 8–11.

Vasquez, M. J. T., Bingham, R. P., & Barnett, J. E. (2008). Psychotherapy termination: Clinical and ethical responsibilities. *Journal of Clinical Psychology: In Session, 64*, 653–665.

Webb, N. (1983). Vacation-separations: Therapeutic implications and clinical management. *Clinical Social Work Journal*, 126–138.

CHAPTER

23

Ending Therapy

Endings matter, and in therapy endings are a process, not a moment. Don't underestimate the power of your relationship just because it was purchased or has been short term. Impermanent does not mean insignificant. You can try to prepare for each ending, but despite all the emotional rehearsals, you can't be certain how you will feel until it happens. Much of it depends on the particular nature of your relationship with your client.

Charlie

Nora was concerned about filling her days now that she was retired at age 55. As we discussed retirement, it became obvious that she faced a far more significant life transition: the declining health of her husband of 35 years. Nora tearfully related her fears that her husband's failing vision made his night driving dangerous. Equally upsetting was the pain that she would cause him if she called attention to his decline. Together, we worked through the losses and fears that surrounded the inevitable changes in her life, and Nora became better able to address these alterations head on. In so doing, she became more accepting of certain circumstances and was also able to take firm action when appropriate.

Eventually we both knew that it was time for therapy to end. This process was eased because, in many ways, we had rehearsed this termination in all the work we had done with her other losses. I asked, "Next week will be our final session together; what do you imagine that will look like?" Nora said, "Well, I think we will continue to talk about these meaningful things in my life, but at the end if we don't end with a good hug, then everything else will have been for nothing." We ended with a good hug.

Many of the topics we presented in the previous pages are subjects that can be raised throughout the course of therapy. However, some issues are directly, primarily related to the course of therapy itself. Termination, by definition, happens at the conclusion of treatment, and as such, raises specific and very important questions about endings. Perhaps the most important question that arises during the final days of treatment, just like it inevitably appears in all of life's endings, is shared by client and therapist alike, when you both wonder, "Did I do all that I could?"

Some questions are common to all therapy terminations, but others are evoked by the manner in which treatment ends. Some therapy terminations are carefully planned, such as in psychoanalysis. However, most of us are not doing analysis and know that terminations can range from careful, thoughtful endings to a surprise one-session announcement, or worse, a brief phone call or a no-show, no-call disappearance.

There are also different ways in which termination is initiated. Termination discussions can be launched by your client, by you, or by mutual agreement. Client-initiated termination may indicate a premature ending to therapy. Counselor-initiated termination occurs when the clinician believes that the client's goals are met, no progress is being made, the counselor leaves a setting, a training commitment ends, the client needs services that the therapist or agency cannot offer, or artificial time limits are imposed, such as managed-care restrictions. Obviously, the most satisfying termination is that which is mutually agreed upon by counselor and client because both believe that it is a good time to end. We will cover questions that are raised in all of these situations.

Termination has never meant that psychological work ceases; it only marks the point where psychological work continues without the physical presence of the therapist. All endings, whether they are about therapy, school, relationships, or life itself, raise similar salient underlying, usually unspoken, questions that include: "Did I accomplish what I set out to do?" "What is going to be left incomplete and imperfect?" "How do I feel about unfinished business?" "Can I go it alone?" "Why do I have such mixed emotions?"

Clients rarely ask these questions directly, but the sentiments are embedded in those that are spoken. They are serious questions that we ask ourselves at various points in life when we experience important endings. Terminating therapy is one of those times. Termination also inevitably brings up other endings that have occurred in your client's life. It may evoke other memories of loss and abandonment, success and failure, creations and reunions, the desire to tie up loose ends, and emotions of sadness, anger, and gratitude. If you are willing to sincerely engage with these mixed emotions and ideas, you often have a chance to make termination a significant period of learning. Be aware that, even with preparation and rehearsals, endings can be intellectualized until the day arrives. Some emotions, such as anger or disappointment, may only come into existence at the very end of treatment.

Some of the following questions are about actual endings, and other questions are those that occur near or at the end of therapy and are evoked by the possibility of terminating treatment. A few questions may also arise at earlier points in therapy.

QUESTIONS

The following questions are answered in the Responses section:

"How will I know when to stop?"
"I don't have anything to talk about. Should we stop?"
"I decided that today is my last time coming here. What do you think?"
"I still have problems. Does that mean I can't stop?"
"Can we stay in touch? Can I have your cell phone or e-mail?"

"May I come back?"

"Can we be friends?"

"How do we end? What do we do?"

"Can we celebrate with cake/drinks/party?"

"Here is a gift. Will you take it?"

"What do you think about my progress?"

"Now that we are ending therapy, can I finally know more about you?"

"If finishing up is such a good thing, why am I sad and angry?"

If the therapist initiates termination (e.g., when the clinician is a student who must leave the placement), then other questions may also arise, including:

"Why are you leaving?"

"Can I go with you?"

"Where are you going?" "Will you be back?"

"Why are you throwing me out?"

"Don't you like me?" "Did you like talking to me?"

"Who will I talk to after you are gone?"

Clients' questions during termination offer us another chance to understand their worlds more fully and to go into realms where the experience of ending is generalized, is worked therapeutically, and can have a lasting impact. Before answering these questions, it is important to acknowledge that each of us has our own personal history of endings. Each ending brings up the possibility that our own feelings, thoughts, and behaviors can unknowingly creep into our clinical work, so, in our answers, we will also address the knowledge that clinicians' emotional reactions are alive and well at termination.

In answering questions at termination, we hope for a lot. We strive to empathize with the strong emotions; acknowledge loss and change, specifically in relationships; address issues of separation and individuation; appreciate gains; prevent avoidance of the feelings aroused by ending; encourage compassion in lieu of perfection; review the work done; address rejection, if needed; and clarify post-therapy contact.

Linda

I come from a family that didn't believe in separations. We rarely went on vacation because it involved leaving home for a week or two, and if we did, then we snuck out at 5 A.M. to avoid saying goodbye. Every one of my mother's brothers lived within two blocks of our home, and all of them believed that every important relationship had to last for forever, at the minimum. One of the most valuable, strange lessons that therapy has taught me, as both client and psychologist, is that relationships have limits in time and saliency. Even significant, vital, creative, loving relationships may end, and impermanence doesn't reduce that importance.

RESPONSES

"How Will I Know When to Stop?"

We answer this question directly: "We will both have an idea when it is time to stop. Actually, it becomes pretty clear when things are winding down. You will feel like you got what you came for, even if we never spelled it out exactly." No final bell is rung to signal termination. Sometimes clients stop for practical reasons, such as moving, money, having contracted for a set number of sessions, or schedule changes. Usually, the reasons to end therapy are more vague than that. Some signs of impending termination are when you and your client recognize gains and do not see additional emergent problems, or therapy sessions begin to feel lighter and there is less to talk about for awhile, or clients have clearly gotten healthier and are functioning better.

For most of your clients, ending therapy is both exciting and distressing. It is exciting to feel growth and new capabilities, and it is normal for clients to want to try out their skills on their own in the real world. It is also distressing because termination signals the end of a key relationship that has offered understanding and support.

Linda

When I look back on my six years in psychoanalysis, I think that on some level, I spent the last five years of it slowly learning how to separate. I'm slow about leaving. At the very end of analysis, I had a dream that told me I was ready to go. In the dream, I was sweeping out the garage at my childhood home. When my analyst asked me about the significance of the garage, I told him, "When you have done everything, all the chores, all the fix-ups, all the cleaning, and there is nothing left to do, you sweep out the garage. It's the last thing you do."

"I Don't Have Anything to Talk About. Should We Stop?"

When a client has "nothing to talk about," it is time to entertain several questions. Specifically ask yourself whether your client is unknowingly holding back on a difficult topic, or if you have spent your previous sessions resolving crises and are now able to shift beyond those pressing matters that upset lives but are not always the most important. This is the time to suggest, "It's good that nothing urgent is going on. Let's take this opportunity for you to tell me about the feelings and thoughts that come to your mind as we sit here." It is also an appropriate time for you to suggest a conversation about topics that have not yet been discussed. This might include ways in which this client approaches his life or specific personality variables. If it really is time to stop, then that will become apparent.

"I Decided That Today Is My Last Time Coming Here. What Do You Think?"

This question comes up with unpleasant regularity. "Well, that comes as a surprise. I haven't had time to think about it. Tell me how you arrived at this idea, and we can figure out what to do." After the discussion, you are better able to say, "I can see why you want to stop. I respect that decision, and let's schedule one (or three or six) session to review our work and wrap things up." Or you might choose to say, "I understand, but I don't agree. I think that we still need to discuss (whatever issues remain outstanding)." Keep in mind the idea that clients will often flee from therapy if their feelings of attachment or dependency become uncomfortable.

The statement of "I want to stop now" raises our general rule about instant endings. The first time a client suggests stopping, we treat it as a significant point in the course of therapy, but not usually the end to therapy, and we try to examine the circumstances that surround the comment. Discussion of "why now?" can lead anywhere and is usually productive. However, the two preceding questions, "I don't have anything to talk about. Should we stop?" and "I decided that today is my last time coming here. What do you think?" raise another clinical matter. Is your client avoiding feelings? Is your client afraid of becoming dependent? A speedy exit is one sure way to not experience the myriad of emotions that surround detaching from therapy and you, the therapist. Don't let the client rush you. Don't get swept up in the client's avoidance, discomfort, or urgency.

"I Still Have Problems. Does That Mean I Can't Stop?"

Linda had a client, Bob, who said it best when he announced, near the end of treatment, "Now I have normal problems." We answer, "Life is complicated and has legitimate suffering. We can't stop that; we just got you ready to deal with it more successfully."

Ending treatment provides yet another chance for clients and therapists to remember that they are not perfect. The recognition that therapy has prepared your client to go out and live a human, imperfect life may be the most significant gift she receives from treatment. Understanding that therapy has limits, people have limits, and life has limits prepares clients to give up the tormenting nature of perfectionism in favor of compassion for themselves and others.

"Can We Stay in Touch?" "Can I Have Your Cell Phone or E-mail?"

This can be tricky because therapists do different things and agencies have different guidelines. Most students change agencies yearly. After school, clinicians move on to other positions, and even in private practice, you have to think before responding. First, familiarize yourself with agency rules; it may be against policy. Next, consider if it is advisable to keep in touch. If it is not advisable, you can say, "The policy here is that we do not stay in touch." You can add, "It may interfere with your continuing work with someone else." or "I want to say yes, but I know that I won't be able to."

If staying in touch is possible and you believe that it is a good idea, clarify the request: "What does staying in touch mean?" The important element here is, do you want to stay in touch, even a little bit? Don't let guilt rule your answer. Be honest and respond accordingly. You can always get some sense of your client's thoughts by asking, "What do you have in mind?" but think about your honest wishes, too. Depending on your goal, you might say, "Here's my card. I would love to hear from you sometimes." or "The agency prefers that we do not stay in touch, but if you ever want to come back in treatment, I'll be here." If you do not believe that your client is ready to end, you might say, "We have done some important work here, and I believe that you would benefit from another therapist's expertise to further the work in the future." Sometimes you may feel guilty and want to stay in touch, but six months later, at a new job with an entirely new set of responsibilities, this may reveal itself to be a bad idea.

Whether you plan to stay in touch or not, the question reminds us that clients want to know if they will be able to keep us. Don't be tempted into a distancing lecture on internalization of you as the therapist. Just remind them, "We have worked together long enough and hard enough that you will hear my voice when you need to make a decision. You will remember me and I will remember you."

"May I Come Back?"

Before you answer this one, ask, "Are you worried about something in particular?" This question is usually a query about what happens if the client runs into trouble in the future. Address that underlying concern first. Then, you might respond, "Of course. I don't know that you will need to come back, but if you are confused or upset and want to talk things out, for one session or for an extended time, please call me." If you are planning to retire, leave the agency or practice, or move away, or become a tap dancer, this is the time to say so with the reassurance that the agency will be available to them.

"Can We Be Friends?"

This question is asked frequently when you work with adolescents, but any client might inquire. Friendship is almost impossible to achieve because the power balance has been skewed by one person (the client) revealing much vulnerable information and another person (you) revealing little personal material. Therapy is not a relationship of equal status, whatever your theoretical view. Also, transference lasts forever, even if you don't believe in it. It seems more reasonable to respond, "This is a unique relationship that doesn't lend itself to a regular friendship. I'm better off being here, being in your corner if you ever need me again." or "I don't believe that this relationship can be transformed into a normal friendship." or "You have good friends. I want to remain available to you as a special confidant if you ever need to talk again." or "We have worked on ways that you can have better and stronger relationships with your regular friends." or "I would love to hear from you and keep in touch, but this relationship doesn't translate well into a let's-go-to-the-movies friendship."

"How Do We End? What Do We Do?"

It is always different, so think about your particular client and the unique relationship. One thing that ought to be included in the last couple of sessions is review. Reviews consolidate growth and give both of you an opportunity to see your client's progress. Before the session, reread your notes, then talk together about the presenting problems, other concerns that emerged, the client's progress, the highlights, and the rough spots. If it is appropriate, don't forget to include a discussion of your relationship with each other. "I like to take time to review our work together. I want both of us to look backward so we can see what has changed, and I want us to look forward as preparation. Maybe we can make some predictions about the future and get you prepared."

"Can We Celebrate With Cake/Drinks/Party?"

We have rituals to mark many important life transitions and endings, so this question is less strange than it seems on the surface. Think about funerals and graduations. Rituals give form to experiences because they untie us from one stage of life and ease us into the next. Therapists who work with children often have ending celebrations where they draw pictures or take photos that the child can keep. With adults, you might inquire clearly, "What do you have in mind?" The final session still has work to be done—important work—so you might consider, if they want a party, "We have lots to talk about, so why don't you bring in some (coffee, tea, cupcakes, something simple) and we can talk while we snack."

Linda

No one has ever brought food to a final session with me. Only once did I have a couple come in with a camera at their last session. We all trooped next door to the dentist's office and had him take our picture together. Then we had a very ordinary termination session. With another client, we took a few moments of the session to destroy some written reminiscences of abuse. I was skeptical because therapy rituals are foreign to me, but I was very aware that this client carefully marked events and turning points in concrete ways. For her, it was a freedom ritual; she was happily ending that part of her life. I've never done it since.

"Here Is a Gift. Will You Take It?"

Clients do not generally announce that they are bringing you a gift at the end of treatment; they just show up with one. When clients have been seen for free or at a significantly discounted rate, they are more likely to bring termination gifts. Often the gift means, "I have something to offer you, too." or "Here is something that will remind you of me." This is not the day to inquire or to analyze; it is the time to be gracious.

Neither one of us has ever been given an inappropriate gift, although Linda was once surprised with a horseshoe-shaped flower arrangement that looked like it was stolen from a funeral parlor or a racetrack. Even then, our general policy is to accept and say "thank you."

Linda

When I was ending analysis, I told my therapist that I thought I deserved a gift because I had worked hard. I was half kidding, but I think I wanted to take something away with me. He asked, "Oh, you want a memento?" I responded, "No, I was thinking of something bigger, like a Mercedes."

"What Do You Think About My Progress?"

This is a golden question because it opens up a dialogue and joint reflections. We usually answer with, "That's a very important question. Let's take a look and compare observations. Why don't you begin and I'll jump in."

"Now That We Are Ending Therapy, Can I *Finally* Know More About You?"

Adolescents can be relentless with this type of questioning, but whether it is a child, adolescent, or adult, clinicians have very different reactions about how much to answer. The important point is to be careful to not overwhelm the client with information, not burden the client, and not be withholding. Usually your client just wants to stay connected, and a more complete image of you helps maintain that attachment. Don't say too much, because the danger is that your work will be altered by any quick change in the relationship that takes place: Your client may also feel confused, cheated, or beleaguered if you now start to tell your life story. Additionally, opening this door with the client may mean that future therapeutic interaction with you is out of the question.

Here's how we answer the question, "Can I *finally* know more about you?"

Charlie

Recognizing that we don't always have the luxury of writing, re-reading, editing, and re-editing what we actually say in response to these kinds of questions, I usually make some brief approximation of this statement: "I think that you are asking to have some tidbits about my life to take with you, and I can appreciate that. Rather than a bunch of brief facts about my life, though, I think you do know me in a way far deeper than these tidbits would reveal: We have shared some very intimate moments together in a way that both of us only do with a few people in our lives. I am hoping that you take with you a sense of the professionalism that we have created, the great respect we have built between us, and the sense of privilege that I feel to be part of your life journey."

Linda

I am more likely to see this question as a final request for genuine connection and some knowledge to take away. I generally reply: "Okay, what do you want to know?" Usually the information requested is minor—a concern or interest about my life. If it seems benign, I am glad to answer honestly. Clients are rarely inappropriate at the end of treatment. If, in my opinion, the question is too personal or calls for an answer that might overwhelm my client, I say something like, "I don't think that is a discussion we want to begin on our last day, so I'll just pass on answering." Whether I answer with details or not, I often say, "I think that you probably know me very well. You may not know a lot of cocktail party details, but we have talked together honestly, and I'll bet that you already know the important things about me."

In considering personal questions that are posed in the final sessions, keep in mind the same guidelines laid out in Chapter 9, Personal Questions, and add the knowledge that you are providing a lasting image. There will be no follow-up and no time to correct your disclosures.

"If Finishing Up Is Such a Good Thing, Why Am I Sad and Angry?"

Therapists must give clients the opportunity to work through their reactions to terminating. You can say, "Losses often evoke sadness and anger. Ending our relationship is a loss," and that may make it understandable, but it is still a loss. We have to allow each client to experience all of the reactions to termination: sadness, anger, satisfaction, gratitude, and pride in work well done. All of these feelings are best dealt with directly. We validate all of these, the emotions we enjoy and those we dread. Terminations are not easy for therapists either. It is tempting to be inappropriately humble, distant, desirous of wrapping it all up neatly with a bow, or to overlook the swirling emotions that surround an ending because we are also experiencing the conclusion of a relationship. How you handle termination depends, in part, on your own comfort with endings and losses and with your relationship with that particular client.

Damon Krohn, M.A. and researcher for this book

In my first placement during graduate school, I worked with Anthony, a 16-year-old Hispanic student. He was extremely depressed and angry about his parents' divorce and the ensuing loss. After approximately seven months of therapy, his mood and behavior had improved. Although I had always let Anthony know that our time was limited, with three sessions remaining, I reminded him that we would have to terminate shortly. The next week, Anthony was suspended from school for fighting, and he missed our session. He missed the next one, too. I tried to contact Anthony, and he finally showed up for our final meeting. He admitted that he got into a fight and missed two sessions because he was scared to lose me. I had helped him feel better about his parents' divorce and had been his support system. After our discussion, I realized that his fight and missed appointments resulted from my reminder that we would terminate. Anthony's acting out was his way of demonstrating that he was being forced to deal with too many losses. Particularly with adolescents who have suffered through multiple losses in their lives, conversations about the number of sessions remaining will have been part of many conversations. This is simply the final one.

The final questions come up when the therapist has ended the treatment. If you have been working in a nontraditional setting, you might be part of a team, so other people remain to provide constancy, but you will still be missed.

"Why Are You Leaving?" "Can I Go With You?" "Where Are You Going?" "Will You Be Back?"

These are questions to answer directly. They occur when the therapist, often a student, goes on to another placement or graduates. It also happens in agencies or private practices when a therapist takes another job or moves away. Before you tell clients that you are leaving, decide on your answers to the types of questions posed here. Don't wait until you are sitting in the room swamped with guilt to formulate a response.

Not surprisingly, these questions, "Why are you leaving?" "Can I go with you?" "Where are you going?" "Will you be back?" speak to the sense of rejection when one person, not both, has initiated the ending. Therapists, especially newer clinicians and those who have initiated the end of treatment because they are leaving an agency/school/town, feel overwhelming guilt and worry about abandonment. This leads to a desire to give, give, and give more at the end of therapy. Often, the therapist gives too much information and too many answers, leaving clients buried under their therapist's gifts and without an opportunity to process all their feelings.

"Why Are You Throwing Me Out?"

Even if the ending has been discussed, you may still hear, "Why are you throwing me out?" Empathize with your client's feelings, but also reiterate the real reasons for ending. They can run a wide gamut, for example, "I know that it feels like I'm throwing you out, but it is me who is leaving the agency." or "We do 13 weeks of behavior modification here. That is our policy." or "You need to be seen by a clinician who can do a different type of therapy (prescribe medications, hospitalize). I cannot do that." or "I have told you several times that I cannot do my work if you come into therapy stoned and you continue to get high, so we have to stop. I haven't thrown you out; you have fired me."

If you are moving out of town, the answer is simple. "I'm sorry, but I'm going to another agency that doesn't allow me to bring you." or "I'm sorry but I am leaving town/retiring/joining the circus." or "I am leaving to go to (some other named place) because I am continuing my training/have an opportunity for a good job." or whatever the honest answer happens to be.

On the other hand, if the option to continue is available, "Can I go with you?" can be answered, "Yes, it may be possible." This answer necessitates a clear discussion of the pros and cons. There are different policies everywhere. Talk it over with your supervisor or clinical director. You have to think about agency policy, whether you can reasonably take this client with you, whether the client will make a successful transition (people often do not), whether you have the resources to take this client with you, and whether you want to take this client. When you have answered those questions, you will have your answer.

"Don't You Like Me?" "Did You Like Talking to Me?"

Leavetaking can bring up feelings of rejection. It is important, whatever circumstances surround termination, that you take some time to reflect on your client's unique work and speak to that.

Charlie

During my internship at a college counseling center, I treated a client who made great progress in the first semester I worked there. Both she and I were disappointed that our work needed to stop at the end of the semester because she was going to graduate. In my head, I cooked up a scheme where she could sign up for some academic activity for the spring semester in order to stay eligible to receive services from the counseling center.

I was smart enough to take my thoughts to my supervisor before sharing them with my client. My supervisor looked at me and said, "Do you really want to get into a pattern of scheming with your client in an ethically questionable manner to continue her services?" I was shocked back to reality by how easily I considered compromising my ethics to avoid my own and my client's fears of moving on with our lives. My supervisor's comments have resonated with me many times since, when clients have proposed dubious arrangements to avoid distressing emotions.

These inquiries are questions that only adolescents and children are brave enough to ask. Endings, even when they are explained and understood, have the capacity to bring up fears of being unlovable, old losses, and painful rejections. At this point in the therapy, the questions deserve honest answers, even if those answers are, "Some days were very hard." or "I didn't enjoy all of our conversations." or "I didn't always enjoy talking when you were so angry/stoned/silent, but I like your honesty, your guts, and I'm proud of the changes that you made." For some teenagers and adults, the answer is simple, "I have totally liked talking with you, and I like you and I'm proud of the work you did."

"Who Will I Talk to After You Are Gone?"

This question is troubling, particularly when you have been working with an adolescent or adult who has experienced multiple losses, or has no real support at home, or who has no further options for continued treatment. Hopefully, in anticipation of termination, the two of you have worked on building new outside supportive networks and have strengthened the existing resources available at home or in the community. This is the time to show confidence, support, and remind your client that he has learned new skills and attitudes that can be used in the days ahead.

Individual and cultural differences are apparent at termination. For some clients, therapy was a business transaction, and they say goodbye to you in the same way they leave their dentist. Others can experience it as the final departure of a family member. Most people treat termination as leaving a dear confidant. Whether clients are able to discuss the ending of therapy fully, give you a hug, or express gratitude varies with personality, culture, age, and the relationship. If we have tried to understand and work with each client's uniqueness during the course of treatment, we shouldn't be surprised or disappointed to see their individuality appear at the leavetaking.

FURTHER THOUGHTS

"In your life also, caterpillar endings are butterfly beginnings."
—Laura Teresa Marquez

Our identities as therapists are tied up in our clients' mental health, however it is defined, measured, or subjectively assessed. We join people at difficult periods in their lives and get very close, work hard, and then we separate. Therapy is created to be a temporary relationship, even if it lasts for years. Its impermanence does not diminish its significance. In fact, treatment is sweetened by appreciating the finiteness of the relationship. We are subtly reminded over and over that there will be endings in the future.

Each therapy experience belongs uniquely to that client and to that therapist, and so it is also with termination. Most endings will have the flavor similar to the way treatment was engaged in: serious, business-like, emotional, satisfying and proud, deeply searching, denying loss, or any imaginable combination of content, tone, and emotion. Termination is another time when therapists and clients have parallel concerns—you, the therapist, wonder whether, and to what extent, the therapy worked and will hold. Clients also wonder if their gains will hold. Both of you are sad, and both of you are excited for the client to try her wings. Clinicians ask themselves: Have I helped, do I understand what transpired, and what have we done together? The client has similar queries: Am I better, am I ready, and what will I take with me?

As treatment concludes, therapists and clients react to the ending based on their previous experiences, past losses, personality characteristics, whether and what work was accomplished, and what we see for the future. In the final phase, the therapist's job includes helping the client to acknowledge the loss of the relationship; work with the feelings aroused by ending; encourage compassion in lieu of perfection; review the work done and gains made; address rejection; acknowledge and enjoy successes; and clarify post-therapy contact.

Clinicians still in school have additional tasks because they terminate based on school calendars, not on clients' timetables. They may carry guilt about selfishness and abandonment, concern about transferring clients into good hands, and about effectiveness and adequacy. But during the last sessions, we address all the feelings, review the process together, and look at the highs and lows, the growth accomplished, and the vulnerabilities that remain. But treatment (as with a book about therapy) was never meant to fix everything; therapy remains a human relationship with all the attendant strengths and weaknesses.

SUGGESTED READINGS

Baum, N. (2007). Therapists' responses to treatment termination: An inquiry into the variables that contribute to therapists' experiences. *Clinical Social Work Journal, 35,* 97–106.

Gross, B. (2006). When enough is enough. *Annals of the American Psychotherapy Association, Summer,* 27–40.

Jakobsons, L. J., Brown, J. S., Gordon, K. H., & Joiner, T. E. (2007). When are clients ready to terminate? *Cognitive and Behavioral Practice, 14,* 218–230.

Joyce, A. S., Piper, W. E., Ogrodniczuk, J. S., & Klein, R. H. (2007). *Termination in psychotherapy: A psychodynamic model of processes and outcomes.* Washington, DC: American Psychological Association.

Kibel, H. D. (1980). Ending human relationships: Problems and potentials. *Journal of Religion and Health, 19,* 18–23.

Pinkerton, R. S., & Rockwell J. K. (1990). Termination in brief psychotherapy: The case for an eclectic approach. *Psychotherapy, 27,* 362–365.

Roe, D., Dekel, R., Harel, G., Fennig, S., & Fennig, S. (2006). Clients' feelings during termination of psychodynamically oriented psychotherapy. *Bulletin of the Menninger Clinic, 70,* 68–81.

Schlesinger, H. S. (2005). *Endings and beginnings: On the technique of terminating psychotherapy and analysis.* Hillsdale, NJ: The Analytic Press.

Siebold, C. (2007). Every time we say goodbye. *Clinical Social Work Journal, 35,* 91–95.

Todd, D. M., Deane, F. P., & Bragdon, R. A. (2003). Client and therapist reasons for termination: A conceptualization and preliminary validation. *Journal of Clinical Psychology, 59,* 133–147.

Concluding Thoughts

The power of therapy lies in the freedom it offers clients to discuss anything and everything. One consequence of that freedom is that inevitably, therapy does not follow a script—clients surprise us with their experiences, their insights, and sometimes with the questions they ask. That novelty keeps the work endlessly interesting. Throughout your career, there will be more questions and more experiences to process. There will also be some clinical interactions that will keep you awake at night. Whether we admit it or not, all good therapists experience anxiety, worry about making mistakes, and second-guess how they have handled a specific situation or interaction.

The uniqueness of each therapeutic encounter brings up uncertainty and anxiety that can make therapists feel intimidated and wonder if they are up to the challenge. That uncertainty often becomes acute when a client puts us on the spot (intentionally or unintentionally) by asking a question. In the responses we have proposed in this book, we hope that we have conveyed our belief that, although there are guidelines to consider, there are no right or wrong answers. You have the framework for approaching questions, and when you stay connected to and curious about your client's experience, you can relax and stay focused on the interchange between the two of you in that particular moment.

Uncertainty is inevitable. We all have different levels of tolerance for ambiguity. We can't tell you what to say in every situation. We can't create certainty. We haven't provided certainty with this book. However, by giving you examples of how real therapists handle real questions, you can think about what approaches resonate with you and you can try them. That process can build your confidence, allowing you to be less unsettled by the unexpected event and better able to use the surprise to learn more about your client and yourself.

In *What Do I Say?* one thread that runs through all of the theory, topics, and suggestions is that of being seen. Our anxieties and concerns about being seen are why the issue of self-disclosure comes up repeatedly as you make decisions about how to respond to questions. When clients ask for information or direction, they look to us for advice. When they ask questions that are about us as nontherapist people, or questions that ask for an opinion, we feel them looking at us. Either way, they invite us to step into the light. Clients already know about exposure and vulnerability. It takes courage to be a good client (and a good therapist).

In therapy, clients are usually the people being seen and therapists do the seeing. Perhaps people gravitate to clinical work because they are comfortable being participant-observers, and then training does the rest, enforcing the importance of not being seen too much or too often. When we respond to questions, we show more of ourselves and become vulnerable, a feeling that is not normally associated with sitting comfortably in the therapist's chair. Client questions ask for disclosure, and our personal selves peek out in the answers. There is another situation: occasions when our personal selves don't peek out, they leap forward. Many therapists get into trouble by talking too much, saying too much about themselves, their opinions, and their experiences. Remain thoughtful.

The questions we decide to answer, the information we provide when we do answer, and the words we choose that convey our thoughts can bring us closer to ourselves and to our clients or can act as a barrier, separating us from them and from ourselves. At its best, the role of therapist is an authentic combination of person and skills that allows us freedom to do our work within necessary boundaries. At its worst, the role is a defensive hiding place filled with false professionalism and fancy psychological jargon that might sound good but doesn't help clients move forward.

The reality is, we disclose all the time. In therapy, as in the rest of life, it is never a decision of disclose or do not disclose. It is how to disclose, the purpose, and *how much* to disclose. We disclose important information about ourselves every time we open the door to our offices. We are seen. Our greetings to a client, the clothing we wear, our demeanor, our office, our choices about which topics to follow enthusiastically and which to let slide, our words, our tone, and all the rest all reveal who we are. Disclosure isn't about telling your age or whether you have ever used drugs; we let people know about us constantly by what we do and don't say. When we are most effective, we work to connect with our clients, be present, and also not contaminate the relationship too much with our own messy internal lives. Even with that goal, however, we don't control every bit of what we say and certainly not how we are seen and heard.

Just like when you encourage clients to examine and learn about their personal worlds, in this book, we have tried to encourage you to not be afraid of your interior life. Personal therapy is the best place to learn about yourself so that you don't have to worry about being surprised; you will already have discovered much of the interesting stuff. You will be able to be present because you don't have to censor, edit, and, most importantly, worry.

Every clinician who participated in this book by sharing experiences made the decision to be seen. All of our guest clinicians who wrote about their ideas or clinical encounters understood that other people would read about them. A few thought long and hard before agreeing to contribute. Therapy is usually a private experience. Many clinicians hide their less-than-perfect interactions. Our guests showed real confidence. We have also been present in this book, with our mistakes and successes. You have learned about us; in fact, you probably know each of us pretty well from reading about our work and our beliefs about doing this work. The same thing is true for you and your clients. They come to know you while you work to understand them.

Writing this book turned out to be deeply personal. We both learned much more about why we do what we do. Although we were each originally trained in a strong psychodynamic tradition, we have always answered clients' questions more than that theory recommends. That is not to say that either of us discloses easily, because we don't. But we don't generally rephrase the question or return it to the client without contributing something of our own. We usually answer something, and whatever we actually say, we work hard to maintain our focus on understanding the clients' needs and experiences and providing the responses (whether we say something about ourselves, give direct advice, or ask questions for clarification) that we believe will be most helpful for their growth. Whatever we choose to say, it is essential to keep in mind that ultimately therapy is not about us. So, the writing made us think about what we believe and has revealed the way we think and the work we do in the privacy of our offices.

We hope that this book has helped you to feel more competent and more skilled so that you can set aside some disquiet and relax into the work. We understand the anxiety in this work. We feel it now as we complete the book. Apprehension is mingled with joy as we eagerly wait to see the manuscript printed and all dressed up in a cover. During the last two years, we have focused our curiosity on what we needed to do in order to connect with our readers, have you understand our ideas, not be overwhelmed by challenges, and be excited about possibilities. Preparing our book has also connected us in new ways to the clients who have contributed to our development, the students who have helped us think more clearly, the richness of the research literature, and with our own professional aspirations.

References

APA Presidential Task Force on Evidence-Based Practice. (2006). Evidence-based practice in psychology. *American Psychology, 61*, 271–285.

Atkinson, D., Thompson, C., & Grant, S. (1993). A three-dimensional model for counseling racial/ethnic minorities. *The Counseling Psychologist, 21*, 257–277.

Feldman, T. (2002). Technical considerations when handling questions in the initial phase of psychotherapy. *Journal of Contemporary Psychotherapy, 32*, 213–227.

Freud, S. (1912/1959). Recommendations for physicians on the psychoanalytic method of treatment. In *Collected Papers*, Vol. 2 (pp. 323–333). New York, NY: Basic Books.

Glickauf-Hughes, C., & Chance, S. E. (1995). Answering client questions. *Psychotherapy, 33*, 375–380.

Greenberg, J. (1999). Analytic authority and analytic restraint. *Contemporary Psychoanalysis, 35*, 25–41.

Greenson, R. (1967). *The technique and practice of psychoanalysis* (Vol. 1). New York, NY: International Universities Press.

Langs, R. (1973). *The technique of psychoanalytic psychotherapy: Volume I.* New York, NY: Jason Aronson.

Prochaska, J. O., DiClemente, C. C., & Norcross, J. C. (1992). In search of how people change: Applications to addictive behaviors. *American Psychologist, 47*, 1102–1114.

Rogers, C. (1946). Significant aspects of client-centered therapy. *American Psychologist, 1*, 415–422.

Wachtel, P. (1993). *Therapeutic communication: Principles and effective practice.* New York, NY: Guilford Press.

Index

About the Authors

Linda N. Edelstein, Ph.D., is a clinical psychologist in private practice, as well as a teacher and author. She has written *Maternal Bereavement: Coping with the Death of an Older Child*, *The Art of Midlife: Courage and Creative Living for Women*, and *The Writer's Guide to Character Traits*. She teaches at Northwestern University and was previously a Professor at The Chicago School. She maintains practices in Evanston and Chicago, Illinois, and has recently begun a blog, www.lifeaintforsissies.com, in order to talk about psychological ideas.

Charles A. Waehler is an Associate Professor in the Collaborative Program in Counseling Psychology at The University of Akron. He has been with this program, at times serving as Training Director, since receiving his Ph.D. in Counseling Psychology from Northwestern University in 1989. Along with publishing more than 35 articles and 5 book chapters in his career, he turned his dissertation into the book *Bachelors: The Psychology of Men Who Haven't Married* (Praeger, 1996). Waehler is a practicing psychologist with Cornerstone Comprehensive Psychological Services in Medina, Ohio. At various points in his career he has taught classes in personality, abnormal psychology, personality assessment, and different aspects of professional service delivery, as well as supervising practicum training. Dr. Waehler lives with his wife Tracy; together they have three daughters: Sage, Casey, and Kailee.